The Magic Of Being

By Nilofer Safdar

Copyright Notice

© Copyright 2016 Nilofer Safdar

ALL RIGHTS RESERVED. No part of this book can be reproduced or distributed in any way without written permission of the authors.

DISCLAIMER AND/OR LEGAL NOTICES:

The information presented herein represents the view of the authors as of the date of publication. Because of the rate with which conditions change, the authors reserve the right to alter and update their opinion based on the new conditions. The book is for informational purposes only. While every attempt has been made to verify the information provided in this book, neither the authors nor their affiliates/partners assume any responsibility for errors, inaccuracies or omissions. Any slights of people or organizations are unintentional. If advice concerning legal or related matters is needed, the services of a fully qualified professional should be sought. This book is not intended for use as a source of legal or accounting advice.

You should be aware of any laws that govern business transactions or other business practices in your country and state. Any reference to any person or business whether living or dead is purely coincidental.

CONSUMER NOTICE: You should assume that the authors of this book has an affiliate relationship and/or another material connection to the providers of goods and services mentioned in this report and may be compensated when you purchase from a provider. You should always perform due diligence before buying goods or services from anyone via the Internet or offline.

TABLE OF CONTENTS

INTRODUCTION 1

PHENOMENAL BONUSES 5

CHAPTER ONE: BE YOU AND BREAK THE RULES OF BUSINESS 7

CHAPTER TWO: RECEIVING THE JOY OF BUSINESS 27

CHAPTER THREE: CURING THE INCURABLE 55

CHAPTER FOUR: HOW TO GET THE RELATIONSHIP YOU
    REALLY WANT 77

CHAPTER FIVE: ARE YOU ADDICTED TO THE ILLUSION OF
    RELATIONSHIP 103

CHAPTER SIX: LEARNING TO LIVE AGAIN AFTER GRIEF 125

CHAPTER SEVEN: HAVING YOUR CAKE AND EATING IT TOO 143

CHAPTER EIGHT: LIVE BY DESIGN NOT BY DEFAULT 167

CHAPTER NINE: BE THE LEADER OF YOUR LIFE, BE YOUR
    OWN BEST FRIEND 193

CHAPTER TEN: BEING DEFINITELY DIFFERENT 215

CHAPTER ELEVEN: THE ART OF CREATING BUSINESS
    FROM THE EDGE OF POSSIBILITY 227

CHAPTER TWELVE: MY BODY BEAUTIFUL 251

CHAPTER THIRTEEN: CREATING YOUR LIFE FROM CHOICE 269

ACCESS CONSCIOUSNESS COPYRIGHT NOTICE 291

THE ACCESS CLEARING STATEMENT 293

CONTACT OUR CONTRIBUTORS 295

WHO IS NILOFER SAFDAR 297

SESSIONS WITH NILOFER 299

MAKE YOUR BOOK AN AMAZON BESTSELLER 301

WHAT NEXT 303

MORE BOOKS BY NILOFER SAFDAR 305

UPCOMING BOOKS 307

INTRODUCTION

❖

I started doing my first telesummit in November 2011. It was a year long telesummit with interviews scheduled twice a week. At the same time I found Access Consciousness while listening to another telesummit. The tools intrigued me and I started playing with them. I started following Dr Dain Heer, the co founder of Access Consciousness, on various telesummits. On one of them he spoke about the Bars. At that point there was no one in the UAE teaching the Bars. So I started being in question about learning the Bars.

One day I read a status update on Facebook from someone that they had just finished facilitating a Bars Class in Muscat, Oman. I remember feeling so disappointed to have missed a class right on my doorstep. I wrote to her immediately asking if she facilitated classes in the UAE. She said she didn't but would be happy to if I would invite her. She had flown Etihad Airways from Malaysia to Muscat. She later told me that on her stopover at Abu Dhabi she had asked what it would take to facilitate classes in Abu Dhabi. Wow! Talk about Ask and you shall receive.

Thus began my journey with Access Consciousness. As I started using the tools, my whole life started to change. I remember waking up early in the morning to do an interview for my telesummit, and I was sitting there with no reference points. I felt as if my whole life had been deleted and I didn't know anymore why I was doing the telesummit. It started becoming very heavy for me to continue with the telesummit in the form it was at that point. I had completed seven months and over 65 interviews till then. I had Speakers booked to speak for the remaining 5 months as well. One day I was receiving Bodywork from my friend Alexandra, when I realised that I just couldn't continue with the telesummit anymore. So I made a different choice and cancelled the rest of the event.

That summer I travelled to the USA with my family on a holiday. I went to San Francisco to attend a Level 2&3 (now COP) with Gary Douglas, the founder of Access Consciousness. I attended the Specialty classes with all these brilliant Access Facilitators. I started playing with the idea of doing an all Access Consciousness telesummit. But it wasn't yet time.

When I came forward to Abu Dhabi in September, while speaking with VanithaSubramaniam to organize the second round of classes in the UAE, she asked me, " Why don't you invite Gary to an online interview to invite people in the UAE to Access Consciousness?" That was Thursday, and in the next 3 days I had invited and set up a telesummit with 10 Access Consciousness Facilitators. Where the first telesummit had a very definite Form and Structure, this one had none. It ran over 5 days, had interviews at all different times of the day, I broke all the rules and I had so much fun doing it.

Where before I would struggle to have 3-4 live callers during the interviews, in this one I had 30-40 live callers and sometimes even 80-100. It was phenomenal. Way greater than I could have imagined in my wildest dreams. I started getting emails from people all over the world how much they loved an all Access Consciousness telesummit and how much of a contribution it was to their lives.

Today as I write this Introduction, I have done 3 more all Access Consciousness telesummits. And while I couldn't interview Gary Douglas in my first one, I have interviewed him 4 different times, including on a TV Show.

This year since January I have been playing around with writing a book. At one point, I suddenly went," Wait a minute! I have all these amazing interviews with all these amazing Access Consciousness Facilitators! Aren't those books waiting to be created!???? What if I could create books like the Chicken Soup For The Soul series by Jack Canfield and Mark Victor Hansen.

THE MAGIC OF BEING

I thought it would be really easy to do that - get the interviews transcribed and then edited and voila my books are ready. Talk about having projections and expectations and solidifying the energy. Also I got into this whole thing of how the book has to look like, how it has to be edited and structured. Talk about Form and Structure! Cute but not bright like Gary says. I had some really interesting points of views.

After simmering in this cesspool for a few months, I suddenly saw the light of the day. I destroyed and uncreated all my book projects. I went to question - Book, what would you like to be like? How would you like each chapter to be? Who would you like to contribute to? Who would you like to edit you? How would you like to be edited?

I was struggling to get editors for the books. I had one who was working on another book project by me. She is fantastic! And I was looking for more editors so that my books would get completed at the speed of space, yesterday :)

I spoke to a friend, Apeksha Mishra, who was an expert in branding. I shared my struggles about finding good editors. She asked me a question, " Do your books want to be edited?" My jaw just dropped! Not edit the books? She explained to me how Unabridged and Unedited books were more valuable and how people would pay more to have those than polished manuscripts. The energy just expanded out and I felt light and joyful. I realised that I finally got the energy of the book.

This book is a compilation of all the interviews I did in September 2012, with 10 Access Consciousness Facilitators. Yes. It is edited. We have removed all the fluff from the interviews, the oohs, aahs and umms and the specific references to events within the telesummit. I have kept the language of the speakers and the language of the questions as much as possible. Except in places where it just didn't make sense. After each chapter was edited, I sent it to the speaker to look through it and add and enhance to it in any way.

As I read through each chapter doing the final edits, I am in so much gratitude. To all the speakers for their unique awarenesses and brilliant facilitation, to all the listeners for being a part of this wondrous creation, to all those who sent in questions or asked questions during the telesummit- you asking questions created a new reality which has never existed before. I am aware these tools and processes shared within these pages are evergreen. I feel like I'm reading something totally new which I've never heard of before. Am I touching deeper layers of stuff? You bet!

I wonder what else is possible now that has never existed before?

What physical actualization of an unreal, unbelievable, fantastic, phenomenal, unfathomable, magical, miraculous reality totally beyond this reality are you now capable of generating, creating and instituting?

Nilofer Safdar

PS: Did I mention that the book has a life force of its own. And it gets created when it gets created! This was probably the second book I started playing with. Apparently now is the time for it to be actualized :) I probably wrote this introduction a couple of years ago. When I was reading through it just now, it just felt right somehow. So I'm not changing it.

Just one little footnote. Most of the interviews are from the first all Access Telesummit I did. A few are additions from other interview series. They just asked to be in the book. What can I say :)

PHENOMENAL BONUSES

Please send your purchase receipt to www.magicofbeing.com to get these phenomenal bonuses-

1. Audio Clearings From Each Chapter
2. Fabulous Questions From Each Chapter
3. Other fantastic bonuses

Visit www.magicofbeing.com for more…….

CHAPTER ONE

❖

BE YOU AND BREAK THE RULES OF BUSINESS

By Cory Michelle

CMFW, CF,

Founder Crazy Possible Experiment™

Creating Big Classes

"*I met Cory for the first time when I was in San Francisco attending the Level 2 and 3 in August 2012. She talked about this tele-call series that she was going to do called "Accessing Your Thriving Business". I signed up for it. She said she was going to offer the first seven people who sign up a free session with her. I was the seventh person to sign up hence I received a free session with her and I was wondering how many more people are going to sign up for that. We started the tele-call series in 3 weeks' time and there were 35 participants! I said this woman definitely knows what she is doing.*

She's been there, done that, so she's gone from just surviving, like a lot of us are doing to actually thriving and she has this amazing capacity to actually actualize 35 people in her tele-call series in 3 weeks' time. And I felt lucky. Can you tell us how did you do that?"

We ended up with 41 sign ups. Some people like to sign up and then either listen later or never listen to it. I just Keep Going, Keep Promoting. When I create an event, tele-call or a class I tap into the energy and ask the question "What can this be?"

The number I was getting was between 40 and 50 people for this particular tele-call class. I thought, "Ok great, so what's it going to take to have that many people in class and what energy can I be to be the invitation to have these people choose it, sign up, pay for it, and then actually come to class?" Right there, that's the energy. And those are the questions I asked. Then I took action and asked: "Who can I connect with? Where else can I present? Is there an email I can send out? Is there a call or connection I can catalyze? What else can I choose to have more people come to class?" And then the awareness starts to pop in and my job is really just to choose and take action.

The Beginning

When I started creating using the tools of Access Consciousness®, to me it kind of came out of nowhere. I was probably asking for something to shift in my life but I never would have expected to become an Access Facilitator or choose to do an Access Business. I had a whole other business that I had created and had a vision for. So when I dove in at first it looked like about five months of me just facilitating Bars classes and having some random sort of clients show up for private sessions. After about five months it was like I got hit over the head with a clarity of the vision of what this could be. And that's really when I started taking action.

I also asked the same type of questions: "So, what is possible here? What is possible for this business and what would be fun for me?" I realized I needed to get a website up because I was already doing large classes. I was already on my way to becoming a certified facilitator but back then I didn't even know if I was going to facilitate Foundation Level 1 classes. All I knew was that the energy was light, so I kept taking action in the direction that was light. Some might want to call that direction, but that wasn't so necessarily. I was being the invitation for the light choices to show up, for me to be aware of them and to keep taking action.

When I started I'd never been coached before and I had a totally different business. I didn't have private clients or anything like that. At that time, I really wanted to create some revenue that would sustain me and grow and actually let me thrive. And I said, "Ok, what can I actually do here?" I'd seen all the other coaches give away little free sessions so I thought of the same. I saw that it would create buzz for me and a way for people to know about what I'm doing. It was kind of a way of announcing the business to the world. I also saw that it would create some testimonials. But what I really wanted to know was what could I do for people in twenty minutes? What kind of change can we create in a 20-minute "laser session"? – That's what I called it.

"Was this before you became an Access Certified Facilitator or after you became an Access Certified Facilitator?"

It was after. But I wasn't facilitating Foundation Level 1. I didn't really have a client base. I facilitated a bunch of Bars classes but I hadn't really chosen that yet. I gave away these 23 sessions instead. I created a system to where they could sign up online and to give away 20 and when 20 were sold out then I would announce the same. And I used it as marketing on Facebook. I used phrases like "There were only so many available." and "Get yours now." I created urgency and people were noticing me. People started asking questions about my work. And when I did those, it was really great. But I didn't upsell anybody into any packages. So I didn't end up creating more business for me.

I created a buzz and I showcased my work and I was amazed. People were digging it! Then I needed to make money. I decided on a price of $44 and I decided to sell 21 of them. So I did the exact same thing except that I sold them instead of giving them away. I sold all 21 in 48 hours.

So at this point in the story, I'm catalyzing a lot of really major results. And I'm making money. Now was time to ask: How do I get these people continue on this coaching with me?

"So when you actually created this buzz and you were actually selling your sessions, so what energy were you being when you were doing that? Or what was the behind-the-scene energy work that you were doing?"

It was just following the lightness by just choosing what's light and without any force. Actually there's not really a lot of force in my business at all, even now. There's more: This is what I'm going to do and the following the energy was the fun.

And: "What invitation can I be to have people come and work with me?"

But it's not doing business from the point of view like: "I've got to do this. I have to do everything." It's more "inspired action" or "light action" where when you take the action it will actually catalyze way more than just doing a to-do-list.

"Yes. It's like putting together this tele-summit has been like that for me and it's been incredibly light and joyful doing it. And there is a lot of work that goes into it but it's just that I breeze through it. But it's that lightness and that joy of doing it, so that's fabulous. "

So these classes, I started facilitating them and I realized I was never really in sales and that I didn't know how to close people using the old rules of business. I was just expecting that if people want to work with me they'd ask me. And I'd get through 17 of those sessions and nobody buys the package. I was just asking people that if they like the idea I can e-mail them the details. I was pretty much using the most not-powerful invitation ever. Nobody was signing up for anything.

I was holding onto that amazing result, from my actual invitation; to purchase more with me; to continue with me; to create more results with me… and it was just completely ruined. So I thought of some possible changes.

I asked: "What other information do I require to have better results?" I knew more was possible and I knew that what I was choosing wasn't working so I asked: "What do I need to know that would actually make this work?" I then watched a video put by some marketing people that said: "invite them to work with you". It made everything click. And my next 4 calls were great. I told people that I wanted to invite them to work with me and boom: greater results. I asked them what areas of their life they would like to work on and they signed up.

I thought I could have done that from the beginning. The biggest takeaway in there was that if something is not working it doesn't mean that someone or something is wrong or that it will not work.

"That's really the energy that comes forth from you – the invitation – it's not a hard sell, nothing, it's just the invitation."

People run away when I hard sell. In the world of sales, I've made every single mistake possible and I still wouldn't consider myself an expert in sales. I'm more of an expert in being an invitation for people to come and play with me.

I used to be an event planner and I would to plan big events. Actually I started planning events when I was about 15. We'd have family fun nights and all these people would show up and then later, when I started planning events for non-profits, we'd have 1500 people show up. Being the invitation is part of the natural energy for me, but now I choose it intentionally.

I choose to intentionally be that energy. I also choose to attract all sorts of things to me. For example: I be the invitation for more money and the invitation to good looking men around me.

Being The Invitation

I really just ask the question. Even before I had the Access tools, and a true knowing that I could ask these questions, I was already pulling energy by just seeing what's possible. Or by choosing that choice that could catalyze. There's a lot of stuff out there. I often asked: "If I choose that would it change things for me? Would it create more?" There are a lot of things in my life now that a couple of years were sitting right in front of me that I just never chose. I even knew some of them that if I would have chosen them, it would have changed everything… and I never chose them.

Now I use these questions: If I chose this would it change, would it generate and create more for me? Would it be fun?

Most of my questions are like that. I think it got to a point where the questions where I could perceive the energy, and that as you ask the question you start being the energy. So while I definitely ask questions, there's also almost like an always-on switch for being the invitation that I now I have to turn off sometimes! For example, when I go to the grocery store, I don't really want to talk to people. Here I turn it off. Otherwise everybody turns up and talks to me. And I want to get away from them.

It comes with the energy… how much are you willing to engage and receive?

Being Seen

Often if I'm at the grocery store I'm in yoga pants, with a ponytail and no makeup. And I don't really want to talk to anybody. I'm not really one of those women who are made up all the time. I look like a normal person. So sometimes I don't really feel like talking to anybody or even being noticed. Instead I turn my invisibility on so that nobody really sees me.

There are so many people who come to my classes who have that but it's *always* turned off. What if we could turn it on? What if we could turn the invisibility cloak off and turn you on? What are the possibilities there that actually do this?

If you are asking to be the invitation but you are not willing to be seen, then people won't find you. They'll know there's something but won't know what. They won't know that it's you and your thing.

THE MAGIC OF BEING

If you have your invisibility on it's not a superpower but it's something that we create so that we are not seen intentionally. Often it's because we believe if we are seen then something not so great might happen. And maybe it happened in the past. When we are asking all these questions like "What would it take to receive more clients or have more people in class or be the invitation?" Then you are not willing to be seen, or you haven't shifted that – and it's not a large shift, it's more of an asking "What would it take for me to be seen right now?" And if you don't do that then people who want to be will be attracted to you, but they won't be able to see what to choose!

"Dr. Dain Heer, co-founder of Access Consciousness, had 2 questions – "If I were to stop hiding, how would it change the world?" and "If I were to stop hiding, how would it change my life?

You turn on and off your invisibility and then depending on whether it's turned on or off, you are either visible or you are not.

"I know a woman who has learnt the Bars. She did 3 classes and now she's creating huge classes for herself. I was wondering what is that she has that she's able to create these huge classes for her and it is that she is willing to be seen. Can you clear it a bit? Everything that doesn't allow me to be seen or allow everyone to be seen."

You are recognizing that she's doing something different. Whatever is in my own way of being seen like her or asking for more than that... do you get that you can just have that energy of that?

Everywhere that you've decided that you don't want to be seen, it's not good to be seen, for whatever reason, through all time, space and reality, will you destroy and un-create all that. <u>Good and Bad, Right and Wrong, POD and POC, All Nine, Shorts, Boys and Beyonds.</u>

Wherever you hid that switch, that you would never find it, the ability to turn it on and off by choice, will you destroy and un-create anything that doesn't allow you to know, be, perceive or receive, what would it take to be at total choice with your on and off? <u>Good and Bad, Right and Wrong, POD and POC, All Nine, Shorts, Boys and Beyonds.</u>

You take somebody like Madonna or presidential candidates; they have got to be willing to be seen, no matter what. Through all the Goods, all the Bads, all the Everything. They have got to be willing to be seen, no matter how they are seen. It is through the lens of the person who is observing them. They are going to be seen for the truth and they are going to be seen for not the truth as well.

All the places where you only want to be seen for what's true or the façade you like to present and nothing else, will you destroy and un-create that? <u>Good and Bad, Right and Wrong, POD and POC, All Nine, Shorts, Boys and Beyonds.</u>

It's one of the things that have been coming up. The Willingness to be Vilified. The willingness to be made wrong, to have lies said about you, to be seen as not the energy that you are presenting. People are going to see you in whatever way they want, no matter what you do. The willingness to let them have whatever point of view they have is huge. But often we go around trying to have everybody like us.

What if they could just have whatever point of view they have? Some people have very interesting points of view. If we are only letting in the people who can really see us then we are missing out on so many other places where people could see us in whatever light they see us. It also filters out a lot of other people that might actually bring us money in the business world. Or be on your tele-call. Or participate in whatever you are doing. This applies *even* if you are hiding out, and even if you have a job; if you are going invisible to your job, that might be a good thing, but you also might get looked over for promotion. Or if they bring doughnuts to the office, they might forget one for you. That sort of thing used to happen to me. There would be a birthday or cake or whatever, and they would forget to invite me.

THE MAGIC OF BEING

"I have an awareness I would like to share. I've been doing the energy pulls and nobody turns to look at me and I just realized I have my invisibility switch on."

You are pulling energy so people are confused. They are looking around. There's a point of connection for them. If you have the invisibility on, they think "Something's going on here but I don't know what it is."

Energy Pulls

I love using energy pulls. I like to engage the energy of the whole operating Universe – all the molecules of the Universe, to work for me; to contribute and to work for me.

All the places, whatever doesn't allow you to have all the molecules in the Universe contribute to you all the time, will you destroy and un-create it all? <u>Good and Bad, Right and Wrong, POD and POC, All Nine, Shorts, Boys and Beyonds.</u>

What an energy pull will do is pull energy from the whole entire Universe through and then you fill in the blank here. For example, if you are looking to build your business, have more people coming up as clients, you pull the energy through everybody who is interested in coming to class who doesn't even know that they are looking for you, and who you could make a difference with. You pull energy through all of them. I always visualize it like a stadium of people and beyond – like the biggest stadium you could ever imagine. Pull energy through all of them, like every molecule of their bodies, their being, and then pull it all through every molecule of your being and body and have it keep washing through like a river running through you. I start with that for a minute. And then you trickle the energy back to all the people, like a little trickle. And connect with all of them! So that whenever there's an energy flow they are being drawn to you. That trickle can help them identify what your energy is. What I find with this energy pull is that people will say they've been watching you over Facebook. Or they'll say, "You're exactly what they've been looking for." Or "It's like I know you for years."

Take it out of business and into dating like I always like to do. You can pull energy through whomever you are dating or if you are on an online dating site. Or maybe you are just a lot in public. The point is, when you pull the energy they'll feel connected to you. They'll feel so easy to be with you. That's an obvious bonus for the clients as well.

Dating

"When you are dating, how do you know who is going to contribute to you? If you are just pulling energy from all the people, then how do you know that who's going to actually be a contribution to you? That means, you are going to be a contribution to them and they are going to be a contribution to you."

Let me explain that in a story that happened to me. I was dating somebody who was not a contribution to me. However, a huge contribution to me came at the end of our relationship. I kept asking: Would he like to stay in that particular agreement? It was always yes but then it got heavy. So when it got heavy, I thought: "It's time to go." I knew it wasn't going to work out, but for whatever reason the energy was still light. When I ended it, the next day I saw almost like a movie of my whole pattern of what I was doing and choosing men for relationships. I saw how I go in and I be superior and I go in and I pick guys that I think I can pick, and they are never ever good enough for me. Doing that and choosing that enables me to always have the option to leave anytime. I always have a back door. I saw this and I thought that I've never actually seen it like this before and I demand change to the Universe. I demanded of myself not to engage in this pattern anymore and asked the Universe to show me something better. I was being a demand.

You ought to look at it like, what are you actually asking for? Because what you are asking for and the contribution created for you are built to be in alignment with each other. So, if you are not asking for better, and are asking what could be a contribution, you never really know what you are going to get. You might get something that's a contribution in a totally different way. For example, this guy was a huge contribution;

what we created together enabled me to see the pattern I was creating. I'm grateful even though the relationship was terribly tumultuous. Before Access, I would have very different things to say about it and probably wouldn't have been able to see what a huge contribution he was to me.

Sometimes contribution does not look all-nice. Or feel joyful. Sometimes, contribution is to make us realize the heavy choices. And that's where a lot of people will finally get that they've been asking for contribution; they get to see all the not so awesome things they have been choosing for their life and they don't really want to see that, so then they finally realize that choosing all of that is what's not working. This is where they see that what they've been asking for is what they just created.

"What would it take to create something different, to create something better, and to create something fun and joyful?"

The next thing that happened was three days later, after this break up, there was this gentleman that I met somewhere and it was a really good connection. I liked that. I was talking to him on the phone and he was saying that he needed a life coach. In that moment, I normally would have said that I'll coach you if we can go for a date, which totally was discounting what I do with people. I saw it and refused. I told the man that he can pay me if he wants, but it would not be a date. That he can buy a session with me.

I made it really clear to myself, and to the Universe and to him, what was that I was choosing. I could have chosen to engage with him more in a dating sort of capacity but I realized that that's the same energy I was choosing before that got me what I didn't want. I was not interested in that. I'd like to have something different so I had to choose different. So, if you find yourself in a similar situation and that's not what you'd like to have, you have to demand of yourself to choose something different… which is exactly what I had to do.

I would start to think "This is familiar and it feels comfortable," and that's when I saw that even telling him that I was having that that awareness would have just created the same thing. I could literally see the future of it and I was not interested in that. That would not have worked for me. I felt like I should create something different. You got to choose something different.

Breaking Rules

"Can you talk about breaking the rules in business and being you? And talk a little bit about the things that you have done different, the places where you have broken the rules and what that has opened up for you."

I break the rules in all areas of life. Breaking the rules in business is very easy for me. I be all of me and sometimes that means breaking the rules. For everyone reading I wonder what it would be like to have more of them available? More of you bringing more of you to the table? To do this, I ask a couple of things.

What I would ask myself is "Where does this business and this world not work for me?" and "Where am I trying to buy into that 'that's the only way to do it'?"

Everywhere that you have decided through all dimensions of time, space and reality that's the way that business is done is the only way and the way you have to do it, will you destroy and un-create that? <u>Good, Bad, Right, Wrong. POD, POC, All Nine, Shorts, Boys and Beyonds.</u>

In terms of what I choose to do that's different, when I get an idea or a vision that I like, I start going after it. Even in my coaching business, coaching and facilitating with Access tools is very different. It's not your normal set of coaching tools; it's not therapy. When people come to work with me, that action alone is doing business differently. All of us, (the facilitators and just other people who would like to use the tools), we create a willingness to do things different.

Anything that doesn't allow you to have total choice in your willingness to do things different, to choose different and to be different, will you destroy and un-create all that? <u>Good, Bad, Right, Wrong. POD and POC, All Nine, Shorts, Boys and Beyonds.</u>

There's a TED video where this thirteen or fourteen year old kid was asking us to stop learning; stop learning and start thinking. But what he was really talking about was being aware. He was saying that when we go and learn from this reality we are learning what other people's points of view are. Even a map is somebody's point of view about how we do things in this reality. What he was saying was that when you stop learning and stop buying into everybody else's point of view about this reality, then you start to tap into what would actually be fun and would work for you.

Everything we've been doing our entire lives and everything we've been trained is valuable and real, will you destroy and un-create it? <u>Good, Bad, Right, Wrong. POD and POC, All Nine, Shorts, Boys and Beyonds.</u>

The kid was saying that when he stopped learning and started to believe in what he was thinking, he tapped into all this amazing stuff that had never been brought through before. It was a whole new theory of something. He was really brilliant kid; pouring in with ideas like quantum physics formulas and stuff, which he really had no idea about and had never even learned of before.

What I would like to do is extrapolate what works that other people are doing; I don't need to reinvent the wheel. Like email marketing for example. Take constantcontact.com, or any one of the other programs you use to send out emails to your list. Ask: What would you put in those emails? How would you like to create it? Mine are still definitely in formulation stage. I haven't come up with something I would really love to send out to people but I invite people to what I'm doing and share cool thoughts. And when I see what another person's creating, and I really like it I think, "How could I change it to make it mine?"

Sometimes there's a change and sometimes there's not. And this applies in all marketing, especially now with how online marketing really works; that people are seeing more things and creating more.

Instead of being a follower, would you be willing to be a leader? Anything that doesn't allow you to be a leader that you truly be, will you destroy and un-create that? <u>Good, Bad, Right, Wrong. POD and POC, All Nine, Shorts, Boys and Beyonds.</u>

Leaders may not have a lot of followers necessarily, but a leader is almost a new thought leader; a new idea leader. They ask: What else is actually possible here? What else wants to come through right now?

And that alone is breaking the rules of business, because if you're like a current business out there, everything is done in a particular way. There are rules and you have to be professional and you have to do it this way or that way and you better not be in pieces, etc. But instead, if you think, "How else can I do this?" That way of thinking might work. Not to throw the baby out with the bathwater but what works for me was that incorporates some of those ideas I liked, and what else is there?

I think in terms of being you and a success, asking questions and breaking the rules; asking questions in business is key. But then also it's about who you be in your business. One of the things I always had trouble with was, I never wanted to drop into super-professional-looking. I always wanted to have kind of a casual style and I kept seeing all these gazillionaires who were totally casual – jeans and cute clothes, but not super-fancy, like a three-piece suit, etc. My body was never quite comfortable in that kind of stuff, so I thought of not doing that. I just want to look nice, presentable, professional, but I don't feel I need to be wearing suits. Because it just didn't match my energy and it looked weird on me. I just did a photo-shoot the other day and they had a three piece for me – a suit – and I was not comfortable.

Even when I was having it on, I was just changing poses. Questions to ask are: How can you bring your own style? Your own flavor versus

THE MAGIC OF BEING

thinking what other people do when they want to be on front page, go to a networking event, or have head-shots done, etc. Like real estate agents always have a suit on; bankers always all have a suit on.

What if somebody did something a little different? How much would they be appreciated for truly being who they were versus what the real estate, insurance or the banker world thinks that they should be?

Everywhere we've aligned and agreed with what's appropriate, will you destroy and un-create all that? Good, Bad, Right, Wrong. <u>POD, POC, All Nine, Shorts, Boys and Beyonds.</u>

Sometimes it's like: Who do you be? What's your natural energy? I was talking to a girl the other day and she was telling me that she wanted to be a marketing brat. I told her it's nice because when you think about a marketing brat, it's somebody who's going to break the rules and they're going to do whatever they want. So when we follow the rules, how original is that?

Fun Being You In Business

"I'm looking at the things that I've done in the past and it has been those things which I have created which didn't fit into any particular rule where I was successful and it was exhilarating for me."

There's a large amount of fun you can have by just being you! Just being you is breaking the rules, especially by being you in business. How much more of you can you bring to the table? We were talking about that girl getting lots of people in her classes, How much of her is she being? When she's talking to people and when she's inviting people? A lot.

I think that the whole "breaking the rules" thing is that it's really just unlocking someone from who they think they should be and who they think everybody else thinks they should be. Sometimes it's just our perception of what everybody else wants and then we try to live that way. Then, the minute we get judged or somebody gives us a funny look, and we happen to be doing what we would like to do, everything becomes a contraction. What if instead of contracting we asked: "What if I could expand my receiving of judgment from other people?" One thing that I've noticed of myself is that the less I judge myself and the more I see me, the less other people judge me. Because I don't have any judgment about myself for them to perceive!

I'm sure people are judging me but I don't judge myself. When I don't judge myself I don't get triggered by their judgment and they can judge me all they want. What most of us are used to is reacting and expending themself, resisting and fighting with those that judged them. Even getting into screaming matches with them about it. When we finally realize that that's actually what we believe about ourselves and how we're choosing to operate, it can change. The person judging was just pointing the truth out. It actually wasn't a judgment at all. It was the truth that you didn't want anybody to see but they saw it. And you were trying to defend yourself.

Truth Versus Judgment

"I experience sometimes a judgment that when somebody is judging me, I feel a hit in my chest like a little tiny arrow. Is it when I'm resisting and reacting to it or aligning and agreeing to it? That's why I experience it as that?"

Is there anywhere in the judgment that's actually true? Is there any part of the judgment that's true?

"Yes. Some part of it."

If some part of it is true, then is it really a judgment?

"It's I'm resisting the truth there?"

Yes.

"That's not really a judgment then."

No. If there's any truth to it, whether it's you or someone else judging, it might not be very bad. There were some things I was choosing that

I thought were wrong and then I tried to hide them. If you try to hide stuff people can see through it. They'll see it and they'll say it. And then you'll be shocked. It's sometimes something that you don't even want to know about yourself. For example, I didn't want to know what I was actually choosing with money. I was hiding it from myself so much that I was resisting, reacting, blocking and hiding like a kung-fu ninja move. If there's any truth in the judgments that you perceive just ask: Are they really judgments or is there something underneath there? The more you look at those things that you are hiding from yourself, the more you begin Accessing Your Consciousness, Accessing Your Awareness About You and Being Willing to be Honest with Yourself, you will see that the judgment is true. Then ask: "What can I do to change that?"

After you see the truth, you will see that nobody ever says anything about it. You will have acknowledged that you have a judgment about yourself and that you're no longer trying to hide it. Suddenly the charge would dissipate.

At that point, if someone was cursing at you or if somebody said things that weren't very nice in that world, would it affect you?

"No. It won't."

Right, because it's wouldn't be the truth. That's their judgment, their points of view and there'd be no charge there for you. Whenever there's a charge, you just want to look and ask: is there anything that's the truth that you haven't been willing to see? Then you can ask: For what reason is this triggering you? And clear all that stuff! The more willing you are to be brutally honest with yourself, the more you can clear.

All the places you haven't been willing to be brutally honest with yourself and fear of what you've been actually hiding from yourself, that would actually give you total freedom, will you now destroy and un-create all that? <u>Good, Bad, Right, Wrong. POD and POC, All Nine, Shorts, Boys and Beyonds.</u>

When we're willing to be brutally honest with ourselves, totally, completely brutally honest with what we are choosing, *we can change anything.* The places we are making choices out of judgments we create all the things we perceive as bad in our life. What if instead of judging those "bad" things, you asked: How did I get so lucky? That last piece on judgment is really key. A lot of people will come to me and they'll say that they are being judged and then they've started to shrink because of it.

"You asked me before that if something's not true, does it stick me and even though I said that it doesn't but somewhere I think it does stick me because today I have my laptop open in front of me, since morning, I've had two or three emails from people who are subscribed to the list asking me to delete them from the list. I asked them to press the unsubscribe button and not to write to me. It's been sticking me. What's going on there?"

Do you have an expectation or a conclusion or an answer about what you would like to have people think about you?

"Yes. I think I am not good enough as they are unsubscribing."

It means you are taking on their judgment.

Everywhere you are connecting to everybody else's choice is having an effect on you, or something about you, will you destroy and un-create that? Good, Bad, Right, Wrong. POD, POC, All Nine, Shorts, Boys and Beyonds.

I've tried some of the weirdest stuff and I remember being unsure of whether it'll work but I wanted to try. I would do it and then it felt lighter and I was good! I learnt this a long time ago when I started planning spiritual events for people. I had created these events, really amazing ones, and invited all my friends. One of my friends came and in that moment when one of my friends showed up to my event and there were another 20 other people who were not my friends, who just found out about it and were interested so they came, I noticed something: I had become so unattached from who came, who subscribed to my list and who unsubscribed, who liked what I was doing and who didn't like it… I was able to really pull in the people who are interested in what I've got. And a lot of the time it is not our friends and families. It's not the people we think that are going to be attracted to or benefit from what we've got. We have to go beyond that. Expand out beyond your circle of people and ask, "Who else can contribute to this?" or "Who would like this?" That includes your list! I often get emails from people that say they don't know how they got on my list, and I have to go back and check and tell them that they opted in. Some of the ways people are functioning from is really interesting. What if their point of view could just be really interesting?

Any time you are having a reaction to anything, you can always ask a question. The question is an action. So asking allows you to get out of reaction and into action.

It's a great place to practice "Interesting Point of View, They Have this Point of View."

I do "Interesting Point of View" a lot with people who tell me they want to unsubscribe versus just clicking the bottom of the email. Anybody who is receiving email marketing these days knows that there's an unsubscribe button at the bottom. A little bit of judgment in that one but the point is interesting.

WHO IS CORY MICHELLE

Cory Michelle, CMFW, CF is one dynamic Unicorn! She's the founder of the Crazy Possible Experiment™, creator of Unicorn CEO™, a renown certified Access Consciousness® facilitator, a gifted speaker, coach, and visionary on a mission to empower life and business entrepreneurs with tools for success. In addition to hosting a popular radio series and being a top-selling author, she creates and leads virtual and live programs & events for people who are ready to experience lives of ease, abundance and joy.

Cory is committed to raising global consciousness by transforming the way life and business entrepreneurs -those expanding their personal lives and those expanding their businesses- relate to themselves, each other and their communities. Experience has taught her that true success, in personal development and in business, is based on the triple gems of collaboration, connection and contribution. This revolutionary paradigm has given her an edge in helping entrepreneurs monetize their businesses, attract tons of clients, create inspiring brands and launch killer products, all while benefiting their communities. It's also the foundation of her work with clients who desire a a true shift in developing their personal lives and relationships.

Clients soon discover that Cory's laser-guided, fast-acting coaching opens their lives to the changes they truly desire in a matter of days, even hours. Part of this involves learning how to Ask & Receive what you truly want and need. As a certified Access Consciousness® facilitator, Cory utilizes and shares Access Consciousness® tools and techniques for quickly clearing away hidden obstacles and unlocking doors to success far beyond expectations.

Some say Cory Michelle makes 'magic'… but what she actually does is teach people how to activate and harness the intuition and magic that resides within. She is the original Unicorn Whisperer.

5 SECRETS TO LIVING A JUICY ORGASMIC LIFE
By Cory Michelle
Listen to this interview with Cory Michelle.
Visit http://www.magicofbeing.com

CHAPTER TWO

❖

RECEIVING THE JOY OF BUSINESS

By Simone Milasas

A World-Leader On The Creative Edge Of Consciousness

And Has A Deep Yearning

To Make A difference In The World.

Nilofer: When I heard you speaking, I heard you talk about the businesses that you had done and how you were doing things just exactly your way, I remember listening to you and saying, "Oh wow, she's done business exactly the way I've been doing things and I've been making myself feel so wrong for doing things this way!"

I would do things, and I would be wildly successful at things and then I would listen to other people and basically just shut it all down. Listening to you talk I was, "Oh! I've always done that and I never allowed myself to go beyond a certain point." So that was something that really opened up for me. So thank you for that.

Simone: You are welcome. I'm sure that there are a lot of other people listening, who have come across the same sort of thing. So, there are a few things you could do – One of them is that I know when I have so many different businesses and I've been involved in so many different industries, for me it was always about finding out how everything operates. "What else can I know?" or "What else can I find out about my different industry?" So I went from job to job, travelled around the whole entire world doing everything from being a Kamaki in a Greek island (which is talking about trying to get people to come into the restaurant saying "You know, would you like to eat? I'll get you a free glass of wine", etc.,) to being a manager in London in the Tube (They were developing a whole new line of train stations). I've done so many different things. I noticed when I got back to United States how everybody was sort of patting me on the back saying "Well, now that you've got that out of your system, you can settle down!" I never wanted to settle down and do one thing! I always wanted to be involved in so many different businesses, different possibilities. Most of the time in this reality, it'll count against you if you project that you should be sort of settling down, doing one thing, making yourself successful at that.

Now, also what you are referring to is – I'd be incredibly successful at about 4 or 5 different businesses, and what I noticed was I loved starting out with a business. The whole creation thing is really appealing to me. So, we create this business, including my going to India, Nepal, Thailand and Tibet and getting designing, clothing and jewelry and getting all that made up with semi-precious stones, sterling silver, etc. We also developed a surf label called "The Shack" with the whole hat range. We did everything, and became successful with it. But then, I got bored. So I quit and I started to destroy it; until I met Gary Douglas, the founder of Access Consciousness, who showed me that I didn't actually have to destroy my businesses to create another one. He showed me you could actually sell it and could actually get someone in to manage it. You are allowed to have more than one business. That's the thing that's truly off in this reality. Most people think that you are not allowed to have more than one business. The thing I always ask is that how many of you have one document open in your computer at all times? Or do you have many, many documents open? It's the same thing with the amount of projects and businesses that you ran or that you are involved in.

Nilofer: Yes for me it was always about creating new things and I would create these things and just get bored because I didn't want to be doing the maintenance of it anymore!

Simone: The interesting thing is most people think that maintaining a business or institution is the boring part, but what if that was actually creation as well?

Could everything that you institute with your business to maintain it be actually creating a business too? Everything that is, and everywhere that you've gone so wrong with of the creation that you have, will you destroy and un-create it? <u>Right and Wrong, Good and Bad, POC and POD, All Nine, Shorts, Boys and Beyonds.</u>

What do you create from this that nobody else does?

What are you willing to have that nobody else does?

What business are you willing to create that nobody else does?

Are you willing to do something different?

Most of the time, if you start buying into people's points of view about what you should be doing or what you shouldn't be doing, you'll start destroying your business. Then what do you know? Your knowing is where you should be functioning from. You're knowledge is what will actually create something different, doing something different and choosing a different possibility.

Nilofer: I was running this tele-summit for six months from November 2011 and after that we finished with it. So when I came back and I wanted to create this one, I realized that I was no longer going into that place of the wrongness of me anymore. Everywhere I was just asking questions of what would work for me and I just kept creating it without really looking at what anybody else is doing or saying. This has been so light to do it. I've not stuck to the rules I think in any part of the creation of this.

I have around 5 calls this week. I had one call the first week, 2 calls last week and 5 calls this week. I'm going to finish up with this and feel, "Ok, this is what works for me, this is what works for the speakers and this is what I'm going to put forward in front of everybody. I'm doing it my way.

I'm not listening to anybody here. I'm doing it the way it works for me." It's just been so invigorating to do it in this way.

Simone: If we did everything in a logical mind, we'd have everything we ever desired, but it's the same stuff that locks us up and it's also the awareness that we've been unwilling to acknowledge. You are willing to follow the energy and follow what works for everybody else and what works for you, which then is not going to be the best outcome for you.

I really desire that people should be that knowledgeable in business as well, but business is one of those areas that people think they have to have the answer, that they have to go to conclusion. If you look at what this reality always asks for, 'Where's your projection?' Does any day ever work out like you think it's going to work out? Or does it always look completely different? When you wake up in the morning, and you say, "Ok, what joy and glory do you think you can have today?" and your day never works out like you think it would. So, no business ever works out like that either.

What if you are willing to focus on some question and choice and contribution in business, rather than answers or conclusions? This choice creates awareness.

Contribution

Nilofer: I remember recently in one of the newsletters that you sent out, you spoke about contribution and I really want you to speak about how people go a lot into competition. This whole topic of contribution and competition and how does it all pan out?

Simone: So, well contribution is a 2 way street and most people don't look at it like that either. What does contribution mean to you?

Nilofer: Contribution feels really light to me and it's this simultaneity of gifting and receiving at the same time? I've really been in that place of doing service, where I've been so bogged down by that word "service". Since I've been aware of contribution, it's a totally different energy to it. It's so light and expansive. It's willingness to let you receive as well.

THE MAGIC OF BEING

Simone: What if you've been unwilling to receive? I spoke to someone the other day and I started thinking because I realized that in their point of view contribution was about giving and taking a step back and giving to everybody else, but not allowing them to actually receive it as well. But what if contribution was a 2-way street? What if contribution was gifting and receiving simultaneously?

What if you've been unwilling to receive? What contribution have you been unwilling to receive that if you received it, would it make your business easier, and cause the cash flow come in a lot quicker? Everything that is and everything that doesn't allow that to show up, will you destroy and uncreate it? <u>Right and Wrong, Good and Bad, POC and POD, All Nine, Shorts, Boys and Beyonds.</u>

What physical actualization of being a contribution that you truly be are you now capable of generating, creating and instituting? Everything that that is, will you destroy and uncreate it? <u>Right and Wrong, Good and Bad, POC and POD, All Nine, Shorts, Boys and Beyonds.</u>

Business In 10 Second Increments

Plus there's so much to talk about with business as well. I just get so much from people trying to control things or function from the reference point of what they are supposed to be doing well. For example, while you are talking about this tele-summit, it's actually functioning from the awareness. When you wake up tomorrow and you've lost your memory, what would you choose? If money wasn't the issue, what would you choose?

Nilofer: It's very interesting when you talk about if you wake up tomorrow morning and you have no memory, what would you choose? This is exactly what happened to me after I've finished my Foundation and Level 1 class. I was doing the tele-summit at that point and so, I get onto this call and I'm sitting there and wondering "Why am I here?" I felt like "Oh my god, what happened here? Everything has just disappeared all around me and I don't even know why I'm here!"

Simone: That's great. Living in 10 second increments as well. But what if you could choose your business in 10 second increments? What if you forget that you have a business? Then how would you create it? What would you create today?

What if you looked at everything like that? So many people look at business as - It has to exist, it has to exist forever. It has to exist for a certain amount of time. How many points of view are there that your business cannot succeed for a certain amount of years and in truth, what's success anyway? What have you defined "success" as? What is so much fun? What if it was joyful? What if it was just a choice? Everything today that you ask, "OK, it's working for me today" you should do the same thing in relationships as well.

Everything that is, will you destroy and un-create it? <u>Right and Wrong, Good and Bad, POC and POD, All Nine, Shorts, Boys and Beyonds.</u>

"What stupidity are you using to create the lack of contribution you are choosing? Everything that is, will you destroy and un-create it?" <u>Right and Wrong, Good and Bad, POC and POD, All Nine, Shorts, Boys and Beyonds.</u>

How much do you refuse to receive? How many currency flows do you refuse to receive? How many cash flows have you refused to receive? How many infinite possibilities have you refused to receive because they don't match the energy of what you've decided your business as?" Everything that is, will you destroy and un-create it? <u>Right and Wrong, Good and Bad, POC and POD, All Nine, Shorts, Boys and Beyonds.</u>

Now, when I'm saying "stupidity", I mean the lack of awareness. I'm not saying that everybody's stupid out there. It's the basis that you are functioning from a lack of awareness.

I was a $187,000 in debt when I joined with Gary Douglas and I used to listen to Gary and Dain in their money classes. They would talk about all these money tools. I was using Access tools but wasn't using the money tools. I think by my third money class. I listened to them, sat there and went "Huh, well I think I should give this a go. What's the worst thing that can happen? Another $10,000 in debt?" So, I didn't tell anyone and I started using the tools that are actually in the book 'Money isn't the problem, you are'. I think that's just a fabulous title - 'Money isn't the problem, you are'.

It's your unwillingness to receive. So, I started using the tools that were in that book and I can give you a couple of tools today as well, and my money situation changed around within around 3 weeks! I was actually earning money from very random places.

Your Point Of View Creates Your Reality

How many people think that the only way they can earn money is by the amount of work that they put in? What if money could show up in different ways? Different possibilities? Everything that is, and everywhere that you've decided that you will have to put that hard work in and you can only earn money for every hour that you are putting in, your weekly wage, your hourly rate, whatever that is, will you destroy and uncreate it? <u>Right and Wrong, Good and Bad, POC and POD, All Nine, Shorts, Boys and Beyonds.</u>

If you have that point of view, what happens if you see a gold nugget on the side of the road? You actually won't see it, because it won't match the judgment that you've created - That you can only earn money by the amount of time that you work. So I used these money tools from the book and my money situation changed dramatically. I saved probably within 18 months and I had money in the bank account. I wasn't in debt anymore, there was money in the bank account, the credit cards were paid off. I sat there on the computer and went, "Oh, I've got money. I'm not actually in debt!" and I seriously felt like "Ok, so where's the marching band? Where's the big fireworks? Isn't this supposed to feel different?" Then I realized within about 2 weeks, I created myself in debt again.

Luckily I had the Access tools so I started asking questions and realized "Oh!" I was more comfortable being in debt than actually having money. So everything that that is, for everyone of you and all the listeners out there who actually feel more comfortable being in debt rather that actually having money, will you destroy and un-create it? <u>Right and Wrong, Good and Bad, POC and POD, All Nine, Shorts, Boys and Beyonds.</u>

There's one thing about awareness – you can change anything. So, with these stupidity processes, it's about changing the lack of awareness that you are having, because choice gives awareness. You can change anything, if you are willing to be aware of it. You can change anything.

Everything that that is and everywhere you feel that you are the only one and that nothing can be changed for you, will you destroy and un-create it? <u>Right and Wrong, Good and Bad, POC and POD, All Nine, Shorts, Boys and Beyonds.</u>

Uninviting Money

One of the tools that you use is, at the end of every day –

POC and POD everywhere that I have uninvited money today.

We are so quick to ask for money to show up and we are so quick to uninvite it. All it takes is you going to a restaurant and your body saying, "Hey, I want to eat the lobster" but you are thinking "No, I can only afford the chicken sandwich"; you've just uninvited money.

So POC and POD everywhere that you've uninvited money today. I still do that before going to bed.

Nilofer: You are saying that your body wants a lobster but you order the chicken sandwich. But if you really have the money only for a chicken sandwich, what do you do?

Simone: Ok, so you can acknowledge that your body actually desires the lobster. Thank your body for the awareness and also ask your body to contribute to you making more money. It's not going to the unawareness of what your body is asking for. You can acknowledge it. You can still buy the chicken sandwich but acknowledge what your body is asking for. I'm not saying, "Ok, you like a Ferrari and you can't afford to buy a Ferrari, you just uninvited money." No. Acknowledging what is, is a demand to show up in your life, in your business.

Nilofer: So, you're saying that you have to be willing to receive the energy of everything and then you can still choose whatever you choose. You are not going from a place of "Oh my god, I can't afford it! I won't have it so put that out of my Universe." Instead you can say, "Oh, I'll have that and how can I have it?"

Simone: Yes. What would it take for that to show up? Ask more questions, because the second you go "I can't afford this" or "I can't have this", that's a conclusion. There's no question there. So if you ask a question - "What would it take for this to show up?" or "What would it take for me to create this?" or "What would it take for me to have this in my life?" and it can show up in any way. A conclusion is also "I have to be the one that goes and earns the money to actually purchase the lobster." What if someone was willing to buy you the lobster? There are many different ways that it could show up.

What stupidity are you using to create the lack of receiving that you are choosing? Everything that that is, times a godzillion, will you destroy and un-create it? <u>Right and Wrong, Good and Bad, POC and POD, All Nine, Shorts, Boys and Beyonds.</u>

10% Account

So one of the other tools that I used to change so much for me, with money is the 10% account. Now what's the 10% account? It's putting away 10% of absolutely everything that you earn. So, every dollar you earn, 10% goes away to you and putting that away for you. It's to honor you. One of the things that I heard Gary talk about as well was, "Well, I can't afford that because I've got all these bills and I'm this much in debt."

If you say you can't afford it, and you say that you can't do it, if you make money the issue, money will always be the issue. So again, I introspected, "Ok, what's the worst thing that can happen? I end up spending it?" But I have never spent my 10% account and it created so much ease for me. Putting 10% away of everything that you earn for you. But please, if you do this, don't do this because you heard me saying it on the tele-summit, do it because you are choosing to do it. Do it for you, as an honoring to you. If you pay your bills first, the Universe will be "Oh, he loves bills. So, I'll give him more bills!"

So, what if the Universe thought that you desired to honor you? Now, I've got money in the bank account, I've got silver, I've got gold, I've got jewelry. So I've got things that have been fun for me with the 10% as well. I've kept that 10% and it's grown and grown and it's been a lot of fun. I'll say that there's a certain amount to everybody, that when they get to that amount, it creates this sense of peace in your world, in your Universe. Maybe it's an amount that you can live for the next 3 months or 6 months or whatever that is. It will start to create ease in your Universe, using your 10% account. Now what I've also done is put 10% away for any of the businesses that I have, so that is me honoring the business.

10% Business Account

Nilofer: So what if there are people who are healers and their whole business and their whole income overlaps? Would you still recommend that they set aside 10% of the business and 10% personally?

Simone: Sure, do what makes you feel lighter as well. If something is right, it just feels light and if something is heavy, it's usually a lie. Do what makes you feel lighter and ask a question as well – "If I do that, will it create more for my business or less for my business? Will it expand my business or contract my business?" Play with all of these tools and do them because they work for you.

It depends on how you run your business as well. If you actually take a percentage chart of the business, then put away 10% of that for you and then get the business to put away 10% as well, you'll have money. Now there's one thing that I can say is this will not work out logically. You will find that money shows up.

What if money was like magic? What if it just showed up? You'll find that it gets created and shows up in a very different way. So if it feels light to you, put away 10% for the business as well.

Is Business Serious

Caller: "So how can I get out of this serious mode I get in when I'm talking about my practice?" I use kinesiology, but I do exactly the same with Access. I'm a Bars facilitator. I've asked questions about this. I'm also demanding fun in my business. So far just a little result. I want to do it right. Want people to know I take it and them seriously, but it is just boring, both for me and for them. Do you have any suggestions?

Simone: Where did you buy that business had to be serious? What if business was not serious? What if business was light? What if business was funny? What if it was joyful? What if it was magical? What if it was an adventure?

Everywhere that you've created business as serious, will you destroy and uncreate it? Right and Wrong, Good and Bad, POC and POD, All Nine, Shorts, Boys and Beyonds.

What's your judgment of business?

Caller: Marketing!

Simone: Marketing? Ok. I did this question with a lady once and she was saying to me that she didn't like business etc. and hence now she wrote books. I said, "Do you enjoy writing books?" and she said, "Yeah, I love writing books." So I told her, "That's business. It's all business." So what we got down to and what most people have a point of view on is that they don't actually like the petty book-keeping or the accounting or filing side of business. What if they included everything?

A long time ago with my dad, (he used to be an accountant) he had these graphs on the table. It had this slither of a section of graph that was about the creation of business, and this big piece of it about accounting and statements etc. I got cranky and said, "I don't want my business to be like that. I like it to be about the creation part sort of thing."

He looked at me and said "Oh Simone, you can't have this," and pointed to all the creation stuff, "without this" and he pointed to all the accounting and the book-keeping, etc. I knew he was correct, so I knew I had to be aware of everything.

What if you have to be aware about everything and yet you didn't actually have to do everything? What are making so serious about business that it isn't?

What stupidity are you using to create the seriousness of business that you are choosing? How many conclusions and answers do you have in that business which is serious? Everything that is, will you destroy and uncreate it?

<u>Right and Wrong, Good and Bad, POC and POD, All Nine, Shorts, Boys and Beyonds.</u>

How many times have we been told that business is serious? That's what you've grow up with. Just go into any city around the world and go to the downtown area, and look at all the corporates. Just because they are wearing suits and ties, they become serious.

Then look at – 'What is the manipulation?' 'What if the working in the corporate world is a manipulation and you could actually manipulate and create anything within there.' But what if you didn't have to buy that this thing is serious? What if you weren't wrong actually enjoying business and having the adventure of living?

Everything that is, times a godzillion, will you destroy and uncreate it?

<u>Right and Wrong, Good and Bad, POC and POD, All Nine, Shorts, Boys and Beyonds.</u>

What physical actualization of creating your judgment, decisions, computations, conclusions as a reality, are you using to create your business as the judgment, decisions, computations, conclusions that create the limitations of your business as the necessity of this reality? Everything that is, times a godzillion, will you destroy and uncreate it? <u>Right and Wrong, Good and Bad, POC and POD, All Nine, Shorts, Boys and Beyonds.</u>

How much of the stuff that comes up and around is based on this reality? I see other areas of people's lives, where they do function from question, they do function from the lightness and the space. What if people also have this with money and business? It's just a choice.

Everything that that is and everywhere that you've decided that you are going against the brain, against this reality and you are creating your own reality, will you destroy and un-create it? <u>Right and Wrong, Good and Bad, POC and POD, All Nine, Shorts, Boys and Beyonds.</u>

What Can You Add

I was talking to someone this morning about their business, and she's always complaining that it's not working and that there's not anything more showing up. Most people have a lot of things in their business and when you ask "What could you add to your business?" they go, "Oh, my list is already too long. I'm being overwhelmed!"

No! What the question is "What else could I add to my business?" What if it was a new computer system that created more ease and did something quicker? Or it was somebody else that was assisting you with the things that you don't like or prefer not to do?

Now the first thing that she responded was "I don't have the money to hire someone." If you go to that conclusion and you go to that judgment, your business will not succeed. It will not move forward. You've got to ask more questions. You've got to be willing to have to change what can occur.

What if you could hire someone for 2 to 4 hours a week and you swap sessions a few times a week? Maybe just some body work or give them free classes etc? Start it off like that. Somebody who is great at doing things on Facebook, at doing marketing in 2 or 4 hours a week can create a miracle. But if you have the point of view that you don't have the money and you'll never be able to afford to do that, then guess what?

You'll never have the money and you'll never be able to afford to do that.

Where are you limiting your business by all the judgments, decisions, computations, conclusions that you are creating your business from? Everything that is, will you destroy and uncreate it? Times a godzillion? <u>Right and Wrong, Good and Bad, POC and POD, All Nine, Shorts, Boys and Beyonds.</u>

I'm driving right now in a car with some friends of mine in Miami, going to a hotel. But I'm doing business anyway. Someone was saying to me "You need to take a photo of you doing business everywhere!" Because I'll be on a boat on my computer doing business. I'm in the back of the car at the moment, on the tele-summit. It's hilarious. The business is never serious for me. There's always something that is possible and it's always an adventure.

Business can be included in everything. So many times people work Monday to Friday, 9 to 5 or they have the weekend off, what if we never turned off? What if you never turned off from your business? What if it was included in everything you did and were?

So many people sort of switch off or contract or become in serious mode or actually become anything that's you. Everything that that is, and everywhere that you are functioning from anything like that, will you destroy and un-create it? <u>Right and Wrong, Good and Bad, POC and POD, All Nine, Shorts, Boys and Beyonds.</u>

Closing Down Your Business

Nilofer: You were talking about "What can I add to my business." So many times I've been in this place of looking at things going on in my business and (of course at that point I did not have the tools of Access and I wasn't really into asking questions or whatever) I kept doing things and they were not working out. So at what point do you actually say that "Ok. This isn't working out and I need to let go of this and move on to other things?"

Simone: Good question. There are a couple of things for that as well. Tell me, how many people out there who create their business, think that they can't actually close their business down? I'm in the midst of closing down one of my businesses. Now that business was fantastic, I had a lot of fun. It changed a lot of people's lives and I'm in the midst of closing it down. It was not working for me anymore and so much of my time, energy and choices are taken up with Access Consciousness - The joy of business, which is what I would prefer. So have a look at what makes you feel lighter with changing your business. You are allowed to change your business. If you want it, you can have a business every year.

But one thing that I will ask is that the thing that we mentioned earlier on is – don't destroy your business because you'd like to actually start another business. If you are one of those people who actually likes to create businesses like a start-up business, which you love getting involved in how that looks, it doesn't mean that you have to destroy a successful business to move onto something different. You can hire someone, you can sell it, etc.

Ask the business questions as well. That's definitely what I would be doing. Ask the business "Would you like to move on now? Can I sell you?" or "Is there another possibility that's showing up?"

Business Creating Itself

Now a lot of people misidentify that when their business starts to create itself, it has this sense of space, some people go to the place of "Oh, the business is not working" which is a conclusion. So you conclude that the business is not working and you misidentify the space that the business is actually starting to create itself. So what if business was easy? What if making money was easy? So when business starts to have this space about it, ask it, "Ok, so will you make me money?"

Is that the point at which it appears to be as if nothing is happening? Is it the point where it's getting actualized and you kind of misidentify as "nothing is working"?

At that point too, ask the business, now that you have to tools, "Ok, are you creating yourself now?" "Will you make me money?" I just start asking the business questions.

And ask also, "Is this the point I've decided I can't receive anymore?" Everything that that is, and everywhere that you've decided that you can only receive a certain amount, will you destroy and uncreate it? <u>Right and Wrong, Good and Bad, POC and POD, All Nine, Shorts, Boys and Beyonds.</u>

How many of you out there, have a point of view about how much money you are allowed to create or how successful your business is allowed to be? Are you allowed to be more successful than the rest of the people in your family, than the area where you live, the city you live in? What is considered right? Correct? So everywhere that you've bought into the judgments, projections and limitations and complications and decisions of that, will you destroy and un-create it? Is that this reality again? Right and wrong, times a godzillion, godzillion, godzilion. <u>Right and Wrong, Good and Bad, POC and POD, All Nine, Shorts, Boys and Beyonds.</u>

Question. Choice. Contribution. Demand.

So how many of you create your business that you can create the confinement of you, the contractedness of you, that keeps you in this reality? So everything that that is, will you destroy and uncreate it? <u>Right and Wrong, Good and Bad, POC and POD, All Nine, Shorts, Boys and Beyonds.</u>

What if you are willing to receive like we were talking about before the contribution of the questions, the choice, the demand? So everything that that is, will you destroy and un-create it? <u>Right and Wrong, Good and Bad, POC and POD, All Nine, Shorts, Boys and Beyonds.</u>

Lemon Tree Story

Some of the time, during business, I see people cut off the future possibilities rather than allow them to show up. One of the stories in my book is called the "Lemon tree story" because, what if you decided that you wanted to have a business creating orange juice? So you go out, you've got some land, you buy the orange tree seeds and you plant the seeds. You water the seeds, you watch them grow. You are creating your whole business and it's going to be orange juice. You are going to make lots of money. It's going to be great. It's going to taste good. You are nourishing these trees. You are getting excited about it. The trees finally grow bigger and begin to fruit and they are not oranges. They are lemons! Then you see people go, "Oh! Well that didn't work!" and they chop the lemon tree down.

I say "No!" Businesses so often look so different than what you think it's going to be. So what if you were willing to change and go, "Oh, we've got lemons! Excellent! What can we do now? We can do lemonade. We can do lemon meringue pie." So many people destroy the possibilities that are showing up because they haven't met the judgment of what they've decided it to be - the orange juice business.

"What possibilities could show up for me today that I've never even imagined possible?"

Infinite Possibilities

Nilofer: I've been wanting to say it, I love the questions! I love the questions that you've given in your book. One of my to-do list is to record all those questions and listen to it every morning when I wake up!

Simone: Great! With questions, you can have anything. You can create anything. There's infinite possibilities available for all of you, for your business, for your money flows, for your life, for everything. The second you go to conclusion and answer, you cut it all off. You close down all those open doors and windows and everything.

For example being a beautiful sunny day and the wind blowing, knowing you get that weather that's very nurturing; the sun overhead, the wind's blowing, maybe you can smell flowers, you can hear the birds chirping. What you do is you shut all the windows and you shut all the doors so that you can have none of it.

How many times have we done that in business because it didn't look the way it was supposed to look? What if you are trying to make business hard rather than have it easy? What if you've made making money hard rather than making it easy? What if money was way easier to show up in your life than what you've ever perceived possible?

Nilofer: I remember reading in one of Gary's books, he says you have to really work hard to keep money away. You use a lot of energy to keep money away. For a few days I've been asking that question, "What are the ways in which I've been keeping money away today?" and I've been PODing and POCing my way through it.

Money, Now And In The Future

Caller: "What can I do to generate money now and in the future?" I do not get how. I do get impulses but it doesn't generate money right away.

Simone: Ok, so great question and the first part you said, for now and in the future. Ok? Then the last part that you just said was it doesn't create money right away. So if money is not showing up right away, are you actually slamming the doors on the future possibilities? You are asking the question for money to show up now and in the future. So what if when it doesn't show up right away, that you've actually closed the doors for the possibilities to show up in the future.

So, the first thing –

Can we destroy and uncreate everywhere that you've uninvited money to show up in the future? What you create today, create your life for tomorrow as well and create the future possibilities for the money flows, the currency flows to show up. So everything that that is, will you destroy and uncreate it? <u>Right and Wrong, Good and Bad, POC and POD, All Nine, Shorts, Boys and Beyonds.</u>

If you run your own business, one week you may get huge amount of money and the next week you may not get as much. Ask questions like "Have I created something new for the future?" But what have you decided success is? Are you calibrating it with the amount of money you have in your bank account?

Because if you are, then you can actually ignore and avoid anything else that can show up, that would add to your business, even if it doesn't show up in the form of money in your bank account. So everything that that is, will you destroy and un-create it? <u>Right and Wrong, Good and Bad, POC and POD, All Nine, Shorts, Boys and Beyonds.</u>

Now the question that this person asked, the first part of it, was brilliant. It's pretty much leaving it at that because it's not a "how". It's not how does money show up. It's like saying that you've got the impulse, "Ok, cool" but then ask the question about those and say, "Will this make me money today or in the future?"

One of the suggestions that Gary Douglas had was to get a little book and write down all the ideas that you have and ask questions every day. For example "Ok, so truth – will you make me money today or in the future?" "Is now the time?" Don't destroy all the places that you've gone to with the ideas that you have that shut the doors of the future possibilities.

So everything that that is, will you destroy and un-create it? <u>Right and Wrong, Good and Bad, POC and POD, All Nine, Shorts, Boys and Beyonds.</u>

Those questions that she asked too are great questions to start with. Keep asking questions. It may show up today, it may show up next week, it may show up next month, it may show up next year. But the second you go to the place of – "It's not working" you've gone back to conclusion. You've gone to conclusion and limitation and the judgment and then you'll stop the flow of what can actually show up. You'll stop the possibility.

I mean even for example what we are doing right now – the tele-summit.

What can you create that would create more possibilities for the tele-summit? Everything that doesn't allow that to show up, will you destroy and uncreate it? Right and Wrong, Good and Bad, POC and POD, All Nine, Shorts, Boys and Beyonds.

Nilofer: One of the questions that I have been asking with the tele-summit is "What physical actualization of a tele-summit beyond this reality am I now capable of generating, creating and instituting? That's been really so amazing for me. The one I did before towards the end, the energy was getting to be so heavy. With this, it's just so light, so light and things just fall into place. Click in place and all the places where things don't work out, where I would have just gone into conclusion before, I'm continuously asking questions. It's just shifting the energy. It's been so much fun to play with it this way.

It's totally different and I can almost feel like the energy of it. It's almost alive and it's taken on this energy of its own and for the first time I can experience that with my business going on. I perceive I have more money, even though I don't physically actually have it. I feel I can get the energy of more money and it's not yet showing up in my physical Universe and I kind of tend to contract myself getting into that.

Simone: Yes. It's also how much energy you would have to use in order to create the density of keeping money, rather than what you are acknowledging now is the space of money that you have in your reality. It is the possibility. This is space of the business that we are talking about. Choice is how you create awareness. Everything that that is, will you destroy and uncreate it? Right and Wrong, Good and Bad, POC and POD, All Nine, Shorts, Boys and Beyonds.

Now with knowing when to choose not to do a business too, when asking a question, you can also ask, "If I quit this, what will it create?" Questions will always give you the energy of what is light or heavy.

Success

Nilofer: That's a great question - "If I quit this, is it going to give me more or less?" It's really how we look at the word "quit" or we look at the word "close" and we've already gone into conclusion that we only close down because we have not succeeded. It's a total different possibility opening up in my Universe because of that.

Simone: You've mentioned success a few times now too and "What does success mean to you?" Talking about if you calibrate success based on the amount of money you have in your bank account. This is another tool you can refer to business as. What you're actually doing is you are giving the business, the project a job to do – "It's got to make you money." Ok? When you are talking about you tele-summit or talking about your business, you say "Oh, this is one of the businesses I make money from." It's more joy. It's the play of business.

Now for starters what is failure anyway? Can you actually fail? Or like we've been saying, does it just show up different to what you thought was going to show up as?

I once had this lady ring me. She had been married for about 10 years, had 6 kids and every day, her husband used to beat up on her. Someone had given her a magnet that had this "Imagine what you'd do if you knew you couldn't fail" and she had it on her fridge. She rang me and she said, "You know what, I just wanted to tell you that I want to thank you. So I've had your magnet on my fridge for the last 6 months," and she said, "I never thought that there was a different possibility. Every day I'd wake up crying and every day my husband would beat up on me and I thought that this is it. This is what my life looks like."

She said, "Every day for 6 months, I read that magnet. I wanted to tell you that I've now left my husband. I'm living in another house and it's like I have the kids, and I'm really happy and I'm creating my life." I felt like, "Wow, that's a $5 magnet." But to me, I was a success. I'd changed this woman's life, the kids' lives, who knows what else! If I was calibrating my success by a $5 magnet, I probably wouldn't have been very successful. You got to have a look at what it is you're actually wishing to create with your business too. What if this was about making money and changing the world?

Nilofer: When I heard you speak about this story in San Francisco, it really changed my whole Universe about success and all the places where I had been making myself so wrong for not making money and feeling unsuccessful because of that. This story just flipped it around on its ears.

Simone: I mean, how much change are you creating for people. Look where you are. Look where this tele-summit is going. It's like "Wow!" What a change you can create in the world!

Nilofer: Absolutely. I had had all these emails from all these people all over the world, writing in and telling me how much they loved the summit, and I was still in that place of "Who me?! I'm not good enough. I'm not successful" Then I heard you speak about this and I said, "Oh my god! I am superbly successful here!"

Simone: Yeah. Also, anyone listening out there too, what if one person could change the world? What if one person does change the world? Everywhere that you don't think that you can actually be the change that the world is actually asking for, will you destroy and un-create it? Every choice you make today, create the change that we are asking for, and everything that that is.

<u>Right and Wrong, Good and Bad, POC and POD, All Nine, Shorts, Boys and Beyonds.</u>

You can run "What stupidity are you using to create the feeling of never being enough that you are choosing, of never having enough that you are choosing?" Everything that that is, will you destroy and uncreate it? <u>Right and Wrong, Good and Bad, POC and POD, All Nine, Shorts, Boys and Beyonds.</u>

That's the space that you can create business from within. That's where you can create and generate anything.

So now, what are you capable of creating, generating and instituting? Everything that doesn't allow you to perceive, know, be and receive that, will you destroy and un-create it? <u>Right and Wrong, Good and Bad, POC and POD, All Nine, Shorts, Boys and Beyonds.</u>

There is a tool in Access. I use it every now and then when there is that heaviness or that conclusion feeling. Get whatever it is that you are looking at : the business, the project etc and get it to turn 180 degrees. Then get it turn another 180 degrees; and turn it another 180 degrees, another 180 degrees etc. You just turn it. Picture you have a sphere and you are turning it a 180 degrees. Then you are turning it another 180 degrees the other way and another 180 degrees the other way and another 180 degrees the other way. Can you see how it starts to create that place of 'You can't keep anything stuck'? 'You can't keep something inside"? It starts spinning so fast that you don't know what's happening anymore.

So everywhere it doesn't let you function like that – your business, your life, your living and everything, all the time, will you destroy and uncreate it? <u>Right and Wrong, Good and Bad, POC and POD, All Nine, Shorts, Boys and Beyonds.</u>

Control Freak

Yes. That's always to do with the speed of change. You remember, we were talking about at some point and we kept saying "I want change, I want change" and then when it really starts to show up, you dug your heels down and go "Oh no, this is not showing up the way I expected it to, so I don't want it". It's showing up so different, or it's showing up too fast or it's showing up too intense. So can we do some clearing around that?

Simone: What stupidity are you using to create the control freak that you are choosing?! Everything that that is, will you destroy and uncreate it? <u>Right and Wrong, Good and Bad, POC and POD, All Nine, Shorts, Boys and Beyonds.</u>

That's basically what you are being when you are refusing to actually receive the change that you are asking for. You go "Oh, but it didn't show up on time!" "It didn't show up exactly the way I wanted it to." "It didn't show up from this person." "It didn't show up when I woke up at 8 o'clock in the morning."

So what, are you a control freak? Being a control freak when the change is going to occur? When the money is actually showing up? When the currency flows are slipping and sliding in?

What if it was the space of possibility? The visual I get is, there's this spinning ball and then you are on it. The ball starts to spin faster, so the only way you can keep on it is by actually running faster, but we try to slow down thinking that if I slow down, the ball is going to slow down. And off we fall!

But what if you do spin off? What's the worst thing that can happen? You jump back up and then there's something else available. For example there's this thing in Star Wars – One of the characters is holding on to one of the galaxies with both hands really tight and another one of the characters says, "If you keep holding on to that galaxy so tight, you will never be actually able to receive anything that shows up from any of the other galaxies."

Everywhere that you are hanging so tight onto the business that you've created or the conclusions or decisions that you've come to (on what it is that you have to be doing or that you should be doing), whether you are a man or a woman, whatever age you are, wherever you live or whatever that is, what if everything was possible? What if you could do, have, create, generate anything? So are you willing to let go of everything? All the answers and the outcomes? Truly?

Ok, so let's do some change here on 3. Everything that doesn't allow you to do, have, be or create that space, just let go of everything on 3, all the answers and the outcomes. 1-2-3.

How does it get any better than that?

Uncomfortable With Change

Nilofer: Ok when things are changing and it's starting to become different and you are feeling a bit uncomfortable about it, what can you do at that point? What tool can you use?

THE MAGIC OF BEING

Simone: Ask a question. "How does it get any better than this?" "What else is possible?" This is a simple, quick, easy phenomenal tool of Access - These questions. Most people ask, "How does it get any better than this?" when something quite bad is happening. Or it is "How does it get any better than this?"

Ask it when a difference is showing up too. Ask it when a change is occurring. Ask it when something great shows up. "How does it get any better than this?" If you have sex, can you decide that that's the best sex you've ever had? What if, then you ask, "How does it get any better than this?"

Same thing in business. If you receive the most amount of money that you've ever received in a day, how does it get any better than this? What if that was just the beginning? What if that was just the tip of the iceberg?

It's so simple!

Nilofer: When I talk to people about Access and I tell them that if you go away with nothing more than just one thing, take this question. "How does it get any better than this?"

Simone: So, let me tell this story of this friend of mine that was in Paris. She had a lot of business to do there and she had decided that she was going to go and stay at this lovely 5 star hotel the night before she left. She didn't make a booking. She went into the hotel and the guy there said, "Can I help you?" She said, "Yes, I'd love to get a room for tonight." He says, "I'm sorry ma'am, we are full."

She looked at him and said, "Well, how does it get any better than this?" because she really had no Plan B. She had decided that she was going to stay there. The guy then said to her, "I'm sorry," and she said "How does it get any better than this?" He said, "Well, let me see what I can do." He went out and got the manager and the manager came out and said, "How can I help you?" and she said, "I'd like to get a room for the night." He said, "I'm sorry ma'am, we are full." She said again "How does it get any better than this?"

Then he looked at the computer and said, "Oh, hang on a second, let me see what I can do." He looked at his computer said, "You know, we've got the penthouse available. I can give it to you for one night at the standard room rate, but you can only have it for one night." She says, "Great. In fact, how does it get any better than this?" So she ends up being in the penthouse suite for the standard room rate and they send a bottle of champagne up to her room! How does it get any better than that?!

That was from simply asking the question of "How does it get any better than this?" You can't be focused on the outcome when you ask these questions. You are asking a question and you're asking the whole entire Universe to assist you on what can show up for you. What are you willing to receive?

Nilofer: I have a similar story about this too. My friend was actually booking a hotel room for an event that she was doing. So emailed the people at the hotel and they gave us a price. So she got the price and she was really happy with it, so she wrote below that saying "How does it get any better than this?" They came back to us and they offered us free snacks and tea!

She wrote that just because she was acknowledging "Oh wow, we got such a great deal, without even expecting anything would happen from there."

Simone: When you don't have any expectations, anything can show up. When you create from the joy of business, you create from the joy of money, you don't make anything significant. You can change anything at any time, without a point of view. How much ease could that create? Would you be willing to have that ease? How does it get any better than that? What else is possible?

WHO IS SIMONE MILASAS

Simone Milasas is a dynamic world leader, author, international speaker and founder of Joy of Business. She is known for demonstrating how to do global business from a place of joy and has been at the forefront of cutting edge business creation and development for over a decade.

Educated in Sydney, Australia at an elite private school, Simone started traveling around the world from a young age working in many diverse industries and businesses and being involved mainly in director and leadership positions of several different companies, at one stage 16 different companies simultaneously.

She has always looked at creating greater possibilities for the future with every choice she makes and has always held a very strong desire to see how we can change the world with and through business.

Simone Milasas has always followed an unconventional approach of exploring as many different avenues of business as possible to make them successful before moving on, and this had led to her vast experience in many areas of business. The Benevolent Capitalism and Leadership approach in business has also been a strong point in her choices - working with Tibetan refugees, Nepalese, Thai and Indians in ways that allowed them to control (and improve) their income streams.

As the worldwide coordinator of Access Consciousness® she has developed a global view, and insight into the way the world currently works, especially in capitalist areas, and how we can go beyond it. As a driving force for greater possibility, Simone is also a leading developer in the Access Possibilities School - an online school offering a different possibility for child education as well as El Lugar, a biodynamic land development project for the creation of a future where sustainability is pre-relevant.

The difference Simone brings to her work is her willingness to look at things differently, contribute to others, and continually make new choices. Simone has developed tools and techniques to dissolve the barriers that can stand in the way of creating success in business and in life. Her global teleconferences and live workshops allow her to reach a wide variety of business people, helping them to build their business from a foundation of joy and openness to create and generate businesses that both sustain themselves and thrive.

HOW TO BECOME MONEY CALLS

By Nilofer Safdar

Do 100x to get 100 million ~ Gary Douglas

Join us http://www.howtobecomemoney100x.com/

CHAPTER THREE

❖

CURING THE INCURABLE

By Liam Phillips

Reality Rebel

A Gentleman Changing Realities

I had my mother visiting me last year and just the day before she had to fly back to India, from where she was visiting, she had a fall in the restroom. She actually had a hairline fracture in one of her ribs. She was in a space where she just couldn't move, she was totally in agony. As her visa couldn't be extended for more than a few days, after 5 days she had to travel. She actually traveled and went back to India. She had with her Liam's book, Curing the Incurable and I was a bit worried about her, as to how she was going to manage. When she went back, it was unbelievable; she was up and about and walking within a month! To have seen her at that point and then in a month she was walking, doing everything normally. I had two of my cousins visit her after a month and I was talking to my cousin, who is about 25 and she said "You know your mom is unbelievable. I get tired walking the whole day and she has so much energy". So, Liam, really, I am in so much gratitude for your book. It is just an amazing book and it has completely, changed my mom's life. Thank you so much.

Thank you. How does it get any better than that? That is one of the reasons I wrote the book. It may be a small book, but it is a powerful one and I often get people talking about how it has changed their lives. I am just so grateful for the tools of Access that allowed me to write that book in the first place. Thank you yet again for acknowledging me, the book and for the Access tools that is just amazing.

From Incurable To Curable

I have found that quite a lot of people come to Access with an "incurable disease", I was always interested in consciousness and when I did get sick I wanted to see how I could change this by becoming more present, more conscious and more aware of what was going on with my body. That book was really like a journal. When I completed Level 2 and 3, I started writing the book and I started getting some really great changes with my body. It was amazing that I also got some really great changes with the way that I was showing up. Being more present and not being bothered by all those thoughts, feelings and emotions that can often be associated with disease. Feelings of 'Oh, poor pitiful me!' and 'What did I do wrong?' When any physical symptoms came up or any emotional symptoms came up, I would use the tools that I had learned in Foundation Level 1, 2, 3 and just write about how they were changing. It was a really great journey for me to write that book.

Who Does It Belong To

When you are in that space where you have a lot of pain or intensity going on in your body, what would be the first thing that you would use? What would be the first tool that you would use?

Let us take a look at that part, the pain! We had a bars swap this evening and the lady that came along asked, "Will this work on period pain?" I said, "Let us see what we can do here". I asked her a few questions like, "Is this pain actually yours?" She did not really get the question until I asked her a few times and then I asked her "Is there anyone in your family that has a lot of period pain?" She started giggling. She had got it right there and then. She suddenly recognized that she was actually entraining the way her mother was creating her body. The next question I asked her was, "Have you ever made a decision to not look like your mother?" and she started giggling again. I knew that it was a yes. If you do have pain, the first question I would ask is, "Who does this belong to?" It may not be your pain; you may just be picking up somebody else's. Keep on asking that question until you get some sort of lightness or some sort of awareness around it. Does that make sense?

Are You Invested In The Outcome

I have been in a lot of classes. I asked the question and it seems to lighten up a little bit but then the pain doesn't go away totally. What do you do in that case?

Before the show, we were looking at how could we change, how could we make sure that the technology was going to work well. I asked you a question, "Are you invested in the outcome?" If you are ever invested in the outcome and you want to get rid of the pain rather than receive the awareness, what you are actually doing is not receiving the awareness and you are really just invested in getting rid of the pain. You have to be aware of whether you are really just trying to get rid of something or do you want to be more aware. For me, no matter what it is, my healing journey has always been about being more aware of what my body is gifting me, what my body is trying to tell me, and what awareness that I am not quite getting. If it keeps on returning it just means that you have either got an investment in the outcome of getting rid of it or that you just haven't quite got the question yet that will unlock it. There may be something that you really love about it and hence you keep choosing it.

It is always the 3 things; either you are invested in the outcome or you need to keep asking the question or what do you love about it?

It is always about following the energy or never trying to fit into an answer. It is often going to be one of those three things because if you ever come to a conclusion on anything, like in the Louise Hay's book 'You can heal your life' there is a part that says if you have a lot of lower back pain it can also be an indication that you have money issues. That may work 90 percent of the time but if that is not actually it and you decided that, that is what it is you will never be able to change. With any of the tools I am give you tonight, please play with them and see what you can create and generate with them. Be playful with them and don't ever come to any conclusion and never be in any expectation of how the change is going to show up for you, if you do that you will just stick yourself with the conclusion or the expectation.

This Can Never Change

Where these questions keep coming from is somewhere we buy into this reality or this point of view. The pain, especially people who are dealing with a really long term issue going on in their body, say, "My God, this is never going to change and I have all this going on, I have used so many things and this has not changed".

Let us have a look at that first before I do a clearing on it. I really appreciate you asking me this question because it brings up a lot of energy. If you ever said, "Oh, I am never going to get rid of it," your point of view creates your reality. If anybody has that old record player going in their head, perhaps we should call it a CD going on in your head now. "I can't change this, I have tried everything and nothing works" that is exactly what you are going to create, more of that. Let us do a clearing for that.

What stupidity are you using with the healing you are choosing and everything that is, will you destroy and uncreate it all? <u>Right and Wrong, Good and Bad, Pod and Poc, All 9, Shorts, Boys and Beyonds.</u>

Whatever stupidity (stupidity is where you step out of awareness) you are using with pain, or emotional pain, or victimhood, you are choosing it! When I was sick, there was a point where I would suddenly recognize that I was creating or choosing the disease. People often say, "What disease did you suffer from?" My answer to them now is, "I created ulcerative colitis, I know I created it, I chose it for whatever bizarre reason."

For whatever reason you created a disease for would you now be willing to give up the reason? And destroy and uncreate it? <u>Right and Wrong, Good and Bad, Pod and Poc, All 9, Shorts, Boys and Beyonds.</u>

It is the reason, decisions, judgments and the conclusions that often create the diseases within our bodies. How does it get any better than that?

You are an infinite being you know everything about you and everything that is going on in your life, which is what I like about Access. The tagline is, "Empowering people to know that they know." We get a lot of people who come to Access or Curing the Incurable and they say, "Oh yes, oh I know that, yes". No body has ever told you that perhaps that pain doesn't belong to you. May be if they told you that all the thoughts, feelings and emotions that you are having are not yours. Oh dear! What if you are creating your whole reality based on somebody else's point of view, is no wonder that we get these weird things like diseases occurring in our body.

Can I ask you a question, "Who does it belong to?" in particular? If you have actually created your body based on someone else's reality and you have actually locked it in place in your body, would it be sufficient to actually just do that tool "Who does it belong to?" once or twice and have the disease going on in your body change?

It is absolutely individual. Have you ever noticed how many people when they really want to do something, perhaps they haven't got enough money to do an Access class or perhaps they haven't got enough money to buy a car, but they really want it, they will find a way to get that money to get whatever it is that they desire. That is when you actually make a demand on yourself to choose the change.

If you just get that any investment in the outcome you will stick yourself. If I just say, "Who does this belong to?" My diabetes is just going to drop away, the second part is the investment in the outcome, it is the conclusion. Instead if you go, "Okay. Right, what's it going to take to change this?" and you are going to make a demand, "Whatever it takes I am going to do it and be it to change this."

When you actually ask that question "Who does this belong to?" you may actually get awareness and then you can return it to sender. For some people it could be just like the lady with the period pain today in the bars swap, we had 3 to 4 questions, it took about 2 and a half minutes and then she looked up and she looked at everybody else in the bars swap and said, "Oh my God! It's gone." As she was willing to receive it and was willing to actually let go of it, she was willing to change it. It is really what you are willing to or unwilling to change that if you are willing to change it, will change your reality and your body and manifest as total consciousness. Everything that doesn't allow that to occur with total ease can we now destroy and uncreate it? <u>Right and Wrong, Good and Bad, Pod and Poc, All 9, Shorts, Boys and Beyonds.</u>

I have seen this in action with a lot of people, they've tried something and it doesn't work and they come to the conclusion that hasn't worked. As soon as you come to the conclusion that it hasn't worked, it won't show up as working, it will show up as not working. As soon as you say, "Oh, I have tried that last thing it didn't work" then you are not going to receive the change that you desire, instead turn it into a question, "Oh, I did the Bars, okay? And the change hasn't shown up quite yet, what else is possible?" Go back into question because something like Bars will open you up to more receiving and you may find that the diet or medication or therapist or more Access processes comes into your life, is going to create the change that your body has been asking for and you have been asking for.

Include Your Body

What do you do when after 30 years of adrenal (stage 3 exertion), stomach, digestive system basically does not work at all, female hormonal (low estrogen, no progesterone and no ovulation) challenges, no one will treat you because you are too complex a case; added to that anxiety which makes you think you need to go to the toilet when you go out, so you no longer go out.

The "Doing" doesn't really matter. Let's have look at the energy of that! Is it heavy or is it light? It is heavy, isn't it? All those signs and symptoms that we buy as real are heavy (to the person who wrote in, I am not having a go at you at all!) I was in your shoes exactly and I did so much research, I started to look at things and was filled with so many facts and points of view. Then there were all these conflicting ideas like don't eat fruit and eat fruit etc, I got really confused. One of the things I would ask is "Are you separate from your body or are you in your body or is your body actually part of you?" If you get that your body is actually part of you then what awareness is your body trying to gift to you, because every single sign and symptom is really just your body trying to tell you something, trying to communicate with you.

If you can actually ask your body and start to include it in all the therapies and all the medications that you are on and diets that you are trying then you can have a different possibility. Have you actually ever asked your body, "Hey body, would you like this diet; hey body, do you require this medication; hey body, do you need to go and see this therapist?"

You can then start to actually "do" the communion with your body and that way you will start to understand what it is that your body is trying to tell you, and you will get more freedom from all of those thoughts, feelings and emotions. Those are the things that are locking you up. Ask your body.

Also with every thought, feeling and emotion of frustration, anxiety, start asking "Who does this belong to?" 98 percent of your thoughts, feelings and emotions are not yours and then you will start to get clear that you are picking up a lot of stuff that is not actually yours. You get them off the internet when you do research or from other people's points of view. You know I don't even think we notice when we talk to other people about the sickness we created that we also start to buy their point of view.

Communication

If you are an infinite being you think you might be actually able to communicate in another way other than just talking?

Do you think that bodies might be able to communicate with each other without actually having to talk? How many people out there in Radio Land have walked into a room and there has been an argument there before and you can feel the heaviness and the anger. Everybody has had that. 99 percent of the people on this call have anyway. When your mum is going to ring you, and 5 minutes before you think, "Oh, maybe I should ring mum today". 5 minutes later she rings you, that is because you are aware and you are an infinite being. This is a telepathic communication and is often not cognitive.

A Different Reality With Healing

This happens a lot with me when I go into a place and then suddenly I have this pain show up all over my body and I say, "I don't know where this has come from, I was feeling so good!" Now I have started asking the question, "Who does this belong to?" In the past I would say, "Oh my God, there I go again, back in pain again." But not anymore.

I don't know how it is with you, I am 47 and I had 14 odd years of, "I have got pain in my body" Or I have a sign or a symptom in my body and therefore it means that I am getting the flu, it means I am coming down with chicken pox, it means that I am going to have a back ache now for the next 3 weeks because I just twisted my back. If you are actually willing to ask that question, "Who does it belong to?" and start throwing out all those conclusions and projections that people have projected at you then you can actually have a different reality. What will that be like if you are willing to have a different reality where healing was beyond what they say!

I guess what I am hearing is again that whole conversation about being vested in the outcome and you are just standing there and making a demand that I want this to change and I don't care how the change shows up. I don't even care what the change is going to look like, but it just has to change.

That is the thing, because how many people actually demand a change but they are only wanting to see the change the way they have decided it is going to look like. That is Investment in the outcome.

We just stick ourselves so much with prejudices. We shouldn't. I want this to change and it has to change and this way and that is the only way that I am going to acknowledge that it has changed and any thing else does not count as change.

Where is the receiving in that? You are only able to receive one avenue of change that way. This is why Bars are so cool because it is about receiving. If you are willing to stop being invested and receive everything, even judgments, then you actually have a different possibility show up.

Receiving Judgments

Amazing! You said if you are willing to receive everything including judgment then you have a different possibility showing up. Let us talk about that because a lot of us have this point of view that we don't want to receive anyone's judgment.

How much energy do you have to use to not receive somebody's judgments or how many walls do you have to build between you and another person so you don't receive their judgment?

If you were to lower those barriers and were not to have those walls around you then wouldn't this judgment come and stick to you?

No, because you would be totally vulnerable and open. You would receive it and it would just go straight through you. It is when you put the walls up, they will bounce off that wall and you would not be able to receive anything else from that person. You won't be able to receive money from them, healing from them, anything from them if you've got this wall up.

It is like the judgment! If you let down your barriers, if you let down those walls it is like the judgments just pass through you and just go away. What I am aware of right now is this judgment which a lot of people have about other people who are going through issues in their lives? "Oh my God, you are always down with a headache" or "You are always down with xyz" or "You are always like this". And personally I have received judgment many times and obviously haven't just received it.

What if you were grateful for every judgment that came to you, and used it to your advantage?

How do you use judgment to your advantage?

What is judgment? Judgment is just energy. It can be a positive energy or a negative energy. If you are willing to receive the positive ones, you will be able to receive 50 percent of the judgment but not the other 50 percent. You actually cut off receiving from 50 percent of the judgments. If you are willing to receive all the judgments, that will actually energize you. You could actually eat them, "Oh thank you for that judgment."

Can you give me some more judgment; can you give me some more energy? It is just energy. You don't have to make it right or wrong. They are what they are.

It is just there without any point of view and whatever is coming at you just receive it. I like that.

Point of view. The great thing about being able to receive judgments is that you will be able to see when somebody is going to stick you with some "bad" intention; you will see it a mile away.

You mean if you are willing to receive it, it is just going to pass through you and not really going to stick you.

Yes. Why don't we all of us that are listening to this right now, because it has got real and heavy, what if we just start to expand right out, expand right out across the whole of the Arab Emirates and the whole of

Australia and connect the two, right across the whole of the world and expand right out beyond the farthest region of the Universe, thank you very much! How can it get better at that? If you are that big, if you are that infinite, do you really think a judgment will have any power over you?

Absolutely not. It is just like water off a duck's back, it just disappears.

Right. Judgment cannot stand in the face of total presence, awareness and consciousness.

I like this tool that you shared about judgment, expanding out. How does it get any better than that?

Whenever you start to expand any judgment right out, you will notice that the judgment will start to get smaller and smaller and smaller.

"If it's just changing one's perspective, why do cancer patients still suffer, although eating the proper thing and doing their best?"

What Do You Love About This That You Are Not Willing To Change

You really got to ask each individual themselves. How does it get any better than that? If you are willing to looking at people with out a point of view, they are choosing what they are choosing, would you then allow them to choose whatever they are choosing. If they are choosing cancer, it is not what I would choose. I choose something totally different. Is there anything I can contribute to that and then allow them the choice. If they are looking at making the changes and there is an energetic curiosity, may be then you could ask the question, "What do you love about this that you are not willing to change?"

What is that you love about cancer? That is a great question. That question will throw them a bit and they will usually answer, "There is nothing I love about cancer!" Don't worry about their answer, the question will start to work what ever they say. Then just ask them again, "Is there something that you like or love about cancer? What is the function of cancer?"

Gary once asked this of a lady who had cancer. And he said that, "What do you love about cancer?" And she said, "Nothing". And after asking that question a few times what came out was that she was dying to get out of her relationship. Gary actually asked her, "What is it that you are dying to get out" and when he asked her that, She said, "Oh, I would like to get out of my relationship." He said, "Why don't you get a divorce then". She said, "No, I can't get a divorce because my kids would never be able to handle it." The lady was 74 and Gary said, "How old is your youngest kid" and she said 58! She had some really crazy ideas that her kids couldn't handle the change. You know there are 2 questions that you can ask if somebody is choosing to kill their body, "What do you love about it?" and "What are you dying to get out of?"

Commitment To Healing Others

"My husband has MS and he is having more problems walking, standing, balancing. I run Bars on him when he allows it. What are some interesting points of view that I can be to give him space? I have learnt so many healing modalities to heal myself and others; I am trying not to push (my natural tendency)"

You want to scratch that word 'try' and remove it from your lexical repertoire. Try and stand up, you can't, you either stand up or you don't.

You know the question I love about trying is 'try to get pregnant'. You are either pregnant or you are not.

Exactly. You are either pregnant or you're not, not try. That's really interesting, how many people who would like a baby and they say, "We are trying to have a baby." Yes mate, you actually got to do it, you don't just try. That is one word that I would be eliminating from my vocabulary, and that is all right. With this particular person, maybe you need to look at all the lifetimes that you have had with this person and all the oaths, vows, fealties, commealties, swearing, hexes, vexes and the curses that you had with them and destroy and uncreate them across all our time, in all realities because if you have made a commitment to healing that person when they don't want to be healed then you are going to be, trying.

All those blood oaths, fealties, swearing, committing, hexes, vexes, curses that you had with your significant other, would you now be willing to destroy and uncreate all of those? <u>Right and Wrong, Good and Bad, Pod and Poc, All 9, Shorts, Boys and Beyonds.</u>

I worked with a dog that had a commitment to healing its owner of cancer and I explained to the dog or gave it the energy that the owner was choosing cancer and was going to keep on choosing that no matter what and the dog still chose to take the cancer out of the body because the dog had a commitment to it and I asked it if it wanted to change that commitment and it said "no." I said, alright. I said, "You will probably die, you realize that don't you?" and the dog said, "Yes." It was willing to die for its owner. About 6 weeks later it died. When you have a commitment to healing somebody then you can't see any other possibility, you always have to push that energy at that person, "I have got to heal this person!" They keep on going, "I don't want to be healed, let me live my choice." Then all that time that you are pushing energy at them they are resisting it and nothing changes.

Interesting! That really brought up a lot of heavy energy. How many of us listening on the line have commitments to healing others? Let us do some clearing.

How many of you have got a commitment to healing your significant other? That could be your husband, your wife, your son, your daughter, your grandmother. Would you now be willing to give up those commitments so that everybody can change? Everything that doesn't allow that, lets destroy and uncreate it. <u>Right and Wrong, Good and Bad, Pod and Poc, All 9, Shorts, Boys and Beyonds.</u>

It is heavy as mountain. How does it get any better than that?

Allergies

"Every now and then it seems like I am allergic to everything and it just seems to get worse. Environment, cold weather, pets, dust, some foods; never knowing what will set off the next set of discomfort. Any clearings would be great, thanks."

Am I allergic to my body or is my body allergic to me?

And depending on what answer you get there, whichever one is light is true for you. Let us have a look at the first one, "Am I allergic to my body?" You could expand on that and ask "Who or what am I allergic to?" And "Who or what am I allergic too that if I did not resist it would make this go right away?"

How does it get any better than that?

Keep destroying and uncreating all the points of view that "my body is allergic to…." If you are pushing and shoving things into your body without asking it, what will that create? I used to do the Neti pot; where you run salt water through your nostrils to clean your nostrils? It worked but then I bought the idea I should do it everyday instead of asking my body. I am cute not bright. What do you think that created?

Just before we came on the show, I was watching a TV program where they were selling a juicer and they were telling us all the benefits of ginger or this, that and other about how ginger cures Lupus and stuff. You think your body might actually be having Lupus for particular reason? Maybe it is not wrongness, maybe it is there because you are irritating it. What points of view are irritable to your body? Are you including your body in the decisions that you are making for it? That's a great question.

How many times do we do things which we don't include our body? Just 99 percent of the times I think so.

99 million percent of the time, I'd say. Believe me. I am changing that and I am making more demands. We went clothes shopping the other

day and I said, "My God, everything is on sale" I just wanted to buy everything, all the tools went out the window. Then I stopped. "Okay, I will just ask my body here, which clothes would you like to have body?" And it started to choose clothes that fitted my body really well and usually it is very difficult to find clothes, they just started jumping off the shelves at me as soon as I started including my body.

Communion With Bodies

Liam is there any clearing that you can do so that we can have more communion with our body, so we can listen to our body more?

Just ask that question, "Body, would you like to eat this? Body, would you like to wear that? Body, which way would you like to go on a walk today? Body, do you want to do yoga today?" I am not going to shout at it or push it to do what it doesn't really desire to do.

What energy, space and consciousness can I be that will allow me total ease and communion with my body and everything that doesn't allow that to occur will you destroy and uncreate it? <u>Right and Wrong, Good and Bad, Pod and Poc, All 9, Shorts, Boys and Beyonds.</u>

I have actually got a monthly call series called 'Get to know your body' where we will be running a whole bunch of clearings on whatever your body needs to heal your and whatever it needs to heal other people's body. You want to check that out, you can check that on my website liamphillips.com. The reason I bring that up is because your body is just a most amazing thing, it is a total miracle and how often do you actually acknowledge that? Often? Every day? Every choice that we make with it? Or hardly at all?

What stupidity are you using to avoid your body that you could be choosing are you choosing and everything that is, will you destroy and uncreate all of that? <u>Right and Wrong, Good and Bad, Pod and Poc, All 9, Shorts, Boys and Beyonds.</u>

What stupidity are you using to totally avoid all the communication from your body and everything that is will you destroy and uncreate it all? <u>Right and Wrong, Good and Bad, Pod and Poc, All 9, Shorts, Boys and Beyonds.</u>

Light And Heavy

"How do you know the difference between heavy and fear or resistance and how do you know the difference between true lightness and the energy of joy and wishing that it was true?"

The question here is to ask "Are you an infinite being?" An infinite being would not have any fear whatsoever and I can prove it to all of you out there listening to this. If you were in a situation, let us say a car accident or the like, do you go nuts and crazy, screaming and yelling or do you just get down to business and create whatever energy is required to change that?

Create, create, and create. I go totally calm, I do whatever needs to be done and I am done with it. And I go bonkers afterwards.

You go bonkers afterwards because your brain has been taught to do so. When you actually need total presence and you know exactly what to do, you know what's light and what is heavy. You intrinsically know what's doable and what's not, and you know intrinsically what's heavy, anything that is heavy is a contraction. Ask the question or move on and ask, "Okay, what else is possible here?" Lightness is an expansion and you can practice that everyday just expanding and we did that earlier on in the show where we just expanded out of your living room wherever you are right across the planet and keep on expanding and expanding until things start to get lighter. And get your Bars run.

A lot of people ask me that question, "How do I know what is the difference between light and heavy?"

You know the difference between light and heavy, you knew when you were signing you life away on that house and you say, "This is feeling a bit heavy, I don't think I should be doing this" but you do it anyway. That is when you go against your knowing.

When you make a choice against your knowing you can say, "Okay, that wasn't my best choice." Acknowledge it and move on. What will it take for me to perceive, know, be and receive the difference between light and heavy? And light is not right and heavy is not wrong, it is not a judgment. It is awareness.

Now would you be willing to be in allowance of you and then allowance of your body? And anywhere anyway you are not, can we now destroy and uncreate all of that? <u>Right and Wrong, Good and Bad, Pod and Poc, All 9, Shorts, Boys and Beyonds.</u>

What is light for you is true for you in that 10 seconds and what is heavy is a lie for you in that 10 seconds.

What feels light to you might not feel light to someone else. I am going to ask you a question for all you people. I have got this really nice house out in the Mediterranean and I am going to invite you all for lobster and champagne, for a whole day cruising around the Med. How does it get any better than that? Okay cool. Or my house needs cleaning, and it hasn't been cleaned for the last 2 years and it is full of cobwebs and dust, which one is light for you?

Obviously I will choose the lobster and champagne.

For me it is not obvious, some people might actually feel lighter to clean the house.

Where I was answering that was if you were to ask that question and I were to ask the question. If it were your house to be cleaned then maybe I might feel lighter choosing champagne and lobster. But if it was my house then it would be the opposite.

That is not actually going with the lightness, it's more about your reasons and justifications. Heavy and light is not about reasons and justifications. It's literally an awareness of the energy.

You may get heaviness when you get on the yacht even if you have all the reasons and justification to go. The heaviness may be a Hurricane forming. My grandmother did that, when she was about 22 years old she was to go on a trip to the Isle of Wight, this was from London to the Isle of Wight and it is was about 5 hours' drive in those days. There weren't many cars so it was very exciting, the car was new, hardly anyone had a car. They were going in the car and all her friends were, "Come on, you'll have fun!" and she said no because it was heavy as hell. They all died, she didn't go. You really got to ask "is this heavy or light?"

Are You Overriding Your Body

"How do you know if you are really hearing your body's answers? I feel like my mind keeps overriding my body. I have always had this challenge with muscle testing too."

There are a couple of things there, how will I know I always have this problem with my mind overriding? If you know that you are overriding it then you know you are overriding it. Stop. It is not about getting the right or wrong answer. You know sometimes I get it wrong, then I say to my body "I am sorry body, what can I do to make up for the damage done?" It is not about getting the right answer; it is about asking the questions. That is the key, if you are willing to ask the question of your body, because your body has very few points of view, but if you are actually willing to ask it a question then it starts to create that communion and it doesn't matter whether you get it right or wrong. If you are willing to step out of judging, about going into the rightness and the wrongness of the answer then it really doesn't matter, okay. If you mess up, maybe you will spend a couple of hours vomiting or something, okay next time you will know better. How does it get any better than that? It will just be your body giving you the awareness that is not the way it wanted to be. It's no biggie, you didn't get it wrong, it is an awareness. How cool are you, you just got an awareness.

Infinite Possibilities Of Life And Living

"Would infinite possibilities even mean being willing to receive death? That would be quite a challenge."

Would infinite possibilities even mean willing to receive death? That would be quite a challenge. No I don't think so. I think the challenge would be receiving infinite possibilities to create your life and living. Everything is the opposite of what it appears to be. It is how many people are actually willing to live and actually stepping to living and how many are actually already half dead because they are never willing to create the adventure we call life. How many people are actually trying to avoid death rather than just living life to the utmost? If you are actually focusing on the death then you are creating the death, more death, and more disease. What if you ask that question, "What will it take for me to actually receive the infinite possibility of life and living?" And when death comes along you will be able to go, "Oh okay cool. Ah, there is a choice." What is death after all? Are you an infinite being and does an infinite being truly die?

Can you perceive how the energy totally changed when you started asking the question of life and living? It is like I got this cool breeze flowing all over...

Wow, you mean you can actually choose life and living or disease and pain, you have a choice today. You can choose life, living and joy or you can choose death, disease, pain, suffering. That is your choice today, what do you choose? If you are choosing the death, the dying, the pain, the suffering, it is just a choice. One is not right and one is not wrong; it is just a choice, choice to create awareness. If you want to indulge in the death then do that, really indulge in it, see what that would be like and what that would create in the world. And what would that create with your family, what would that create in all the things, the project that you haven't completed yet and see if that is actually the choice that you want in these 10 seconds. Indulge in it for a second. You could indulge in totally living your life in 10 second increments. In these 10 seconds, I am going to choose this and in the next 10 seconds it is like, "Oh! I think I am going to write my book." You are going to have so much fun doing that you might not want to get rid of diseases. LOL

Problem Solver

If you are a problem solver you are going to have to find lots of problems to solve, don't you? How does it get any better than that? What if instead of creating problems you asked questions?

Heredity

"I have osteoporosis, hernia and blood pressure and I think I have got them all from my family, so can you suggest some process for this?"

You think or you know? I would first of all get the correct information, if you are having a lot of these things showing up and you are not getting the correct information from doctors then I would be asking different questions with different doctors and going to get more awareness. I had a friend who had high blood pressure and they gave him these tablets, so he started taking the tablets and he got the awareness that there was still something not quite right so he went to another doctor for a second opinion. They found that he actually had something wrong with one of the valves in his heart. He had a blood clot somewhere and he had a stent put in and if he had continued on with the thinning of the blood medication, the blood clot would have moved to his heart in the end and he would have died!

When dealing with these sorts of things always be willing to get the correct information and keep asking questions and at the same time if it is termed heredity ask, "Wow, okay so how many oaths, vows, commealties, fealties, blood oaths and swearings have I got with healing my family?" Will you now recant, rescind, revoke, reclaim, renounce, denounce, destroy and uncreate all of that and return it to sender from whence it came, never to return here, to you or your body or to this reality ever again.

Start really asking your body, especially with all the judgments and the separations, expectations and projections that you have picked up from everybody else, will you now destroy and uncreate and all of those, and the way you have reacted to them or aligned and agreed with them, pod and Poc it? <u>Right and Wrong, Good and Bad, Pod and Poc, All 9, Shorts, Boys and Beyonds.</u>

Thank you so much. Just before I leave perhaps before you go to sleep tonight you could destroy and uncreate your judgments with your body. Ask more questions and then maybe you will get a different possibility showing up, for you and for your beautiful body.

WHO IS LIAM PHILLIPS

Cute, funny, weird and occasionally devilish Liam opens doorways to different and new possibilities every day with all that he meets. But this was not always the way! Liam grew up as a shy and uncomfortable boy which later turned to alcoholism, self judgment, intense fear of people and finally disease that almost killed him! With just 24 hours to live Liam opened one of those doors to different possibilities and chose to step through it.

Now the Author of 9 books, Liam travels the world facilitating Access Consciousness classes and inviting people to different possibilities. Liam's message to the world is about having the courage to choose and be the uniqueness of you! And you don't have to wait or create pain and suffering in your reality before you make that choice! What if you could actually live the life YOU know is possible and never have to fit any box of limitation?

7 DAYS OF PAIN RELIEF CHALLENGE

By Nilofer Safdar

Would you like to get relief from pain? Without surgery, medication or other invasive means. Join us at http://magicofbeing.com

CHAPTER FOUR

❖

HOW TO GET THE RELATIONSHIP YOU REALLY WANT

By Dr Kacie Crisp

Author, International Seminar Facilitator,

Creator Of Body Miracles

How To Get The Relationship You Really Want?

"What you've been looking for is guaranteed not to get you what you really want."

This is the reality. Most would be surprised at it. People who might have tried and failed at relationships many times may have noticed this. I am sure my point would seem contradictory at first. I strongly want to mention the fact that attraction is not necessarily our friend in creating a relationship that lasts. When we feel attracted to somebody what we are most often picking up is what they do with energy.

Being attracted to somebody is being aware of someone who pulls energy massively. If you want to know what pulling energy massively looks like, rent the movie The Tourist, with Angelina Jolie. There are some mesmerizing beautiful scenes of Paris, Venice and Europe where she is walking down the streets. She is pulling energy so intensely that she could attract and seduce anyone, even women! That's what someone pulling your energy feels like.

Mostly when we are attracted to somebody we don't see if they are good material for great relationships but that they have this talent to actually pull energy. They may not be great at relationships though. Often such people who have that capacity can pull the energy, attract you but when it comes to actually delivering something that's worth having or continuing a relationship, they might not have what you think you are looking for.

Energy Pulls

It's really easy to pull energy. You don't have to visualize it. All you have to do is just ask the energy to come towards you and through you. You don't want it to stop at you. You pull it towards you and through you, and contrary to what you might think, when you pull someone's energy, it feels good to them. You don't deplete them when you pull energy through them, you get energy from them through you, and you actually pull more energy into them as well so they actually feel energized. So they feel good too.

Negative Energy and Energy Pulls

The energy doesn't stop at you. It just comes through you. So negative, positive or neutral, you're just pulling it through you and it doesn't stop with you. If you just notice that if you have no point of view about it, then what you are calling negative energy is not going to hurt you.

Actually is there really such a thing as negative energy? I know lots of people believe in it, but, does it really exist or is there just energy that we happen to judge?

The truth is, "Can anything be negative or positive except that we judge it to be negative or positive?"

What you are doing is just pulling energy from the person and pulling it through you and going beyond you? What happens after that?

Just keep pulling it. If you want to practice this, just go into your local coffee shop and just stand by the door and pull energy from every single person in the room. Don't worry; they are not going to embarrass you by everyone turning around at once. Just pull until people start to turn around and look at you and they'll just look one at a time. The kids will look first. They'll know you are doing something, even though they won't know what it is. Smile at them.

If it doesn't seem that pulling energy is working, just ask it to pull a 100 times stronger and see what happens. Keep practicing that until you can get everybody to turn around. You can also use this in restaurants. I do this all the time when the waiter is being slow at bringing the cheque. I just pull energy from them not that I want to start a relationship with a waiter; I just want to pay my bill and get out.

Another misconception about who we are really attracted to is a lot of people have an idea who's their type.

Creating A Relationship With Energy Pulls

You mean people are pulling energy from you and that's how you are attracted to them. How do you know if that person is going to be nurturing to you, if that relationship is going to be supportive, nurturing, caring and loving for you?

It's fun to actually play with. You can ask your body to show you who would be nurturing to you. There's a woman I facilitated classes with who had 2 kids of school age and a disastrous history of relationships. I taught her this one tool and she found the man of her dreams, has a new baby, is totally happy. This all happened within a couple of months of doing the Access Consciousness Foundation and Level 1 with me. So this tool actually does work. All you have to do is ask your body to show you who would be nurturing to you.

Body And Being

Are you defining here that your body is separate from you?

Your body has a point of view and we, **the Being,** tend to override our body. Our body does things that we don't necessarily do. We don't eat, our body eats. We don't have sex, our body has sex. We don't wear clothes, our body wears clothes. Doesn't it make sense to consult our body about things that are relevant to the body? Someone being nurturing to you certainly has to include a component of your body. Your body is a little bit more like an animal, than we - the thinking beings-are. Animals are a lot smarter and more conscious than we are. They are not easily fooled. We think they are not as smart as us because they don't think, but they are actually more aware than us because they don't think. You can get more awareness sometimes from asking your body who would be nurturing to you.

You are asking your body to find someone who is nurturing to you, meaning someone who is going to be nurturing to the body. What about **the Being***? How do you find someone who is also going to be nurturing to the being?*

In my opinion, the best way to know if a relationship is going to be satisfying and work for you is to notice how it is in the present. Many people go fast-forward into the future. They think, "the relationship isn't so great right now, but once I get an engagement ring, once we are married, once we move in together then it will be fine." No, the best prediction of what the relationship is going to be is what it is right now. If you feel relaxed, enjoy the person's company, having fun being with them, from my point of view that's the best predictor about whether it will be fun to be with them in the future.

I know what you are talking about. Been there, done that, totally, the futuristic point of view.

What if everything that you've judged as a mistake in your past relationships and every place you are judging yourself for your failures in your relationship and every place anybody listening doesn't have a relationship and are judging themselves for being a failure for not having a relationship, all those judgments, will you please rescind, revoke, recant, renounce, denounce, destroy and un-create all that? <u>Right and Wrong, Good and Bad, All Nine, POD and POC, Shorts, Boys and</u>

<u>Beyonds.</u>

What if instead of all your past relationship failures, because I had my share of them too, what if instead of thinking they were proof that there was something irrevocably wrong with you, what if instead they were wonderful lessons that showed you exactly what you didn't want and were actually creating a possibility for you to create a relationship that would work for you? Everything that keeps you from seeing that will you destroy and uncreate it all? <u>Right and Wrong, Good and Bad, All Nine, POD and POC, Shorts, Boys and Beyonds.</u>

So Called Failures

I realized this when I wrote my book and finally got it through my head that my relationship with David is different than most other people's relationships. I wasn't aware of that for a long time. Then I looked at some of the things that I did thatwere different and realized that the differentness came from what I'd learned in the relationships previous to the current one were what we would call in this reality "failures."

For instance, most people do things that I call fast-forward. They see a guy across a crowded room and all of a sudden, they are planning their wedding. They go way into the future and block off their awareness of what's happening now. Because I hadn't had a relationship that lasted long enough to project a future about, I just didn't do that. He was here, he was with me for the summer, and I was willing to enjoy that without playing it off into the future. What I thought was a failure because no relationship lasted actually allowed me to create something greater.

Every place that you've kept yourself from seeing what you've learnt in your past relationships is giving you valuable gifts that will allow you to create something greater in the future if you would, will you please destroy and un-create it all? <u>Right and Wrong, Good and Bad, All Nine, POD and POC, Shorts, Boys and Beyonds.</u>

Another thing about saying, "Well this person is my type" is how much judgment does that entail? When you say, "Oh, only this kind of person, only somebody who's 6'2" with eyes of blue and blond hair is my type", and if somebody who is wonderfully fun to be, with maybe even rich, nurturing to you, nurturing to your body shows up? But the guy is only 5'8" and he's got brown hair and brown eyes, can you even see him? No! Because you have all these decisions and judgments that the guy that's going to work for you or the woman who's going to work for you--usually it's women listening to me--this person is going to work for you looks like a certain thing, which stops you from seeing anyone else who could be fabulous and wonderful.

All the decisions, judgments, commitments and conclusions you have about what your "type" is and the only person you are willing to receive, care, affection, love and create a relationship or communion with, everything that is, will you please rescind, revoke, recant, renounce, denounce, destroy and un-create all that? <u>Right and Wrong, Good and Bad, All Nine, POD and POC, Shorts, Boys and Beyonds.</u>

There's another thing about being passionately attracted to people.

Firstly, Passion means crucifixion! When you are passionately attracted to somebody and want a relationship with them, a crucifixion might be in your future. Passion might not be your best choice.

Secondly, somebody that you feel that intense attraction to, you look across a crowded room and exclaim "Her! I've got to have her", "I've got to have him", that's somebody that you have oaths, vows, swearings, promises to from past lifetimes, because in past lifetimes you stood up and the church said "till death do you part", which is fine except that do you as an infinite being ever die? No. So, you've got all of these old promises from 4 trillion years ago floating around the Universe and when someone shows up on a plane, in a bar, wherever you meet people, that you have some promise with, you instantly feel that intense, magnetic attraction. Now does that mean that you can't be with a soul mate from your past life? No, it doesn't mean that. You can still be with the people that you loved in the past life, but if you will un-do all the promises you had with them in the past lives, you can actually be more present and available to have more fun in this lifetime.

Think of someone you had a relationship with, maybe a romantic one, maybe something else that you just can't get clear on and you feel like you never have choice.

All the oaths, vows, swearings, fealties, commealties, you have with that person, would you please rescind, revoke, recant, reclaim, renounce, denounce, destroy and uncreate all that? <u>Right and Wrong, Good and Bad, All Nine, POD and POC, Shorts, Boys and Beyonds.</u>

A fealty is loyalty that we promise to a liege or a lord in feudal times and commealty is a fealty that's built into our physical structure, like a blood oath on steroids. When you have that promise with someone, how free are you? Maybe somebody was a king, maybe your hot prospect in this lifetime was a king in a past lifetime and you pledged to die for them. Do you really wish to enter into a relationship where your promise would still exist is "Oh, I'm going to die for this person"? Or would you rather start with a clean slate and have some fun?

Can we destroy and uncreate all these fealties or whatever to all the people that we've had in all the lifetimes?

All the oaths, vows, swearings, fealties, commealties, you did to anyone and in any lifetime, would you please rescind, revoke, recant, reclaim, renounce, denounce, destroy and uncreate all that? <u>Right and Wrong, Good and Bad, All Nine, POD and POC, Shorts, Boys and Beyonds.</u>

All the oaths, vows, swearings, fealties, commealties, you have in all lifetimes, all realities, all dimensions and anything else I haven't named, would you please rescind, revoke, recant, reclaim, renounce, denounce, destroy and un-create all that as well? <u>Right and Wrong, Good and Bad, All Nine, POD and POC, Shorts, Boys and Beyonds.</u>

Some people reading might feel a little space between their ears. "What's happening?"

What's happening is a lot of reference points you've been using for creating your relationships have been erased. Your reference points are those posts surveyors stick in the ground when they are making a site for a road expansion. They tell the surveyors where the road should be. Your reference points are the things that tell you where you should sit and who you should be, but your points of view about where you should sit and who you should be is actually how you create the limitations of this reality. Getting rid of the reference points, even if you feel a little spacey, feels dizzy. It's actually a good thing, not a bad thing.

Another thing that keeps people in the cycle of choosing people for relationships that don't actually work is that they look for that excitement. Part of that excitement is the feeling of having their energy pulled. When we live in this reality, we think of the more emotion, trauma and drama we have, the more real our life is, the more exciting our life is.

Every place you've mis-identified and mis-applied excitement with joy and peace that you're really looking for, will you destroy and uncreate all that? <u>Right and Wrong, Good and Bad, All Nine, POD and POC, Shorts, Boys and Beyonds.</u>

I'm reading this book about this guy who travelled from Newcastle in England, all the way to New Zealand, in a month only using contacts with twitter. About a third of the way into the book, he reveals that he is actually manic depressive, which started to make more sense to me. He talks about missing his new wife and his kids and he cries several times a day. I'm thinking, "Wow, okay, when I travel, I miss my husband but I don't have to go into tears about that." It's just "okay, that's what I perceive. I'm here now. Paris is beautiful. Next."

This guy goes into the intensity of the emotion which made sense to me when he revealed his diagnosis. How many of us without even being diagnosed as manic depressive or bipolar, love that excitement and feel that we are not really alive unless we feel that?

THE MAGIC OF BEING

If you are always looking for excitement, how much does that make your life turn into a rollercoaster? How much does a rollercoaster describe your past relationship experiences? So everything that is, times a god zillion, will you destroy and uncreate it all? <u>Right and Wrong, Good and Bad, All Nine, POD and POC, Shorts, Boys and Beyonds.</u>

As you said, he's missing his wife and kids and wants to cry several times a day. This whole thing, this whole illusion about this romantic love, about Romeo and Juliet, like star-crossed lovers, "I'm going to die if I'm not with you" and all of that, all those illusions, can we destroy and un-create all of that please?

That's insanity! Romeo and Juliet died when they were 15! Is that really what you would like? Everything you've done to make Romeo and Juliet the desired outcome for your love affair, as your ideal scene, everything you have done to create that, will you please destroy and uncreate it all? <u>Right and Wrong, Good and Bad, All Nine, POD and POC, Shorts, Boys and Beyonds.</u>

That is the point of view of this reality.

In this reality, what people think relationships should be does not really work. There are always romantic movies and they are fun to watch, I get it, but who do you know that really lives that way? Even though we don't know anybody that really lives that way, we see those, we get so programmed to buy into them. It's what my husband, David and I called the "fast-forward."

I've heard people say "Oh, I just met this guy. Is blue a good color for the wedding?" It's like when you go to a website and click on the website and it starts talking to you before you even hit the play button. Doesn't that irritate you? I didn't even tell you to talk to me. The program about "Oh, our lives should look like the movies" runs for us non-stop and it seems that we have as little choice in that as we do when we go to a website and it starts talking to us before we tell it to.

Those pictures from movies, from TV, from magazines of what it should be, govern what we think we want to have but it doesn't really fit us. So we have to bend, fold, staple and mutilate ourselves to fit into that picture of what a relationship should look like. In the process, we end up giving away much more of ourselves than needed until the person who is in a relationship is just in a relationship with someone that they didn't even pick. Meanwhile, they are probably giving away themselves too, so you have these images that are relating to each other, and it's not even the real person.

What do you mean by "image"?

It's this false image of who you are. "If I'm going to be in a relationship, I can't fart." "If I'm going to be in a relationship, I have to cook dinner for him every night." "If I'm going to be in a relationship, I can't let myself do this." The list goes on. We have to give ourselves away unkempt times rather than actually being us. The **image** is the false picture we project of who we are that has nothing to do with us.

Expectations

What if the other person's expectations were just their interesting point of view? Everything that keeps you from seeing that, will you destroy and uncreate it all? Right and Wrong, Good and Bad, All Nine, POD and POC, Shorts, Boys and Beyonds.

It's quite amazing to me that so few of us know what we really would like for our life. If I say, "Life is like this humongous Sunday smorgasbord and you can ask anything you'd like in life," but instead of choosing to say "Some of that, I'll choose all of it," what we do is say, "I can't decide if I want salmon caviar or sturgeon caviar. I don't know if I want that kind of oysters." We just paralyze ourselves with choice in not actually choosing what we really like. We find it very difficult to know what we want, I have no idea why, but we do. One way of putting up a smoke screen for ourselves is to constantly take care of what everyone else requires and wants. If the other person wants this, they expect this, it's a lot easier for us to psychically pick up their expectation and meet their expectation and demand than it is for us to actually know what we would really want.

One of my 6 Dos in relationships is 'the other person's point of view is just an interesting point of view.'

David would love it if I cooked dinner every single night. I love to travel. He's not wrong for wishing dinner was on the table every single night and I do what I can when I'm home and if I don't, that's ok with me too. I do it as a gift to him, as a choice, not because it's a requirement, or his expectation.

We spend our lives trying to fit into everyone else's reality instead of choosing for ourselves. One of the reasons I think we are afraid to choose for ourselves is because we think we'll make the wrong choice. We think of always wanting to make the right choice.

The right choice is a judgment and every judgment creates limitations. What if instead of thinking you had to make the right choice, you were willing to just choose for 10 seconds? The catch in making the right choice is you can only know what the choice is going to create after you've made the choice. We want to make the right choice and think that right choice is going to be forever, we want to collect all the information possible. That's an impossible quest.

You can't actually collect all the information possible as the awareness of what the choice is going to create only shows up once you've made the choice. Then you make the choice and you become aware of what's created by the choice and then guess what, you don't have to follow through on that choice. Unless it is getting pregnant and having a kid, you can usually choose again.

Kids are one thing you can't unchoose, you are pretty much stuck with them. You can usually choose. If you commit to marry somebody and then suddenly, your life grinds to a halt, you've got a stomach ache all the time and nothing works as easily as it used to, that's an awareness of what your life might be if you follow through with this choice to marry that person. Guess what? You can change it.

Every place you've bought that you have to make the right choice in a relationship, and nothing but the right choice will do or make you happy, and if you make the wrong choice you are damned to hell forever, everything that is, times a god zillion, will you please destroy and uncreate it all? Right and Wrong, Good and Bad, All Nine, POD and POC, Shorts, Boys and Beyonds.

Creating A Relationship

Question: *"I was wondering how you can know the difference between dreams about relationships you want that are actually limiting you or keeping you trapped in illusive relationships and what is it that you as a being require or desire for a relationship to be right for you and expansive?"*

That's a great question. What I would suggest is to make two lists

1. Make a list of everything you're looking for in a relationship.

2. Make a list of everything you're looking not to have in a relationship.

You might even want to think about it over a couple of days and keep adding to it. Make those 2 lists and then look at which of those is a judgment. Look at which things on the list are actually a judgment, and then destroy and uncreate those judgments. If you know the Access clearing statements, POC and POD them.

If they don't seem to go away or they don't get lighter, POC and POD them again, until you can eliminate anything that's a judgment.

I didn't do this explicitly, I didn't spell this explicitly out when I met David, but I knew certain things weren't going to work for me. I wasn't interested in being with anybody that drank or used drugs . The biggest thing on my "not interested in having" list was someone that watched TV, especially sports 24X7. I wasn't interested in being a widow to

American football or soccer. If David had done that, the relationship wouldn't have lasted, but I didn't have a judgment.

A judgment version of that would be, "All men ever want to do is lie around and watch TV and watch sports." That's a judgment. Mine was awareness. "I'm not interested in living with that noise in the background of my life for my whole life. This doesn't work for me."

The other thing is I'm more willing to be alone than have something that I don't like. If something doesn't work for me, I'm willing to claim that and risk being alone for it, which makes me quite different from most people. Apparently 95% of people would rather be in a bad relationship than in no relationship at all.

My first recommendation would be to make these lists and look at them, be as honest with yourself as you can, which of those are judgments and which of them are something you would like. There is something called the "Pico-Universe". Pico Universes are the castles in the sky. When you were sitting in school, you built this whole fantasy world because you were so incredibly bored in school, which was a pico Universe.

All pico Universes everyone has created, relative to the relationship and what a relationship will be like and what it's like to get married, and everything that is, times a god zillion, will you please destroy and un-create all that? <u>Right and Wrong, Good and Bad, All Nine, POD and POC, Shorts, Boys and Beyonds.</u>

Pico Universes have a couple of characteristics. One thing about the Pico Universe is that it's all judgment. It all goes to conclusion and no part of it is question. If you are going into Pico Universe over somebody, or just marriage and romance generally, you say, "When I'm married, this is going to happen". You notice all that's conclusion, decision, judgment, none of it has any component of question to it.

Whereas with me, as I hadn't had a relationship that had any degree of success before David, I was willing to be in the question, "What is this person like?" Long before I started doing Access, I would ask him what he wanted to do and consider him as a different person rather than just as this cardboard cut-out that was playing a role that I'd already determined would fit into my life.

Basically you were just being present to who he was actually instead of being in a fantasy world?

True. I hope that those 2 tools – make the list, look at the things that are judgment , eliminate those and then look at how much question is there in what you are looking for or do you have it all decided and judged what it's going to look like. The more you have it decided and judged, what it's going to look like is closed-ended and the more you are going to end in a Pico Universe. It's going to force you to be constantly judging the person you are with to see if they measure up to your fantasy, rather than asking a more relevant question, "Oh, is this fun? Is this working for me right now?" As I mentioned, whether something is working for you right now is the best predictor of how it will work for you in the future.

Soul Mates

What you are really looking for? I've already dissed the past life connections, let me talk a little bit about soul mates. Many people are looking for their soul mate. The first thing I'd like to say is look at the odds. There's a more than 6 billion persons on the planet. What if your soul mate was just born in China and you are already 35 years old. What are your chances of even meeting that person, speaking the same language as them or getting together with them? If you've got the idea that you've got one soul mate that's on the planet right now, you've got like a 1 in 6 billion chance of meeting them. Those are not odds I like to function from.

The thing about a soul mate is that you create this ideal picture of what your soul mate would be. You meet somebody and say, "You are the one. The One. Capital T, capital O. Are you really my soul mate?"

When you do that, you have this list or this picture that you are constantly judging or measuring that person against. The first time things get sticky in your relationship which in most relationships they do, you are going to be evaluating that flesh and blood person who's actually been willing to be with you up to now. You are going to be evaluating that person compared to your soul mate. It's so tempting to say, "You did this, that or the other thing that annoys me. If you were really my soul mate you won't do that." You are setting up an impossible standard for this living, breathing person who's actually there and present with you to measure up to and hence they have to fail.

When you hold onto this idea that somebody is my soul mate, you are really setting yourself up to fail in relationships. Every place you've bought the idea that someone is your soul mate, that a soul mate is what you are looking for, that a soul mate would be valuable and all the judgments you have about who your soul mate will and will not be, will you please rescind, revoke, recant, renounce, denounce, destroy and un-create all that? <u>Right and Wrong, Good and Bad, All Nine, POD and POC, Shorts, Boys and Beyonds.</u>

What Is The Relationship Right Now

Now you've dashed the attraction, you've dashed the passion, you've dashed the right type, and you've dashed the excitement? What is it that we are really looking for? Hate to disappoint all the romantics on the call; I've finished you off now. I said that my point of view about what really is the best predictor of what makes a relationship is going to work is, that is it working right now? Are you having fun right now? Are you enjoying the person's company? To me, even if you have great sex and they give you money and let you do what you want, if you don't actually enjoy the person that you're with, what's the point? I would say I'm totally fine being by myself. I can have a perfectly good time. I always kind of laugh when I go into a restaurant and they say, "Just one?" and I say "yeah." But it's one. The only person that's the center of my life is still here. I can be complete and happy by myself and

David always adds to my life. It's not a place where I feel incomplete without him.

That's just so amazing. How many of us are creating relationships from that need.

I'd say just about everybody. "If I have a relationship, I'm complete. He will complete me." No, first of all, you are energy and is energy ever complete? Are you ever complete? No. You won't ever be perfect either. There will still be more mistakes you can make in the future. More opportunities to be wrong and so what? What if it all were just an interesting point of view? It seems to me, what people are really looking for is what we call an Access Consciousness state of allowance, where they want to be with someone who acknowledges who they are without judgment. Someone with whom it is safe, acknowledged and valued to be just who you are without any demand that you change.

We're really looking for someone to see us, but when we do the dance and negotiation of getting into a relationship, we tend to function from this reality to set it up so that odds are totally against us ever getting that, as we always want to put our best foot forward. We always want to show them our good side not our bad side. We do everything to make the relationship not who we really are in our search for a relationship with someone who will love who we really are.

Everything that is, times a god zillion, will you destroy and un-create it all? <u>Right and Wrong, Good and Bad, All Nine, POD and POC, Shorts, Boys and Beyonds.</u>

What if you looked for someone with whom you didn't have to contract yourself? That would be what we refer to as a state of communion rather than relationship. Everybody thinks they are looking for a relationship but actually a relationship is a distance between 2 points. Is that really what you want? If you have a relationship, you always have to be putting distance into it. In a communion, you can have distance or not and the connection in between the 2 of you is still there. Communion is like when you walk in the deep woods or you walk by the beach and the water's not saying, "I'm giving you so many molecules of O2 and hence you owe me carbon dioxide. You owe me; we've got to get even." And nobody is saying, "Those grains of sand, those leaves are out of place. Can you please fix those?" No, you just can be who you are and you notice how when you even think of being in that space, your being expands and gets so much bigger than the boundaries of your own skin? What if you could be in relationship, a communion where you could have that same sense of being? When I come into my house, I don't have to contract who I am. If anything, I can expand it because I'm home, in the place that works for me, that's the place where I can be who I really am. That's what we are really looking for; everything from this reality that we believed is true about relationships is set up to keep us from getting it. How weird is that?

Question: "If you are in a relationship with somebody, if you have someone who is in your life, around whom you do feel contracted, what can you do to change that? What question can you ask?"

You just asked a great question. "What can I do to change this?"

I was asked a very perceptive question "How do you know when you are being allowance and when you are giving yourself up?" I didn't have a pat answer for the question. What I came up with was, "Look at the trait that's really bothering you the most. If that person didn't change at all, would you be willing to live with that?

If the answer is no, then the relationship is really already over. Your choice is to pull the band-aid off fast or pull it off slow, one hair at a time. If it's something that you don't especially like but it doesn't bother you that much and you are willing to live with it, then that's something that you can be in allowance of. Recognizing that it's not something you are willing to live with is also being in allowance of the trait. It's just your choice to say, "This is something they are. They are not going to change it and I am not willing to live with that." That's a great question you can ask yourself about anything that's bugging you.

You can also use a tool saying, "Truth, is this person willing to have more in their relationship?" and whatever is lighter – a yes or a no – is the truth and then you can choose based on that. You can make a list of what would have to change in order for the relationship to work for you. Do not tell your partner this. Make the list for you, then look at it and see if it's something that that person can change or if it's something that's their essential being. If something's their essential personality then asking them to change that is not kind.

Like if a condition of my being with David was that my desk had to be neat, the marriage would be over. I would try. I could try for a week or two but it's just not going to happen. My desk looks the same if I've been in a hotel room for half an hour or I was home. Look at it and be honest with yourself. It's part of this person's basic personality. It would be cruel to ask them to change. Is it something we could change? Is there some third alternative that you could come up with? Like if there's something that you never agree on, you can just agree to disagree and you don't talk about that subject.

David's a carpenter, he doesn't write on things that are thinner than wood. So he thinks papers are irrelevant. One of the things that I love to do is to write and to read, I have papers around me all the time, kind of like pig-pen in Charlie Brown. We are never going to agree about papers. We don't talk about them. There's no possible good outcome that could come from a discussion about it, why bother to torture each other with the conversation?

Question: "My husband would like to have sex sometimes but I have not had sex for about 5 to 6 years. Hence I go into the wrongness of me when he asks me to and I have hernia which is not healing which could be a convenient excuse also."

Truth, are you willing to actually have sex with your husband? Ask yourself that question. It's my point of view that sex is receiving in this reality and to have a relationship that doesn't include sex unless there's some medical reason for it, like the guys have prostate surgery or something, there's going to be something that's flat or missing about it. That's just my point of view about it. Ask yourself these 2 questions again and again.

What does sex mean to you? What do you mean to sex? <u>Right and Wrong, Good and Bad, All Nine, POD and POC, Shorts, Boys and Beyonds.</u>

Sex means something to you that you're been making wrong? What if you're willing? You've been saying no to it for 5 or 6 years and now you've created this identity in you where you have to say no to it. What if you just made choices for every 10 seconds? And there's a fabulous book by Gary Douglas and Dr. Dain Heer, "Sex Is Not A Four Letter Word But Relationship Often Times Is."

It has great suggestions about how to create great sex. If you are willing, you could start again from there and create something different.

That's a beautiful book. I was just talking to my friend today and I said that that's a book each of us should have been given, when we were growing up. We have all these fantasies and insane ideas about what sex means and it screws us up really bad.

The Access Consciousness Body Processes, which are taught in the beginning classes and Foundation Level 1 and then we have a 3 day class on them. These are fabulous about changing your relationship with your body. There's one that's in Level 1 that changed everything about receiving for me. I realized after receiving one session of this Body Process that it was like my nerve endings had stopped inside my skin and after one session of this MTVSS they connected with my skin and it was incredibly more pleasurable to be touched.

If there's anyone in your vicinity that can do that Body Process for you, that's a fabulous way to start it. The other thing I've noticed is the lighter the touch, the more enjoyable it is. If it is so light that it is almost making the hairs of your arm reach up towards it, which can be incredibly more stimulating than something that's much more forceful. You could just try playing with that and start initiating the touch without making orgasm the goal.

That's another trap we fall into. I got an email from somebody, "We didn't finish." She was talking about having sex with her boyfriend and she said, "We didn't finish," and I realized, in her Universe, finishing is having an orgasm. Everybody has to be evaluated by whether he has an orgasm and whether she has an orgasm. What if instead of that being the goal, which traps you, it was "How much fun can we have being together and the time we have including our bodies"? Doesn't that create much more possibility?

What contribution can we be to changing the face of relationships on the Earth?

Question: "My question revolves around sharing the responsibility my wife and I have around our kids. We particularly get into arguments over the way we think they should be taught. For me a positive way to encourage kids is so much more powerful but my wife sees things very differently. It can frustrate me to see my kids pick up negativity that to me seems not a place they should have to go to. How do you look at this?"

That's a really difficult one, as this man knows. It is so infinitely much easier to raise kids if your values are energetically compatible in the first place. If they are not, just tell your kids how it is and without putting the parent down. If you are with your wife or if you are separated, either one, just talk to them about what is. You could almost even say what was in the question, depending on the age of the kids. Some people look at the glass as half full and some people look at the glass as half empty. I like to look at it as half full and this happens when I do that. What have you noticed? Your mom has a different way of looking at things. It doesn't make her wrong, she just looks at things different. You can choose.

Look at how she looks at things and look at what that creates in the world. Then at how I look at things and what that creates in the world.

Then you can choose how you wish to look at things and what that will create in your world. Empower them to make the choice, without putting your wife down. They're smart, they'll figure it out.

These tools work infinitely much better if you are not vested in the outcome, as the outcome never looks like you think it is going to look.

What are the possibilities of her changing? You can't make anybody change. As soon as you want them to be different, they have to resist.

Every place that you have decided that your wife has to change in order for things to work with you, with the kids, will you destroy and uncreate all that? <u>Right and Wrong, Good and Bad, All Nine, POD and POC, Shorts, Boys and Beyonds.</u>

The way this works is as soon as someone requires that you change, you can't. When anybody tells you to do anything, what happens? You dig your heels in and say, "No, I'm not doing that." It's the same with the wife or anybody else. As soon as someone requires you to change, that's the last thing you'll consider doing. It's only when you get to a place of no point of view about the person's negativity or whatever else you think should change, it's only when you get to a place of no point of view that they then have the freedom to change. As long as you have a 1% point of view about what they should change, they have to resist you. This also works with your kids, especially teenagers.

You could also ask questions over here, "What is this?" "What can I do with this?" "Can I change this?" and "if so, how can I change this?"

Even simply "What would it take to change this?"

3 Traps To Avoid If You Would Like This Relationship To Last

Control, blaming and **trying to change the other person**. Those are 3 of my 6 don'ts in my "6 dos and 6 don'ts to create a relationship that is easy and fun". The first thing is trying to control the other person. If someone controls you, what happens? You resist. Same as when you try and change somebody, what happens? You resist. It never works. You really have to get to a place where, "Wow, it's amazing that she continues to create this negativity". You can stand there and watch it not work but until she's willing to see that it doesn't work, she's not going to change it. It never works to control the other person. It never works to try and change the other person.

The third thing that doesn't work is to blame the other person. It's so tempting when something in our life doesn't turn up as we would like it to, to make it not our fault. Of course, we never want to be wrong. It's always easy to say that it's the fault of the person that's closest to us, which is blame. Whenever you say "Anybody" made you do "anything." – first, you are lying, because nobody can make you do anything. Second, you are actually living something that we call as "distractor implant". A distractor implant is something that is like a dog chasing its tail. It will chase that tail forever but it'll never catch its tail. As long as you are in blame you won't ever solve a situation that you'd like to change. Trying to control the other person, blaming them for anything that happens, never works.

Anything that happens in your life is your creation – the good, the bad and the ugly. The good news is, if you can create the disasters, you can actually create something that's more fun and working better as well if you'd really like to have it. Takes a little brutal honesty. Some people just love the disaster that their lives are and they like to complain about their relationships more than they like to change them. Not your best choice, but honestly, that's where a lot of people do live from. Do you have any more questions?

Question: "What to do to be sure that he or she will be yours forever?"

I learnt that from my husband, David. He's a smart man. Gary Douglas, the founder of Access asked, David what it was that he must have adored most about me. David said that I never required or expected or demanded that he be anything other than who he is, which the model of allowance is.

THE MAGIC OF BEING

So many women, I would say 99.9% of women, have this idea that they know better than a man how a man should be. They have the point of view that they should control the man; train him, to get him to put the toilet seat down and to do everything that they think a man should be. It doesn't work. Because none of my relationships had lasted very long, I didn't have the point of view that I knew what a man should be. It didn't make any sense that I, as a woman, should know what a man should be. It seemed to me that a man should know what the man should be. But that's not most people's – most women's – point of view.

There's no sense of my trying to control my husband David in my Universe. We were on vacation in France and we found this beautiful set of antique crystal and we brought it home. One of the pieces in that was this beautiful pitcher and he put it in a place that I don't like to put the crystal. I knew that it will get knocked off when you put it there and it got knocked off. It was broken and this was antique, one-of-a-kind crystal.

He said, "I broke the crystal but you are not holding it against me." It's not a consistent fighting point. "It was a beautiful pitcher. I'm sad it's gone. Ok, it's gone. Next." So, I'm never trying to change him, I'm never blaming him. I'm never anything but present. "What's happening right now?"

I just had a conversation with someone who met a mutual friend of ours. When she found I was friends with this person, she told our mutual friend something I did that was stupid and thoughtless. It was stupid and thoughtless, I admit, but it was in no way malicious, that I had done 4 years ago. This person was repeating to this new friend of mine.

I'd also done all kinds of incredibly generous things for this person, none of which of course were remembered, just this one stupid, trivial thing that I'd done 4 years ago. I was just floored that someone would be repeating to a third person something stupid that I did 4 years ago. I thought, "Why? What is the value of holding on to that?" That's the opposite of what you need to do to be sure that he'll be yours forever.

If you can create a space where everything he or she does is acknowledged without judgment, you'll have him. You'll have him because so few people can offer that. There will be a sense of being at home with you and between you, to try and create that with someone else is just too much work.

That's what people want a relationship for. "Someone who really loves me for being myself." We put all these roadblocks on the way to make sure that we don't get exactly what it is that we say that we want. It's just illogical. I can work in this field as long as I would like to because there will never be a shortage of insanity. What would it take to change that? <u>Right and Wrong, Good and Bad, All Nine, POD and POC, Shorts, Boys and Beyonds.</u>

Question: "What about sexual attractions to other people even after you are married? How does one resist it?"

How does one resist it? Why do you want to resist it? I'd say you'd want to keep it going.

My husband is attracted to all kinds of people. All kinds of women. We talk about it. I know about it and the thing is I let him have fun. Hug them, kiss them. I don't care because he comes home with me. What if instead of making that wrong, which is the point of view of this reality, she was to use that increased sexual desire with her husband? What would that be like?

You don't have to tell him. Just say, "Honey, look at that guy that's really hot. I'm really turned on, let's go home." Think he's going to say no to that? I don't think so. Unless he's insane! Because the alternative to that is to cut off your sexual desire, the healing, caring, nurturing energy of life itself. To cut that off every time except when you are in bed with a person. It's not a faucet. It's the energy of life itself. Our kids are sexual. We should be able to feel our sexual energy with our kids as well. This doesn't mean we have to copulate with them. It doesn't mean you have to have sex with them. If you can allow yourself to feel this sexual energy with your kids, then your kids won't judge that in themselves and they'll be willing to be much more aware than we were hopefully. It will actually create a change on the planet. It's really the judgments of the attraction; not the attraction itself that's the problem.

Judgment Of Attraction

There's different ways of looking at sex. There's sexuality, which is always a judgment. "I'm a married woman; I can't receive the flow of sexual energy from anyone except my husband. That's bad." That's a judgment. That's sexuality. Sexual desire is having the caring, nurturing, expansive energy of life itself. When we confuse those two things, we think, "I'm married. I can't have that sexual energy anywhere else in the Universe." Why would we limit ourselves in that way? That's so foolish.

Every place that you've misidentified and misapplied sexualness - the caring, nurturing, energy of life itself – as sexuality, which is a limitation and a judgment, everything that is, times a god zillion, will you destroy and un-create it all? <u>Right and Wrong, Good and Bad, All Nine, POD and POC, Shorts, Boys and Beyonds.</u>

All the ways that you've told yourself, all the decisions, judgments, commitments and conclusions that it's not possible to have the energy of sexuality except with the one person that you are committed to, will you destroy and uncreate it all? <u>Right and Wrong, Good and Bad, All Nine, POD and POC, Shorts, Boys and Beyonds.</u>

You could also just run, "What does sex mean to me? What do I mean to sex?" It sounds a little nonsensical but it will bring energy up and it may or may not have words to go with it. Just feel the energy go, "<u>Right and Wrong, Good and Bad, All Nine, POD and POC, Shorts, Boys and Beyonds.</u>"

Just keep saying that over and over again to clear that.

WHO IS DR KACIE CRISP

Dr. Kacie Crisp has been involved in facilitating others' lives and bodies for her entire working life. As a therapist with emotionally disturbed children, chiropractor in the US and Findhorn spiritual community, and now as a licensed facilitator of Access Consciousness, her great joy is to watch clients expand their lives.

She is the author of The Little Black Book on Relationships about her 28 year relationship with her husband, David Caddy. She and David have presented classes on relationships all over the world. She has facilitated and continues to facilitate classes all over Europe, the USA, and Australia. In addition to facilitating the Access Consciousness core classes (Bars and Foundation), she was one of the first four facilitators of the Access Consciousness Body Class. She also offers classes on money and wealth and Right Voice for You. Her classes on relationships and money are available worldwide, via telephone and internet, as well as in person. A longtime resident of San Francisco, CA, she recently moved to Belize, where her husband is building a house on a river surrounded by trees and birds.

She was the first to bring the Access Consciousness Core Classes and others to Scandinavia, Ireland, France, the Netherlands, Lebanon, Russia, and South Africa. She has a blog and a newsletter with a very different perspective on relationships, one that actually works.

She and David have one 26 year old son who continues to amaze and delight them. She is at work on a book about parenting teenagers, which was easy for her.

CHOOSING TO HAVE IT ALL

By Dr Kacie Crisp

Get clear on YOUR CHOICES about money, relationships AND your body with these dynamic products.
http://www.magicofbeing.com

CHAPTER FIVE

❖

ARE YOU ADDICTED TO THE ILLUSION OF RELATIONSHIP

By Susan Lazar Hart

Author, Motivational Speaker, Relationship Counselor

Executive Director Right Relationship for You

Radio Host: Ask Susan Now

CFMW, MFA

I want to know what people have decided. They are addicted to the illusion of relationship. And most people I don't even know where it that they are addicted to the illusion of relationship is.

Illusion Of Relationships

Illusion has to do with form and structure, everywhere we stuck ourselves with a thought, a feeling or an emotion.

One can really go from illusion to illumination, only if you ask questions.

You have nothing, but questions.

Everywhere you have bought into all the Form, the Structure, the Limitations, the Decisions, everywhere you bought into Separations, Projections, Expectations, of Illusions and Illuminations, would you all be willing to un-create and destroy that all? <u>Good and Bad, Right and Wrong, POD and POC, All Nine, Shorts, Boys and Beyonds.</u>

What do we decide illusion is? What do we decide that it isn't? How much have we bought into the illusion of a relationship and created a form out of that, a structure out of that?

What are illusions? I will have the perfect marriage. If I meet the right guy, my money is supposed to be great, my body will be great and my life will be great. I will have the wealth and the children I have always wanted. The illusion of whatever my parents did was totally wrong and I am going to go the opposite way and choose totally opposite because that would give me what I want. How we buy into a form and a structure or something? Are there any questions in any of that?

We are totally addicted to form and structure. And the moment we step out of that form and structure, and we are standing on thin air. You think that's so uncomfortable and you need to go back to form and structure, to create something around it and go back to it.

Even that is an illusion. We decide what space is. Even that in itself is an illusion because it has to look a certain way. What a relationship should look like and shouldn't look like.

And we are stopping us at creating the relationship that we really require and desire, in order to access all of us. Would you all be willing to uncreate and destroy that? <u>Good and Bad, Right and Wrong, POD and POC, All Nine, Shorts, Boys and Beyonds.</u>

Illumination In Relationships

Question: "What are some of the questions that you would ask to actually get to the point of illumination?"

You can ask the question- Does this work for me? Holding on to an idea or to an illusion. You are actually not in the computation of your life or your relationship. You could ask- What do I love about this? How people always say, I do not understand, it does not work and I have done everything I am supposed to do. I have gone to the right school, I have married the person. I just do not get it. What is it you are not willing to be aware of?

What am I not willing to be aware of that even in the face of total awareness, I won't change it, I won't choose it, I won't lose it. What do I love about this? There is something you actually love about it. We love the illusion. Can I have or meet someone who consistently doesn't choose for them?

If you don't choose for you, you can really be sure of illusion, that you will never be the success. You are always sure you couldn't be. Everything that is, will you destroy and uncreate that? <u>Good and Bad, Right and Wrong, POD and POC, All Nine, Shorts, Boys and Beyonds.</u>

Would that even create a story? In which everything is already settled, because it is an illusion. When you look through a veil, you ever walk up, you know pass a store, and there is the curtain or veil or pass the house.

I used to run in the morning, I loved it because I could always see what is going on in everybody's house. Or walk my dog at night. But the lights were on behind, you have an illusion of something going on. And then you make up a story that it is not illusion. And once you make up the story you end up buying it real.

How much does that stop you from generating and creating the amazing orgasmic juicy joy of relationship? A lot or a little or a mega ton? Mega ton. Everything that brings up for everyone can we un-create and destroy that? Good and Bad, Right and Wrong, POD and POC, All Nine, Shorts, Boys and Beyonds.

Four questions you can ask. What is it? Is this an illusion? What can I do with it? Can I change it? If so, how can I change it?

And everything that does not allow it, uncreate and destroy that. <u>Good and Bad, Right and Wrong, POD and POC, All Nine, Shorts, Boys and Beyonds.</u>

When you are living in the question, you are actually living the possibility of something else turning up. You are living in a possibility of uncreating illusion and moves on to choice, question and possibility. How is that landing for you?

When we go to limitation we are going to an illusion. We are only limited by our imagination. An illusion is an imagined story. It is elusive it can never quite get there. We always have to make ourselves better. We always have to create something more to match what we have decided that illusion is. And how much limitation is set in that.

"What we can imagine is always based on our past, on what we know. It is not going in that realm of possibility at all. "

We stick ourselves with that. Then we decide that is the limitation we can deal with. And that is why the illusion is so elusive. You can never catch them because they are not real. They don't actually add to your life. When you are in the grocery stores, and you see they have all the magazines and you always see the same magazine from past 30 years. It is the same woman. She could be Black or White Caucasian, European, Chinese. But she is the same with the big eyes looking at you. And they are air brushed and no one's real. But it is the exact same magazine cover since last forty years. They are showing illusion. If you like this, you will get him. If you act like this you will get her. It is all an illusion.

It has nothing to do with what you truly are, and you are buying into you as wrongness, which is another illusion. When you buy into an illusion you are not actually, in the complication of your relationship or your life that is where we are addicted. We are addicted to correcting the illusion. Is there any such thing as fixing anything? You are going back rather than creating possibility, choice and question. What possibilities are here? What question can I ask? What choice is there for me? And what contribution this is to my relationship? Because an illusion is never a contribution to a relationship.

Trying To Be Someone You Are Not

Question: *"When we are trying to be someone that we are not, we end up attracting people who are exactly trying to be someone they are not and how does that work?"*

Yes. There's a story. A gorgeous woman with shining hair, beautiful skin meets a beautiful man. They end up having a very bad job because both of them have had so much plastic surgery. They were representing themselves as an illusion of who they thought they should look like. And then they have a kid who doesn't look like either of them. It is living life as an illusion rather than happily.

What is right about me, I am not getting? Anything that brings up for everybody. And everybody is saying what do you mean I don't get it? Can we uncreate and destroy that? <u>Good and Bad, Right and Wrong, POD and POC, All Nine, Shorts, Boys and Beyonds.</u>

Reformatting And Reprogramming You

Question: *"I was talking to someone about relationships one day. I asked him where in his life he could be himself. With whom. He said just my kids who are three and five years old."*

Seeing a five year old you have no expectations. You have no projections and separations. They get you and it is amazing, there is no judgment there. And that is where we bought into the illusion. Where at some point in our lives we start to be reformatting to set somebody else's illusion, of what you should look like.

My mom had three boys and then she had me. All she ever wanted was the girl, and I should be really grateful to them. My brothers were born before me. And I can remember her pulling me off the hockey ring. She had a lot of illusions of what I was supposed to be like. I was supposed to be this little thing that she could dress etc. But it didn't work out that way. She had this illusion of what I was supposed to be like. Was she ever really willing to receive who I was, in her later years. Yes.

How many of us are raised by parents who have an illusion and they reformat us to fit their illusion, which vibrates to the illusion that their parents brought them up with. Everywhere we are reformatting ourselves. Everywhere we have been reprogrammed. Everywhere you have been implanted and explanted to be who truly you are not. Would you all uncreate and destroy that? <u>Good and Bad, Right and Wrong, POD and POC, All Nine, Shorts, Boys and Beyonds.</u>

I was with Gary the other night.

Gary and Dain had the awareness that we actually make ourselves stupid, by choosing the lack of awareness. And when we make ourselves stupid, that is what we vibrate to. We choose from that place of making ourselves stupid, because we are really bright, we are really fast. How much did you ever slow yourself down in order to fit into this reality?

That is an illusion. You don't get it.

I have got a great manipulation. I didn't realize that, until Gary pointed that. He said that is actually a great way for me to get people do everything for me. And I liked that. But, that is a choice. It doesn't have to be an illusion. It can be a choice.

Mindscapes

What stupidity are you using as the invention and artificial intensity of the mindscape you are using? With that in mind we get a sense of how to create artificial intensity.

Is an illusion a mindscape? That you created in your mind? You have the whole picture there. You know what somebody's supposed to look like, what they are supposed to smell like, what the people should look like? How should I look at them? You know how is she?

We create these pictures in our mind. There can be somebody who lost hundred pounds and then looks in the mirror and still see himself as heavy over weight person. That is the mindscape they are dealing from.

Have you ever met somebody who is always looking for a fight with their partner? What kind of mindscape did they grow up with? Did they see parents who fight all the time? And they decided that I am not really worthy unless somebody's fighting with me. I have to prove my point. I am holding on to "You have to live to respect me. You have to respect my point of view." You got the illusion that actually creates relationship and he agrees with you. That is the mindscape that we live in. I will pretend that I am right. Even though I have decided I am wrong, which is why I am fighting with you. To agree with my point of view.

How much does that give you the artificial intensity of it? Do you know how intense we are? That we got pick a fight with somebody to have them prove that they love us. A friend of my daughter got married and then the wife returns in about three weeks, four weeks, a month and three months into it and he said that he is going back to his parent's home. She refused to talk about it and then a week later she picked up the phone and yelled that he did not fight for her. That is mindscape.

She had a picture in her head. If she picked a fight, what would happen, what it would be like. And he would come on his white horse and crave her but the guy was brilliant and he said that's over. It is the peak of the universe we live in.

Temper Tantrums

Question: "I do this all the time with my son. He wakes up in the morning and he throws the tantrums. I wake up programmed with the mindscape that he is going to."

How much of a manipulator is he? You can ask him, what does he love about the temper tantrum? Why does he love that?

Could you please tell me what you love about it? That is a great question to ask him. What do you love about temper tantrum, what do you need? Well, I know so much you I am just curious. What do you love about temper tantrum?

Ask him what does temper tantrum mean to him. What do they mean to him. What does he mean to the temper tantrums. When I ask we often talk about the meaningful stuff, which is the willingness. If you are talking about an illusion, it is the addiction to the illusion of relationship. How many people are addicted to not asking a question? How many people are addicted to non clarity?

If you are actually willing to be clear inwards with your child, with your boss, with your partner what do you love about this? How cute could you be? What do you love about the temper tantrums, because actually it does not work for me. But, I am curious what better works for you. Would you be willing to step into that state?

It is for a lot of people.

What stupidity are you using the invention and artificial intensity like a temper tantrum of the mindscape you are using? And everything that brings up will you uncreate and destroy that. <u>Good and Bad, Right and Wrong, POD and POC, All Nine, Shorts, Boys and Beyonds.</u>

Another great question to ask is what story am I buying? That I am making so real. That is creating the artificial intensity of the mindscape I am using.

It can also be other people's stories. Somewhere we bought into their stories as true and real. And we go to vibrate these and that is the addiction. We are addicted to fitting in. Do you ever try and fit in somewhere once you were expected to say a straight no to?

That is again the illusion we saw ourselves. I want to fit in and that is the form and the structure. Our whole life we have been taught that there is something wrong with us. If we just buy an illusion of losing ten times we can even buy an illusion of generating more money. If we just buy the illusion of the children. If we buy the illusion of I am never getting married. If we buy the illusion of I have to get married, everything will fall into place.

Everywhere that brings up, uncreate and destroy that. <u>Good and Bad, Right and Wrong, POD and POC, All Nine, Shorts, Boys and Beyonds.</u>

"What stupidity are you using to create the illusion that you are choosing? What stupidity are you using to create the illuminations that you are choosing?

Going To The Future

Question: In my relationship I want to improve things. And in Access there is an idea of being the energy of something to have it. How do I be the energy of having a wonderful relationship with my boyfriend, without being in a Pico universe by visualizing it? As I usually do."

Go into the future and take the energy of what you would like to create as your relationship and bring it into the present. And ask what else is possible? What would it take to create this? What would it take for more of this to show up? And anything that does not allow it uncreate and destroy it. <u>Good and Bad, Right and Wrong, POD and POC, All Nine, Shorts, Boys and Beyonds.</u>

When you get the energy of the relationship you do not even have to know what the elements of it are.

I go out there and I bring it in. Then I think what is it? May be it is Nurturing, maybe it is Caring, maybe it is Generating Five Million Dollars etc. What would it take more of this to show up? I get the energy the juicy orgasmic constantly questioning universe that is contributing to me. And I am contributing to it. Get a sense of that energy.

What if you could create a relationship that matches the vibration.

Anything that does not allow it, anything that does not match that vibration would you be willing to uncreate and destroy that? <u>Good and Bad, Right and Wrong, POD and POC, All Nine, Shorts, Boys and Beyonds.</u>

And it is the willingness to create that. It is the willingness to go out into the future.

What is it that I would like? Can you get sense of that in the future?

What would it take to have more of that?

When you are copulating, there is a special sweet spot you like to snuggle right into. What would it take to have more of that?

And it does not mean right now. It means the gratitude is there, the contribution is there.

What would it take more of that in my life? And the more we ask here, what would take more of that in my life? The more the universe is listening. The universe asks and sends that in. What else is possible? Universe is listening to everything.

And we do not have to say exactly clear, defined to the nth degree what you want in the relationship. It is the energy. If you and I will step into that energy it will expand the energy. Step into that. If you step into that and then show up and ask for the vibration of that, be the vibration of that.

Copulation (putting body parts together)

Two questions to ask are -

"How does it get any better than this and what else is possible?"

The third one is -

I ask to receive from the earth at the same time. When I am copulating, "Earth, can I receive whatever it is that you require from me? Earth, take whatever it is you require from me and earth, what can I receive from you with this copulation?"

And it is the same way when we are talking of Illusion of Relationship. How many people are buying into it to the Illusion of Copulation? He is supposed to be like this, he is supposed to know how to do this. Rather than turning to this body- Body, tell me what is that you require, show me what you require, where would you be like to be touched? You don't have to say out loud, you can say it energetically. And again you get a difference, there is no illusion there.

Would you rather have awareness or illusion? Would you rather have a ten second increment that gives you a space to be in? That gives you the awareness that you are looking for or would you rather have an illusion that you are sticking yourself with?

Everything that brings up can we uncreate and destroy that? <u>Good and Bad, Right and Wrong, POD and POC, All Nine, Shorts, Boys and Beyonds.</u>

What physical actualization of the adventure of relationship are you now capable of generating, creating and instituting rather than the illusion? Everything that does not allow that to show up, can we un-create and destroy that? <u>Good and Bad, Right and Wrong, POD and POC, All Nine, Shorts, Boys and Beyonds.</u>

Situation

Question: "I had an accident disability work for years- looking at settlement now. I do not know which way to go. I do not know what to do. I do not know what to choose. I do not know what they are going to do. I am bored and in a mental tension around this because it could go really good for lack of better words right now."

What stupidity are you using with the decisions, the conclusions, the complications and the correctness that you are choosing? Everything is that is, would you be willing to let that go? <u>Good and Bad, Right and Wrong, POD and POC, All Nine, Shorts, Boys and Beyonds.</u>

Everywhere you are into that, there is a correct way to be with all this. That is actually buying into the illusion. The conclusion will work for you or not work for you.

How can I choose, because I am caught between this decision and that decision, this conclusion and that conclusion? And everywhere you are in the relationship with your conclusions and decisions there is judgment. Would you be willing to uncreate and destroy that? <u>Good and Bad, Right and Wrong, POD and POC, All Nine, Shorts, Boys and Beyonds.</u>

Were there any conclusions, judgments and decisions in anything that you are saying?

You could go to the energy of it.

What's right about this I am not getting? What possibilities are here?

One of the interesting things here is- This is a Situation. Everywhere that we situated ourselves we have actually placed ourselves on a point, on a line. Can the word "situation", situated somewhere in an illusion, that you are holding on to of how things won't work out. Or will work out. How we can stick ourselves with that?

Would you be willing to let go of any situational set point that you have? What stupidity am I using with this situation I am choosing, because it is actually a choice. We create everything, we actually choose to buy into that there is a situation. We have a situation in the kitchen, this is on fire. We have a situation- Jolly has been robbing the neighbors again.

Everything that brings up for everyone, can we uncreate and destroy that?

<u>Good and Bad, Right and Wrong, POD and POC, All Nine, Shorts, Boys and Beyonds.</u>

That is the illusion of what makes us valuable in this reality, that we have a situation. Rather than what kind of a change is this? What else is possible here that I am not even aware of? What is possible here? What question can I ask? What choices do I have? What is it? How can I change this so that it actually works for me?

THE MAGIC OF BEING

Manipulation

Caller: "I spent couple of hours on the phone with my Attorney. He is putting all this structure and he won't let me ask and explore other options. And the whole time I know that I have a way to do this. There is no limiting as the one he is putting it. But, I did not know what to do with that? I knew it inside and he kept trying to put me in a box. And I do not do box what else is possible here that I am not aware of?"

How can I manipulate this to my advantage?

How can I manipulate my lawyer to my advantage?

Caller:"What do you do with the guilt that comes up with the word manipulate?"

How bad could you be? Everything that brings up for everyone, can we uncreate and destroy that? <u>Good and Bad, Right and Wrong, POD and POC, All Nine, Shorts, Boys and Beyonds.</u>

Who did you buy this from, about manipulation and guilt?

Caller:"My mother."

Would things like guilt be a huge distraction? And is distraction nothing more than an illusion that you are wrong? Anything that brings up, can we uncreate and destroy that? Good and Bad, Right and Wrong, POD and POC, All Nine, Shorts, Boys and Beyonds. Anything that does not allow that, uncreate and destroy. <u>Good and Bad, Right and Wrong, POD and POC, All Nine, Shorts, Boys and Beyonds.</u>

I am treasure chest you could open me up. Pick one, two or three of those questions. Run it, use it and abuse it. We manipulate people all the time.

I am facilitating a five days "Change your Life" class. I walk in and could see what is going on. I have a call that I am really looking forward to doing, the room is not set up. Then comes a guy from some country where they all speak English very well. I am in a country where

English is a pre-dominant language. And I say, "Could you do me a favor? Could you give me some pillows, could you give this, could you give me that, could you get me some chairs? And I said, I just want to thank you so much. You know this is so great. I have to go and this just awesome. I asked him to do many things. And when I came back about ten minutes later he was doing that all. I gave him $20. Did I change his reality? Did I manipulate him that night? We do it every day.

Caller: "But I would never manipulate anybody."

If somebody says, "What would you like to do for dinner?" You say, "I would like to do this", somebody else says, "I would like to do that." What do you do? Don't you go ahead and see how you can manipulate so that you get the food that you want?"

We do it all the time. Would you be willing to have that much fun? Would you be willing to change people's life with your manipulation?

I am so grateful for that man in the class. Is there a chance if I walk by him and ask him to do something for me, he might do that for me?

How does it get any better than that? I sat with him and looked at how we could put the chairs. I know how to put the chairs together; I have done it many times before. How many classes have I taught? I have been a facilitator for seven years. I realized it was important for him to give the information that he had. He is not feeling like he is contributing but he is. I am so grateful and he is a part of the game. How does it get any better than that?

Everything that brings up for anyone, everybody that has bought into the illusion with relationships that manipulation must be avoided.

When you want sex don't you manipulate? Manipulate his head. He is lying in the bed and putting on his head- I want sex with her. That is all manipulation. And it is a win-win.

Whatever you do, don't use it.

Choice Creates Awareness

Question: "My question is to do with rejection, or the feeling of rejection which is a constant theme in all my past relationships." Where I have been left with someone else, it leaves me with a feeling of not being good enough or attractive enough. Even if I know these men who are not right for me, they leaving me for another woman are traumatic. How can I get over the lack of self-esteem and this feeling of being rejected?"

What stupidity am I using with invention and the artificial intensity of the mindscape I am using? And everything that brings up to me, uncreate and destroy that. <u>Good and Bad, Right and Wrong, POD and POC, All Nine, Shorts, Boys and Beyonds.</u>

In this conversation she stated that none of the men that she knows she does not want them and they are not good for her. You would have to create an illusion to match that vibration that you actually had something in common.

How common are you making yourself with the illusion of what you are choosing? Everything that brings up, can we un-create and destroy that? <u>Good and Bad, Right and Wrong, POD and POC, All Nine, Shorts, Boys and Beyonds.</u>

Where did you come from? We create ourselves to match someone else's vibration and we create that illusion. Can you get a sense of how exhausting is that for a body?

It is the form and then you have to make it.

Everywhere that you are holding on to someone, and everywhere you are holding out for; who you decided you should be and could be, instead of being the vibration and who you truly be, will you uncreate and destroy that? <u>Good and Bad, Right and Wrong, POD and POC, All Nine, Shorts, Boys and Beyonds.</u>

And all the stories that you are holding on to as who you are, and who you were. When we create a story we buy the real issue of the past.

Then we look to the future, we do not figure out how we created the same thing in the future that we bought into the past. We are actually bringing it to the future and I call it the taste of tomorrow. The taste of yesterday was promised tomorrow. We create ourselves as something that we put into storage for the right moment. Then we get the illusion that there is no such thing as a right moment.

How much have you decided what your reality is like? And what choice did you make as your reality? That truly is not your reality. That is someone else's reality that you are trying to fit into.

What stupidity are you using to try to fit into reality that you are choosing? Everything that is, can we uncreate and destroy that? Good and Bad, Right and Wrong, POD and POC, All Nine, Shorts, Boys and Beyonds.

And all the judgments and conclusions you have it by yourself, what you are and what you are not. What do you love about that? There is something in it, it is the illusion of what you are not. You could ask- Is it even yours to begin with? If I will start asking you now, of what age did you buy into that you were not enough. Everything that is, can we uncreate and destroy that? Good and Bad, Right and Wrong, POD and POC, All Nine, Shorts, Boys and Beyonds.

You can buy the illusion at a very young age that we are not enough. All we are trying to fit in someone else's reality. We are always reformatting ourselves into something that actually does not work for us.

What choice did you make that created the not you? You have decided you are not as the reality that you are choosing. Everything that brings up for everyone can we uncreate and destroy that? Good and Bad, Right and Wrong, POD and POC, All Nine, Shorts, Boys and Beyonds.

What stupidity am I using in the stopping of me that I am choosing? Anywhere you are willing to do something, and let somebody stop you from being juicy, joyous orgasmic contribution that you truly be. Would you un-create and destroy that? Good and Bad, Right and

<u>Wrong, POD and POC, All Nine, Shorts, Boys and Beyonds.</u>

What stupidity am I using with stopping of the need that I am choosing? Because anywhere we buy into illusion, anywhere we buy into limitation, anywhere we buy into judgment we are stopping us. We are stopping any possibility that we have in creating the relationship; that you like to create with yourself, with a partner, a boss or a child. Anywhere you were stopping at, we are creating the illusion. We are now asking other people to buy into. And that we are busy selling. Everything that brings up, can we un-create and destroy that? <u>Good and Bad, Right and Wrong, POD and POC, All Nine, Shorts, Boys and Beyonds.</u>

The willingness actually to choose something different, to step out of the illusion. What you think something is not working for you. Then you could ask what choice did I make to create this as my reality? Everything that brings up un-create and destroy that. <u>Good and Bad, Right and Wrong, POD and POC, All Nine, Shorts, Boys and Beyonds.</u>

Because every time you choose something you are creating a reality. But, what choice did I make here that created this as my reality. And everything that does not allow that to change, un-create and destroy that. <u>Good and Bad, Right and Wrong, POD and POC, All Nine, Shorts, Boys and Beyonds.</u>

And when you ask what choice did I make here that creates this as my reality; you then can follow the energy of possibility, what else is there that I have not been able to be aware of? What choice do I have? What possibility is there? Anything that does not allow that, uncreate and destroy it. <u>Good and Bad, Right and Wrong, POD and POC, All Nine, Shorts, Boys and Beyonds.</u>

We have millions of choices as quickly as we stop ten second increments, as quickly as we stop the energy of the future, something created as we buy into illusion; we also have the capacity to say, "Okay, what else is possible here?" Change that. What else is possible here?" And everything that brings up that, can we uncreate and destroy that? <u>Good and Bad, Right and Wrong, POD and POC, All Nine, Shorts, Boys and Beyonds.</u>

Everywhere that you are waiting for someone to approve of you, will you destroy and uncreate that? <u>Good and Bad, Right and Wrong, POD and POC, All Nine, Shorts, Boys and Beyonds.</u>

Every time something has come up and I buy my own story, I know it's another judgment. With judgment POD and POC, anything that is contracted, anything that is heavy, anything that's a story it is a judgment. It is a limitation. It is an illusion. I am not concerned about it. Everything that brings up to everybody. Can everybody do that? Can we all uncreate and destroy that, rip apart our credit card? <u>Good and Bad, Right and Wrong, POD and POC, All Nine, Shorts, Boys and Beyonds.</u>

Because we wanted it so bad, we are buying on savings, We are buying on hold, on lease. We buy in bulk and bring it all for sure. How is that? Everything that we trying to make right would we be willing to uncreate and destroy that? <u>Good and Bad, Right and Wrong, POD and POC, All Nine, Shorts, Boys and Beyonds.</u>

Because if we try to make something right, that we have already decided it is wrong. Everywhere that we are all trying to make ourselves right, that we have all decided that we are wrong. Would you all be willing to uncreate and destroy them? <u>Good and Bad, Right and Wrong, POD and POC, All Nine, Shorts, Boys and Beyonds.</u>

What stupidity am I using with the rightness I am choosing? Anywhere any point of view you are buying into an illusion.

Question: *"Is it the rightness or the wrongness of me that I am choosing?"*

Yes. We keep going back to the illusion and if that would make it real. Is there something wrong with us? We try and make it real and true. What if there was nothing wrong with it to begin with? What if it was good? What else is possible here? Who also would like to come in and play? What vibration can I be?

You have to put it in a secret and bury it. You have different staging and you have to walk around and try somersault. Then ask what else is possible?

"If you ask what else is possible without doing all that, it is not going to work."

The willingness should be different. It is the willingness that has to be the creative edge of your relationship. Create relationships not at illusion, right in the middle of it.

Question: "Does it mean we can create our relationship all alone? In a relationship isn't it two people?"

Yes you can. We do not create anything alone. We create crap alone, what we could do is be a relationship with ourselves, and add to ask for the contribution of the universe, because everything contributes to us. Plants, trees, chair and the phone we are using right now etc. It is all a contribution to us. It is the willingness to ask that. My whole day has been like that. With contributions from universe it is very good.

What else is possible when you are actually willing to be out of illusion, to step into what you like in a relationship? If you are willing to step into that yourself, it might be vibration that attracts other people looking for the same kind of vibration. What stupidity am I using with this ease that I am choosing? Everything that does not allow that, can we uncreate and destroy that? <u>Good and Bad, Right and Wrong, POD and POC, All Nine, Shorts, Boys and Beyonds.</u>

One of the things that I am just playing with now is the "Ten Keys to Getting Relationship You Would Really Like to Have". May be in ten seconds increments, with no form, structure or significance. It is really fun to see what comes up, and all kinds of stuff like that. It is really great. It has been great for myself as well the people on the call. It has been terrific. It has been really fun.

The interesting thing about it is that the planet is asking for more joy. That is the whole interesting point of view about this illusion. The people are addicted to drama and trauma. If we are intense it means we are in relationship with each other, rather than the lightness and the actually willingness to proceed and to receive everything about that person with no judgment, which probably is another call. We have to do another time.

What stupidity am I using with the lack of fun that I am choosing in all my relationships? What if relationships would add to your life? Would you be willing to give up the illusion that a relationship is your life? What if relationship is a contribution to who you be? And anything that does not allow that, can we un-create and destroy that? <u>Good and Bad, Right and Wrong, POD and POC, All Nine, Shorts, Boys and Beyonds.</u>

Would you be willing to live in the contribution of your life you are living? Anything that does not allow that let us uncreate and destroy that. <u>Good and Bad, Right and Wrong, POD and POC, All Nine, Shorts, Boys and Beyonds.</u>

We have everything all added up. We have created our story, we created our mindscape and we have to spend the rest of our lives matching it. And that is the illusion that we are buying into. That is the situation that we have created.

What stupidity am I using? What is the contribution that I am refusing? Everything that does not allow that let us uncreate and destroy that. <u>Good and Bad, Right and Wrong, POD and POC, All Nine, Shorts, Boys and Beyonds.</u>

How is it getting better than that?

When you buy somebody else's idea of a relationship is true, that is the illusion that you are living to. That is the addiction you have. What if you had a right relationship that worked for you?

WHO IS SUSAN LAZAR HART

Susan Lazar Hart has travelled the world as a radio host, motivational speaker and co-founder of Right Relationship For You. Susan combines the tools of Access Consciousness with her real world experience as a wife, mother, life coach and relationship counselor to introduce people to a whole new possibility in their relationships with EVERYTHING.

Whether you're sorting out issues with your mate, your children, your boss, your body or even your finances…Susan Lazar Hart delivers information that is easy to understand and gets results. A favorite at women's conferences and Natural Living Expos in Canada and the United States, Susan Lazar Hart is a crowd pleaser. Susan is an invitation to intimacy and relationships from a different point of view. Her straight-forward approach and irreverent sense of humor keeps audiences mesmerized as she shares tools that are not only simple to use, they get immediate and profound results.

Here are some comments from a recent class:

Thank you Susan! Thank you for being in my life! It's been now a couple days of total lightness! I have not experienced anything like this for… mmm… I actually don't remember when I had such experience…
GP - Montreal

Susan is the key Right Relationship facilitator…tremendously caring as well as fun.

DL – Australia

"Intimacy and Relationships, like gardens, must begin with seeds that are nurtured, cared for and cultivated with awareness."

Susan Lazar Hart

Susan Lazar Hart is an invitation to intimacy and relationships from a different point of view. Her classes and talks are for singles or couples of all orientations, lengths of commitment, and stages of life.

CHOOSING FOR RELATIONSHIPS THAT WORK FOR YOU

By Susan Lazar Hart

Get to a place where you actually have choice- with the people in your life, with money, with your body. Shift and change what isn't working for you. Create the relationships you always knew should be possible with… everything!

http://www.magicofbeing.com

CHAPTER SIX

❖

LEARNING TO LIVE AGAIN AFTER GRIEF

By Wendy Mulder

Registered Nurse, Founder of Living With Ease

Wendy's first book "Learning from Grief" was written while she was nursing her mother through a terminal illness at home. What was it like?

Well, what I found is that while that person was alive, I enjoyed each day with that person as much as I could. So when she did pass away, I felt such gratefulness that I had been there and known her. It never felt like it actually ended. It just changed the relationship and my question is always – "Would they ever truly want you to be sad? Or would they want you to be actually enjoying and filling your life with lots of joy?" The sadness comes, the tears come but you must move on. That's a wonderful thing about the tools of Access Consciousness. Yes, you allow the tears to come. You allow the sadness to be there but then in the next 10 seconds you think – "What else is possible now?" But don't sit in it. Don't let yourself get stuck in it because that's where this whole grief overtakes so many people's lives. It can be so much easier than I think a lot of people make it.

What really stands out from the experiences of grief that I've had with loved ones passing over is it's been the lack of them being there physically. You were saying before that it's not that they are not there; they are there but the relationship changes. I perceive the energy of the people who are actually alive right now and how that feels to me versus perceiving the energy of people who have passed over and it's almost like they are not there anymore. What would you say to that?

I suppose it's that one of "Yes, if they are gone, do you still have their beautiful memories of them?" They may not be there in the physical form, though you still have those memories. You still have that part of them that always will be with you. This is a fairly big area as well, because I've had quite a lot of different people that I have known who are now gone and even though physically I can't see them, energetically I feel - "What else is possible there now for you to be able to go out?" It's acknowledging that time that you did have with them, allowing those memories and just being willing to actually live your life. Not going into trying to define or put some word or form of structure on that energy of when they passed away is very important.

People in grief are in that place of "It should be like this and they should still be around"

All the thoughts, feelings and emotions around what death is and how it should look and all the significance of all of that, all the wrongness of death and all of the wrongness that people go into when someone has passed away, let's just totally, utterly, godzillion amount of times, destroy and uncreate all of that. <u>Right and Wrong, Good and Bad, POC and POD, All nine, Shorts, Boys and Beyonds.</u>

Kindness

What is kindness? What is the key ingredient to rediscovering you?

A lot of people blame themselves when someone has passed away. There's a lot of, "Maybe I didn't do enough" and they start going into the wrongness of themselves. The way that they still think they are going to be here forever, that they just buy into and that actually allows them to start judging themselves, which we truly don't choose to do. That person who passed away as well would never want you to be like that. So, let's just un-create and destroy all that.

Right and Wrong, Good and Bad, POC and POD, All nine, Shorts, Boys and Beyond

The other thing that I find comes up as well, is that when someone does pass away, a lot of times people almost disappear or exit their life, because then they have none of the thought or emotions of past events. It puts up a smoke wall for you to stay there than to actually move on. I think a lot of people think that if they move on, they are going to forget about their loved ones.

Everything that is uncreate and destroy all of that. <u>Right and Wrong, Good and Bad, POC and POD, All nine, Shorts, Boys and Beyonds.</u>

So, what if you could actually continue to rediscover yourself? Still have the beautiful memories of the person that's passed away and live in the next 10 seconds, and be willing to allow certain tears and be willing to be in allowance of yourself and for the person that has passed away. That's what's so wonderful with some of the Access tools.

It's just about, "Ok, so what can I be and do different right now that could allow for more ease and joy for me and for all those loved ones that I've known?" Everything that doesn't allow that, let's just totally destroy and un-create all that. <u>Right and Wrong, Good and Bad, POC and POD, All nine, Shorts, Boys and Beyonds.</u>

Caregivers

So Wendy, share with us some of the tools, some questions, some clearings that people can do who are actually looking after a loved one who is going through a terminal illness. I have witnessed when my aunt was just around 40 and she had a terminal illness. Her children were really young. Her daughters were in grade 8 and grade 6 and I was perceiving their thoughts, feelings and emotions all the time and I was like, "Oh my god! What is it going to be like for them without a mother!" and totally buying into all their grief and for me what was coming up was, "Oh my god! What if I had lost my mom at that age" Can you talk a little bit about all of that.

Ok. What would it take for you not to step in and validate this reality on how grief is seen based on all you thoughts, feelings and emotions when a closed one has died? Everything that is, let's totally destroy and uncreate all that? <u>Right and Wrong, Good and Bad, POC and POD, All nine, Shorts, Boys and Beyonds.</u>

Let's set one tool of "Who does all this belong to?" which is a great tool to use to about 99% of all of that thought, feeling and emotion. We are so aware, when someone's dying, there can be a lot of stress in people's lives. A lot of stuff comes up. Suddenly a lot of family dynamics come up and if you're choosing to step into that and being connected to all those thoughts, feelings and emotions, it can be very, very stressful. But you can have another choice. You can be willing to be all of what you choose to be. Be aware of how everyone functions around you and not step into that whole reaction of what's going on and actually be willing to ask - "What would work for me here?" "What would be ease and joy for you?"

That's one of the key things to me when I started looking after my mom. It was a choice. It was "What do I choose here? Do I choose to do this or was it under obligation? Or was it something I had to do or something I should do? It was a choice and it was choice of ease and joy. So I set it up for me so that it would work for me with ease and joy and this facilitated so much more ease for me, for my mom, for my relatives because I was the one that was choosing it. I was the one the house or running the decisions of how it should go, and not getting into all of the thoughts, feelings and emotions of what was going on for everyone else.

I have a beautiful tool that you can use. It's basically an *Interesting Point of View* of where everyone else is with respect to what's going on. There's an energy that comes up because grief has so much significance in this reality. When you talk about grief, where does it hit you in the body? It's not a light thing and what I've always been saying is - "What would it take to have a totally different perspective on that?" Allow that person to enjoy those last days with you and allow the people around to have the ease and joy as well, so that we facilitate so much more ease, so much more consciousness and it can be a journey of total ease.

Letting Go Of Grief

I still perceive this whole energy of people who've really lost their loved ones and are just holding on to that energy. How could you facilitate them in letting go?

A great tool is say, for example, with you and your grandmother. You are still holding on to grief there. What if you could actually un-create and destroy your relationship with your mother or your grandmother in relationship to you. Let's just do that now.

Will you un-create and destroy your relationship with your grandmother, even though she's not alive anymore. So everything that is and everything around all of that, let's just uncreate and destroy it. <u>Right and Wrong, Good and Bad, POC and POD, All nine, Shorts, Boys and Beyonds.</u>

I just had this awareness, when you said uncreate and destroy the relationship. It's that interesting point of view of you having to be physically around for me all the time. Literally by doing this, you let go of that and that facilitates ease. That's a beautiful one too. Just by un-creating and destroying, and that's if they are alive or not, that changed the relationship. By un-creating and destroying it, you are allowing for so much more ease in your whole connection and communication with that person. So how does it get any better than that?

Caregivers

There are sometimes people, who are actually nursing and who are caregivers to people with debilitating illness like dementia and things like that. This is a purely cultural perspective, but when I look at the west, I find that still people have a lot of choices in terms of the kind of care that they can offer them, but if I look at what goes on in the east, especially back home in India and so on, it's almost like people in the house who are nursing and caring for people find it a really difficult journey taking care of them. What would you say to that?

Ok, so what if you could actually just change that point of view? What if the people that you are talking about, what if they could be educated on how easy it could be? If you are educated and start to be aware of the words that you speak and the vibration that you are, if someone's saying that this is a really difficult journey for me to look after a certain somebody, then that's what it's going to be. That's the beautiful part of being in the question, "How can I do this?" or, "What else is possible here that could allow me to do what I require to do and do it with total ease?" But we've never been taught that. We've been taught that we aren't allowed to actually have choices. So that, to me is what I would suggest. When I'm with people that are having all these issues, actually re-educating them to say - "Ok, what if start being in the question" because while you are having these conclusions, nothing's going to change.

Questions For Caregivers

The question is – "Is that for the carer we're asking the question for?"

It is a carer for those who are actually looking after a loved one at home. At the moment, things are not working out, so it's actually educating that person to see that they can actually ask questions and that they are an energy already and there's a vibration there. Be willing to see that there are choices here. They can't do this, it's too difficult, and it's too hard. Actually delete a lot of that to allow them to step into other possibilities. Asking questions without any conclusion of what the answer should be, allow what is required to show up for you . Some Questions they could ask. How can I do it with ease ? Is there another choice that would work even better?

Really it comes down to simple choice. Be the question and don't give up on it. Keep going with it. I guess a lot of people think there's no such thing as magic anymore and what if magic was just about you being willing to be more of who you'd be and acknowledge that. That's what Access does. It's actually empowering people to know what they know, and using that with a career. "Well, if I'm going to do this job with this person or if I'm going to take this on, what choices do I have here? What else is possible that I haven't even considered today that would facilitate more ease in this role?" That's a great one that I use a lot of times – "What else is possible here that I haven't even considered?" That just opens it up to the Universe. It's not like you go looking for an answer straight up. It's just allowing that. Maybe later on in the day, you'll get an awareness of something and that's the magic, because nothing's impossible if you're really willing to choose for you.

When you ask the question, you are opening the door for those energies to show up. The energies that you can perceive but you don't even know how they are going to actually come into physical form. Asking the question and not being in anyway invested in how the outcome is going to be. But being willing to trust in yourself to be willing to be the question and ask it and allow for the Universe to actually support you on that. It *is* magic. It's just that we've been taught in this reality for so long and we've been trained for so long that we don't have a choice. That we have to do this and we've got to do it the way that the system in this country says we have to do it. Well I've proven that wrong many, many times, where it's just keep on it and just be the question. That allows for the magic.

I think a lot of people might take a little step then get a little bit disappointed and go "Oh, well this is just the way it is. This is just the way it is." It's a common saying of people. Saying "Oh this is just the way it is. So, we'll just have to accept it." So what I'm saying is what if there was a totally different possibility here that you actually could be the question and you were actually willing to allow ease for the person you're caring for and also allow ease for yourself so that there is joy? Ask the question of yourself as well "If I choose to do this, will this expand my joy in my life?" and it's just that amazing energy of choice and to play with that choice, which then has that beautiful visual effect. What else is truly possible?

Losing Children

So till now we've been kind of tapping into the energy of losing loved ones who are kind of older than us, maybe our parents, our grandparents and so on. Speak a little bit about people who are either going through or who have actually lost their children and I think that's a big one for a lot of people.

Yes, it is and how incredibly aware are children? What if we could look at what an amazing gift that they were here for as long as they were? Where we might get so scarred that we should decide when or not someone goes? What if we could actually just be willing to be in total allowance and be in so much gratitude for having the gift of this person for as long as we did? Would that person, would that baby, would that child want you to be so grief stricken to never be able to have joy anymore in your life? What if you could actually just be so grateful having had that that person, that beautiful, gorgeous, adorable energy of that child who is just so expansive and so joyful in your life for that long?

Yes, of course you will have the tears and of course you will have all that but also be willing to see that you still have living to do now and that's my point of view on it. It's recognizing the gift of the period of time you had them in your life and really what magic can you be now from having this amazing thing being there in your life? However long it was, whether it was for 2 months or whether it was for 5 years or 10 years. Would they want you to be so engrossed in the thoughts, feelings and emotions of the grief and the trauma and drama of that for the rest of your life or for years to come or would they really truly choose for you to start being who you truly be and have the joy in your life and also have some living again as well?

A lot of people when they are actually looking at losing their children or having lost their children, they go into this place of total guilt, "It should have been me and not them" Can you just speak about that a little bit?

That's that whole energy of those thoughts, feelings and emotions of what they pick up or actually stepping into that judgment of themselves in thinking, "Oh my goodness I didn't do it right" That's not only in children, that's in adults as well. People go into this whole guilt thing and it's a space that people step into. When that energy comes up – it's a heavy energy. It's not light. When it's a light energy it's joyful and it's expansive and for them again, being willing to go, "Ok, what do I do for these next 10 seconds?"

Whatever that energy is, everything around all of that, let's just totally, utterly, godzillion, godzillion, godzillion, un-create and destroy all of that energy that's just come up around all that. <u>Right and Wrong, Good and Bad, POC and POD, All nine, Shorts, Boys and Beyonds.</u>

How much does that guilt, how much does that blame actually get you to disappear or exit your life? Do you get the energy of that?

Everything that is and all those thoughts, feelings and emotions and all those great walls that people put up to actually stay in that state, than actually moving forward or changing that, let's just totally, utterly, un-create and destroy all of that. <u>Right and Wrong, Good and Bad, POC and POD, All nine, Shorts, Boys and Beyonds.</u>

What different choice can you make now that will allow you to be more present in your life? With being more present to allow for all of those thoughts and those feelings to come past you but don't get stuck. They are going to come but don't be that rock that gets washed away in the river and then twelve months later, you might wake and go, "My goodness, I'm still here in this place!"

Everything here and everything around all of that and all of those thoughts, feelings, emotions and attachments and everything else around all that, all of the conclusions and all the guilt and all the blame and everything else around all of that, let's just totally, utterly, godzillion amounts of times, un-create and destroy it. <u>Right and Wrong, Good and Bad, POC and POD, All nine, Shorts, Boys and Beyonds.</u>

Everywhere that you've resisted and reacted to it, and everywhere that you've aligned and agreed with all of that, let's just uncreate and destroy all of that as well. <u>Right and Wrong, Good and Bad, POC and POD, All nine, Shorts, Boys and Beyonds.</u>

Grief brings up this energy. People have lost loved ones and grief is a part that comes after loss. So everything that is as well, all of the conclusions around what or how this reality sees all of that, and how that should all function and how we should all function in this reality when some grief or some loss or anything, all the expectations, all the assumptions that we have around grief and everything else around all of that, and all the 'should's' and all the 'have to's' and all the 'got to's' let's just totally, utterly, godzillion amount of times, un-create and destroy it all? Yeah? <u>Right and wrong, good and bad, POC and POD, all nine, shorts, boys and beyonds.</u>

Losing The Breadwinner

It's so fascinating. When I was going into this interview, I said, "Hmm, I don't really have anything to talk about grief" Now I have all these things popping all over the place. I'm getting the energy of this. People in my life are showing up who've gone through grief or who are going through grief.

So the other energy which is showing up is people who actually lose someone who is the "breadwinner in the family". So either their husband or their father and they become stuck in this loop and they've exited from their life and they go through almost their whole life saying that, "Oh my god, if he had been around my life would have been totally different." What they are creating and generating in their life, if the breadwinner had been around? How their life would have looked like versus how it looks now? What judgments they have about it?

How much do we actually choose to blame someone else instead of actually looking at ourselves and looking at what else is possible. How easy is it for us to blame someone else. That means really that we don't have to do anything different. So everything around all of that as well and everywhere that , even in relationships with people who are still alive and the breadwinners out there, it's how much of that as well?

"Well this is not working for me, so, and it's because of such and such and such and such."

Everything that that is as well, all of that negativity that just keeps us holding and just keeps you in that loop really. Let's just uncreate and destroy everywhere in our bodies all the trifle sequencing systems that actually keep us locked into that whole cycle going on. Maybe looking around all of that, let's just totally, utterly un-create and destroy all that. <u>Right and Wrong, Good and Bad, POC and POD, All nine, Shorts, Boys and Beyonds.</u>

It just keeps coming back to us all. What is it that that I can be and do different today? When we say the word "different", it's not different of what this reality says, it could be just a simple little thing. It could be just, "Oh wow, maybe I could just go and have a day of…" whatever that might be. Just total nurturing to you or just enjoying something that could be fun to you, that actually allows you to start being more present with yourself, that allows you to trust yourself more and allows you to be truly honest with yourself, so you can really ask some honest questions. What else is truly possible? Truly? A lot of the times, we judge ourselves.

When we judge ourselves, where is it that we bought that we have to be mean to ourselves? Where is it that we bought that we have to be kind to everyone else and to put ourselves right down on the list? So everything that is, yeah, <u>Right and Wrong, Good and Bad, POC and POD, All nine, Shorts, Boys and Beyonds.</u>

Trifold Sequencing Systems

Trifold Sequencing Systems is just basically what you were saying "Get on that loop" and people just go around and around. You can just imagine this circle that's going around and you being actually able to just step out of that and go, "Ok, so what else is truly possible here that I haven't even considered?" It's probably the easiest way and sometimes it's just getting the energy of it which is what you be and as soon as I've said it, it's clicking out of that. Our bodies and our beings have been so entrained, to what our family will like or how our mother and father were and so, the more aware that we become, we are able to see that we have choices.

Some of these incredible Body Processes like the **Trifle Sequencing Systems** actually allow us to start letting go of some of that in our bodies.

All the trifle sequencing systems in our body and all of that those people are actually willing to let go of that as much as they allow them to, let's just totally, utterly un-create and destroy it all and dissipate it all from our bodies back into Earth. Everything that doesn't allow that, let's just totally, utterly, godzillion amount of times, uncreate and destroy all that? <u>Right and Wrong, Good and Bad, POC and POD, All nine, Shorts, Boys and Beyonds.</u>

One of the things around grief is what if you could actually stop judging yourself? What if you could actually be willing to be kind to yourself and be in allowance of yourself? I remember when someone had been saying that to me probably about 3 years ago, (I was doing a body class), "What if you could just be in allowance of yourself?" and I went, "I have no idea what you're talking about. I mean 'allowance of yourself', what's that?" It was just really, really interesting. Then it was just like, "Oh, so, maybe stop judging myself?" I said, "Oh, what if I could actually just be in gratitude that I'm alive and breathing and I have this amazing body and I'm here now, and , maybe I could enjoy myself. Oh, wow! Ok."

Everywhere that you have always been taught you have to be in allowance of everyone else and couldn't be in allowance of yourself and couldn't be able to choose for yourself or couldn't actually speak up for yourself and you couldn't actually have your own point of view about what it is for you, so all of that, let's just totally uncreate and destroy all of that and allow for some of that to show up in people's lives. <u>Right and Wrong, Good and Bad, POC and POD, All nine, Shorts, Boys and</u>

<u>Beyonds.</u>

I think it becomes so familiar with us, because sometimes for a lot of people or different cultures as well, it can be a familiar energy. Being willing to get out of that familiar energy and truly just even today, with people who are reading, what if you could just take two tools away with you of "How does it get any better than this?" and "What else is possible?". Even if you just use those 2 tools and everything that's going on in your life right now, go "How does it get any better than this?" It's constantly moving into the question. Say I give you an example. You've got a terrible big bill that's like thousands of dollars. But if you went, "How does it get any better than this", it's still allowing for that energy to keep it standing. You're not going into any conclusion and then maybe you get a whole lot of money in your bank. Wow, how does it get any better than this? But that's the energy of it, actually allowing for it to keep moving, to keep expanding, and to keep being in the question and that is such an amazing gift. Even if you could just take that one "What else is possible now?" Or take both of those, you have no idea what it's going to look like, but you're putting the question out there and not stay stuck in that one spot.

Do You Have Choice

So this is bringing up some different energy now and this is one about expectations. So, just recently I was talking to this woman and she was actually looking after her daughter who was autistic and her daughter was about 18 or 19 and basically, she was just exhausted from looking after her daughter and she finally made a choice for herself and she decided to move her daughter into a care facility. She said, " I had my family show up and my cousin and they were making me feel so wrong and they had all these expectations. They asked me what kind of mother I was for sending my daughter away, etc. so on and so forth" So she was of course functioning from a total choice. She was looking at this place of what was working for her and where she really needed to be kind to herself, but I know that there are a lot of people who really can't step into that place and what would you say to that and what tools can you give them?

A lot of people get caught in the obligation and the expectation of what they should do for their family and where did we buy into that? I, having a nursing background, still working in different areas of nursing, I see lot of people who are carers and they take on these roles without really asking any questions and then they get so exhausted. Then they get angry that they actually are doing this, and they are not facilitating anyone themselves or the person they are looking after. So what your friend was doing was, "Ok, what's going to work here for me?" and it's stepping into that. It's actually being willing to step into that. It's a demand, really, to start to be kind to you, and it's different for every person to have what's kind to them and it's starting as well to become aware of the amount of energy, or expectations, of assumptions, of what we're told is a fair amount of what we should be doing. It just feels so heavy. Yet, that's what a lot of people are doing. That's what a lot of people do. Well, I couldn't not do it, because then I'll be judged.

That's where I go back that one step – If you can just make that demandment first up to yourself, that no matter what it takes, I'm choosing. I'm starting today to be kind to me. It might be a little bit of a process, but even starting to make that demandment, it actually gives you more strength to be able to stop judging yourself.

Also being able to be in totally interesting point of view when judgments are coming your way. One really, really great tool is when someone is projecting something at you, it gives you an incredible awareness of how that person is functioning, and for many, many years, people used to project stuff at me and I used to take it on personally and judge myself. It wasn't until many times ago, by continuing this thing – "What would it take for you to get there?" Whenever someone is projecting something at you, they are giving you the awareness of how they are functioning and that was just such a relief!

"Oh, wow, ok, I don't have to take on any of that. I just have to be willing to see how that person is functioning and tell them " Thank You ! Thanks for caring!". Also saying to myself "No matter what it takes,

I'm going to start choosing for me. I'm going to start being kind to me and I have no idea how that would look." You'll just find that making that demandment and putting that question out there allows for something to change.

Everything that is and everything around all of that, let's destroy and uncreate it. <u>Right and Wrong, Good and Bad, POC and POD, All nine, Shorts, Boys and Beyonds.</u>

It's a totally different perspective, yet when we see it, "Oh wow, that's so easy." It's a judgment; it's such it just contracts down so therefore, it doesn't allow for any space. It doesn't allow for any ease. It doesn't allow for any joy. So if you are doing it on yourself and then someone's projecting at you as well, where are you? Where have you gone? You wouldn't want to stay in it like that. So everything that is, lets uncreate and destroy it. <u>Right and Wrong, Good and Bad, POC and POD, All nine, Shorts, Boys and Beyonds.</u>

What else is possible here?

Choice Creates Awareness; Awareness Doesn't Create Choice

People have lots of awareness about things though until they are willing to choose something/anything, nothing will change! Choice creates awareness.... For example, I had the awareness of this telecall coming up though it wasn't until I was willing to choose it could anything different show up around what I am aware of with grief. And it never looks or shows up the way we think it might .

It's choice and also the question. Take for example, you're there and you're looking after someone and things are not going well. You say, "Well, ok, what else is possible here?" We've been taught to look for the answer and to fix it. So this is just totally different. That person has to choose that energy for themselves. They've got to make that demandment and choose, but also it doesn't stop there. It's an energy that keeps moving and you keep going with it. So, it's about "What question could I ask here that would allow for more ease to show up for me?" Be willing to be those questions. It's not, "Ok so I'm going to choose right now, I've got to be kind to me."

That pretty much stops the energy. You're not going very far there. Whereas if you could just go, "Ok, so what else could be possible here today to allow for me to start choosing to be kind to me?" It's a choice and it's being willing to actually play with those questions and play with them and play with the choices and be willing to know that you don't have to get it right. There are many, many choices that I've done that I've lost out on and said, "Oh, ok, that wasn't such a good choice," but if you are living only 10 seconds, it's, "Ok, what should I choose now? Ok, so what other question can I ask here that would allow and facilitate more ease and more choices?" Just play. I just can't stress enough on that, on the energy of playing with your questions and playing with your choices.

We've also bought that, "Well I make this one choice and I have to get this choice right no matter what, because if I don't get it right, my goodness!" So a totally different perspective of changing that and going, "Well, ok, what else can I do now that would actually facilitate more ease for me and facilitate more ease for caring for this person and asking the question of the person" I'll give you a prime example with my dad. A lot of my family had all these points of view that how it should be done, we can't do that, or we should do that, we have to do this, we've got to do it this way. Where are the questions in that? What would work for you, dad? What would you like to do? So how is that working with me? That's my question to myself. "I can do that. Well, it might not work today but maybe in a week's time we can do that. How would that work for you?" There's just this sense of ease in the communication and a sense of ease for him. I don't have a point of view about how he should be living his life or how I should be doing something for him.

Asking Questions Energetically

Sometimes like when the person you are caring for is not able to communicate, would it help just to ask the questions energetically?

Yes, totally. The more present that you can be, the more willing you are to just totally be there with yourself, the more aware you are about what it is that would facilitate more ease for that person that you are looking after as well. What is the kindness of you and the gentleness of you that you acknowledge? What if you could acknowledge that the kindness and gentleness of you was a strength of yours that allowed you to have so much more clarity in whatever it is that you are doing? So everything that is and everything that doesn't allow that for everyone, let's just totally un-create and destroy everywhere that vulnerability, that gentleness and that kindness of themselves. What if that was just such an amazing strength that we would allow that we are, that we could then actually be willing to give out so much more clarity to what it is that we could do to assist that person. We are looking after and to make choices for ourselves. Start having that beautiful gratitude all the way around. So what else is truly possible here that we haven't even considered today?

Last Thoughts

Ok. So probably my question that I'd like to put out to everyone is – "What if today was your last day, what would you choose? What could you be and do differently today that would actually change things right away for you?" Whatever it is that's going on at the moment that's really not working for you and it's heavy or whatever it might be, what would it take for this to change? What if it was that simple? What would it take for us to have much, much more fun and much, much more joy? What if money wasn't the issue, what would you choose?

WHO IS WENDY MULDER

Wendy Mulder RN. BNSc. CFMW is a Registered Nurse, Access Consciousness Certified Facilitator and founder of Living With Ease and Kindnesswithgrief.com.

As a professional and andcarer for family and friends through terminal illness, Wendy shines a different light on grief and loss: "Grief is an area that many people don't like to talk about because it is seen as sad, heavy and significant. I pose the question, 'What if we could see grief from a space of allowance, question, and possibility?'"

Wendy facilitates people world-wide in the arena of living beyond grief through her books, workshops, private sessions and events, and offers pragmatic tools and techniques for moving forward from difficult situations. She has an online radio show, "Moving Beyond Grief" at Blogtalkradio.com

THE EARTH IS PRAGMATIC – ARE YOU STILL DRAMATIC

By Susanna Mittermaier

People in this world love being dramatic, celebrate lack and limitations… the Earth does not: it is pragmatic and does what works, no points of view and judgments. What are the elements the Earth is offering with this and what inspiration can this be to us? http://www.magicofbeing.com

CHAPTER SEVEN

❖

HAVING YOUR CAKE AND EATING IT TOO

By Margaret Braunack

"The Wizard From OZ"

Facilitator of Change, Transformation & Possibility

Work With Inmates Of The Maximum Security Prison

An Access Consciousness Facilitator from Brisbane, Wendy Mulder, who actually created this following the energy of the book she had written, and I were involved in this program. She asked me to join her – originally the plan was that we were going to work with the staff at the prison and then it got changed from that and we ended up working with the inmates. We taught the inmates "The BARS" and the changes that occurred for them within the prison system were phenomenal. My own life changed quite dynamically during and after that time also and I really got to see how the gift of contribution really works. Contribution being a 2 way street, as you gift so shall your receive.

A lot of the inmates in the prison have committed crimes under the influence of drugs and alcohol. We worked with their addictions, as well as teaching them the BARS. A lot of them shifted into peace and ease with their bodies and became totally relaxed. Many of them were on night-time medications, which was a major problem for the prison and so the management was excited to know that a lot of the inmates were coming off their night-time medications because they were a lot more relaxed.

"What about the changes that occurred in the prison system? Did you finally get around to teaching the bars to the staff?"

No. The prisoners were more interested in learning the BARS than the staff ever were. That was very interesting indeed for me to hear. I don't really get attached to anything, it's what showed up and it showed up for as long as it showed up and there have been a lot of major changes with the prison system since. The prison is actually now being run by a totally different organization and at this point, there has been no invitation for us to come back.

Everything shows up as it does, it creates whatever change is required in that moment and just trusting that and not forcing it to be something different is the greatest gift. I know the change that those men received in that time we were there created miracles for a lot of them and what they choose to do with that is entirely up to them. We totally do live from choice creates awareness.

Having Your Cake and Eating it Too!

This is the title of my book. It was quite amazing how this new product showed up. I had been asking questions for quite some time about what I would like to add to my life. Gary Douglas, the founder of Access Consciousness, had empowered me several years ago to acknowledge that I have capacities with food and bodies, and so for about eighteen months after he facilitated me to look at that, I asked a lot more questions and he kept on saying to me, "You know that that's a capacity that you could be making a lot of money from". I was present and aware of what he was saying, and I wasn't sure what that was going to look like. So I just kept asking questions, because owning a restaurant, or studying to be a chef didn't do it for me so I kept on wondering about how to integrate facilitating people to changing possibilities with food and bodies. That is how I came up with the title. I was actually facilitating some classes in Melbourne, Australia earlier and I went to dinner with some old friends. Later that evening after talking about what I was choosing to write about in my first book a friend suggested this title. It is about facilitating people into a whole new world of choice and possibility. It's getting people to see that it's not just an either-or Universe, it's not about this choice or that choice- it's about the willingness to know you can have anything your heart truly desires. It hasn't been created about food and bodies after all; it is all about empowerment to choice. Food, sex and bodies is for my third book.

Four Elements – Hedonism, Opulence, Decadence and Orgasmic Living

Hedonism - The actual meaning in a dictionary prior 1946 of "hedonism" is finding the pleasure in all things. It doesn't cost money to find pleasure in all things. I live in a beautiful apartment on the edge of the Brisbane River and I find pleasure in walking along the river and having a cool breeze and the sun on my skin. I find pleasure in having ducks waddle up to me and I find pleasure and joy in just sitting, watching the city cats (catamarans) gliding along the river or walking at night with the city lights gleaming on the water. It's finding that pleasure and it doesn't necessarily have to cost money. It is a choice to find the pleasure in all things.

"When we actually read these words – hedonism, opulence, decadence and orgasmic living, the first thing which pops into our mind is that it is all to do with money. We always go to "how much money it will cost?"

When you actually get the energy of hedonism, it has been gleaned as wrongness in this reality. It is wrong to be a hedonist. It is wrong to be different. It is wrong to have the pleasure of everything. You have got to fit in and be the same as everyone else.

Everywhere you're working hard at destroying you so that you fit in, to be the same as everyone else will you now destroy and uncreate it all please? <u>Right and Wrong, Good and Bad, POD and POC, All Nine, Shorts, Boys and Beyonds.</u>

To truly be living from hedonism, opulence, decadence and including the orgasmic living in there, you have to be willing to see how different you are and you have to be willing to receive the judgment of others and to acknowledge that you are choosing a life that's different to what everyone else is choosing.

Everywhere you are unwilling to receive the judgments of others, where you put up walls and barriers to receive it all, the good, bad and ugly, will you now please un-create and destroy it all? <u>Right and Wrong, Good and Bad, POD and POC, All Nine, Shorts, Boys and Beyonds.</u>

Judgments

"When you talk about receiving judgment of others, can you tell a little bit more about this? How do you actually receive judgment of others? For me it feels like an arrow through you."

For all of my life, from my earliest recall, I have perceived so much energy and I never really had the tools and techniques to know what to do with it all. I never found it easy to be at school or anywhere for that matter as I would perceive all this intensity of energy and I always believed that everyone was judging me. I never fitted in and I was always different. I actually went into hiding.

I'm aware that a lot of my life has been done from hiding, of not wanting people to see me, not wanting to show up. I'd just go back into hiding again whenever I was willing to show up. It has only really been since using the tools of Access Consciousness that I started to really show up in my life and I am willing to now receive all of that energy and intensity that I perceive, even the energies of judgment. I ask a question as to whether the person is judging me or am I perceiving their judgments of themselves.

I have the awareness that most of the time what I perceive are their judgments of themselves. The greatest gift this has given me is that it has allowed me to come out of hiding. Now I'm willing to show up as me and it doesn't matter what other people think about me. I'm just willing to receive the energies of all of that, all the barriers and the **walls down, and just receive it as an interesting point of view.**

"Does it mean that when we actually get judgments, we tend to put up walls and barriers? If we were to actually become vulnerable and just let down all our barriers and receive all that energy without concern, just allow us to receive that energy and so much more becomes available to us?"

Yes. People don't realize that it is these walls and barriers that we put up to the judgments stop our receiving. If you align and agree with the person's point of view, that is the positive polarity, and if you resist and react to a person's point of view, that is the negative polarity. Either/or, whenever you put walls and barriers up to receiving, you shut out and you stop your money flows. You stop more fun, joy and whatever else you would like to have in your life and you totally shut you out of your own life. You separate you from you, which then separates you from everyone and everything. With the willingness to pull the walls down and receive it all, you're going to have a lot more fun, a lot more ease and a lot more money showing up in your life.

"When wondering whether the person is judging you, you get the realization that he's not really judging you but himself. That opens up everything."

There's actually a lot of freedom in using these tools. When you actually know it's these self-imposed barriers that stop you then everything can change. When you have these walls and barriers it's like putting yourself in prison. "I like that person. I don't like that person. That's good food. That's bad food. That's a good person. That's a bad person." All these judgments that we live in constantly and the walls and barriers that we have in place so that we don't have to receive that intense energy, shuts down our awareness and it shuts out our entire life from ourselves.

For me, the more I'm willing to function from no walls, no barriers, my life just gets more fun, more easy and it's such a sense of freedom in that. And there's a lot more money showing up.

Anything that now doesn't allow you to totally receive the energies of hedonism, opulence, decadence and orgasmic living, and not have a point of view and just keep choosing what works for you, everything all of that is, can we un-create and destroy it all please? <u>Right and Wrong, Good and Bad, POD and POC, All Nine, Shorts, Boys and Beyonds.</u>

Opulence – The literal meaning of opulence is about the power in the world. It's about having the riches and the affluence and in Australia we have what's called the "Tall Poppy Syndrome". We have this sense that if you go beyond what everyone else is choosing, you'll be called a tall poppy and everyone will work to pull you down. It's quite a significant thing that exists in Australia that we should all just be the same.

Those who are choosing so much more and are willing to be seen and are willing to have an opulent life, you have to be willing to receive the judgment. You have to be willing to be called a tall poppy. You have to be willing to do it so different and not have the point of view that people are destroying you with their judgments. You are different and it is ok to be different.

Everything all of that is, will you now uncreate and destroy it all please? <u>Right and Wrong, Good and Bad, POD and POC, All Nine, Shorts, Boys and Beyonds.</u>

Nilofer: "I was in the US in the summer and when I would tell people that I'm from Dubai, they'd believe that I have a lot of money. I found myself really justifying and saying "how do you know, what if I didn't?" I was in the judgment until I actually read somewhere, "Are You Willing to be known as Rich?" and I was shocked."

When people project into your Universe that you have a lot of money, then you're actually allowing yourself to have a lot more money from that projection. It's like someone projects into your Universe that you're wealthy or you're poor or whatever their judgments are of you, then that is often what we create.

You definitely want people to project into your Universe that you have a lot of money, because then more money gets to show up. But you have to be willing to receive all the projections that people have of you to allow that to show up.

Everything all of that brings up, will you uncreate and destroy it all? Right and Wrong, Good and Bad, POD and POC, All Nine, Shorts, Boys and Beyonds.

Decadence - This is a big one for a lot of people as the literal meaning of decadence is about immoral behavior. Immoral behavior would be something like doing something so different to what anyone else is doing that it is deemed as immoral. What if there's no right, no wrong, it's just choice creates awareness? If you were totally choosing something because it was choosing from a rewarding choice or choosing from something that's going to expand your agenda, then with those elements, just because someone judges it as immoral, is that just their judgments and their points of view?

But if it's something that you're choosing that's really working for you, then often what we talk about in Access Consciousness is when you are choosing differently to others, you may require to function from "Just for Me, Just for Fun, Never Tell Anyone."

"We buy into other people's points of view and then we make that our reality. I remember just reading those words, and I was amused."

It's quite interesting to see where people will go with the judgments in this reality.

Judgments are what keep this reality in existence. Every moment of every day, we're constantly in judgment of the Right or Wrong, Good or Bad, and regardless of what it is, whether it is with other people, with the food we eat, with bodies or with our choices, we are constantly locked in that state of judgment which is how this reality keeps getting created. The thing is when you are willing to be you and change the world, when you are willing to choose your reality that works for you, then you have to let go of the judgments and that will allow you to function from 'Choice Creates Awareness'. You make a choice, you'll have an awareness of what that choice brings you and if that choice is not going to work for you, you have to be willing to change it and make a new choice, without going into the wrongness of your choices. In all the work I do with people, most people are paralyzed in the no-choice Universe. It's like they are paralyzed in fear of choosing "The Wrong Thing". You have to truly get that there is no wrong choice. So it's just choice creates awareness.

Everywhere we are paralyzed, in the what if I make another wrong choice - it's just from that place where we go into no-choice, instead of asking a different question. Everything that is uncreate and destroy it all please? <u>Right and Wrong, Good and Bad, POD and POC, All Nine, Shorts, Boys and Beyonds.</u>

What Question Can You Ask To Have The Four Elements Show Up In Your Life Every Day

It's the willingness to be in the question every moment of every day. Having gratitude is the greatest way of allowing these elements to show up. Being more of you and being grateful for everything, judgment can't live where gratitude is living. When you are grateful for whatever shows up, the Good, Bad and Ugly, then you know that you are eliminating judgment from your Universe and it's really the judgment that you have of you or anything or anyone in your Universe that stops you from having these four elements – the hedonism, the opulence, the decadence and the orgasmic living.

It's your willingness to be 'Interesting Point of View' for every single point of view that you have about everything. This is the fastest, easiest way to get to have these elements show up in your life.

Interesting Point of View

I have spoken about the polarity – whether you do the aligning and agreeing which is positive polarity; the resistance and reaction which is negative polarity – both of these are forms of judgment. Mostly people see a reason to give up the negative polarity because everything here is about getting out of the negative and have the positive and that's why the positive polarity locks us up more than what the negative does because we can see a reason to give up the negative. We don't see a reason to give up the positive. We just believe that is supposed to be positive. That's the good thing. We want more of the good. That's why the positive will lock you up more. What the target is with Access Consciousness is to get people out of the positive and negative – the aligning and agreeing and the resisting and reacting. A lot of the spiritual metaphysical communities talk about acceptance – acceptance is positive polarity. It is aligning and agreeing with someone's point of view. The target with Access is to get everyone into total allowance, which is 'Interesting Point of View'.

In allowance, there is no judgment. In allowance, you are being 'Interesting Point of View', and interesting point of view has no charge on it. There's none of that density and contraction of judgment like positive and negative has. The thing is to take 'Interesting Point of View' one step further, you have to be really present and really aware that 'Interesting Point of View' does not mean being a doormat and a lot of people will door-mat themselves to be 'Interesting Point of View' and that's not what this is about.

Gary gives a great example with his son who I think at one point was doing alcohol. He said, "I love you and adore you and don't come to my house when you've been drinking." And the thing is with this is that Gary wasn't making his son right or wrong for choosing to drink, all he was saying was that it didn't work for him for his son to come around to his house when we had been drinking. So that's doing allowance and you're not door-matting yourself to what the other person's choice is.

"That's such a different way of looking at things where a lot of people are just functioning from acceptance of the behavior instead of going, "I don't have a point of view about your drinking. Do what works for you, but what doesn't work for me is you coming and abusing me when you do that."

Becoming Vibrationally Compatible With Hedonism, Decadence, Opulence And Orgasmic Living

Whatever energy you are being is what shows up in your life. So whatever energy you choose to show up in your life or whatever you attract into your life is the vibration of where you are functioning from. If you are a person who does a lot of thoughts, feelings and emotions and a lot of judgment, then your vibrations are what we call in Access Consciousness, the electrical vibration. The process of what I talked about earlier and what I taught in the prison – the bars, which are 32 points on the head: this is the fastest, easiest way of getting people out of that electrical vibration. That's the density and the contraction that the people live from on this reality.

To shift out of the electrical vibration, the target is to get everyone into the acoustical vibration, which is the vibration of nature. How many of us love to be in nature because there's this sense of space and possibility. That's when you are being the acoustical vibration, then as your vibration changes, these elements start to show up into your life. They can't show up in your life when you're functioning from a density of the electrical vibration. The more you get bars run, the more you run the Access clearing statements to clear the electrical vibration from your being, the more you do the Access body processes, the more you shift into that acoustical vibration, which allows these elements to show up with ease.

Question:"Even with all the changes I have made, I still have a problem with my skin. Two small patches of psoriasis on my ankle. What am I resisting about change in my body?"

What are you resisting with change in your body? My question would be, is there someone or something that's irritating you in your life? Who or what is an irritation for you? Everything all of that brings up, wil you un-create and destroy it? <u>Right and Wrong, Good and Bad, POD and POC, All Nine, Shorts, Boys and Beyonds.</u>

What stupidity am I using to create this psoriasis I am choosing? Everything all of that is, will you un-create and destroy it? <u>Right and Wrong, Good and Bad, POD and POC, All Nine, Shorts, Boys and Beyonds.</u>

I'd be asking lots of questions, Ask your body what awareness is it giving you, when something shows up in your body, your body is giving you an awareness that you are not willing to be present with, which is why that energy came up of who or what is an irritant in your life, just asking that and running the clearing lots and lots, you may start to have an awareness of what choices are you making that actually aren't working for you and your body.

"Any pain etc showing up in your body is actually awareness and not really something which is wrong? What are some of the questions that you can ask to unlock this awareness which your body is giving you?"

I would ask, "What awareness are you giving me with whatever it is that's showing up?" Our body is this amazing sensory orgasm, it's constantly sensing and receiving all this information, but then the minute you actually start to label things that show up in it, and then give it some structural significance, you lock it in. Just having the awareness of even asking, "Who does this psoriasis belong to?" is it actually your psoriasis or are you actually facilitating someone else's body with that psoriasis? These are all questions that you have to be willing to ask to have the awareness of what actually is showing up.

A classic for me was a couple of years ago, I had shingles and it took me a month to actually get to a point of picking up the phone to ring Gary and within minutes, he asked me the question "Who does it belong to?" I had been asking this question many times over and it just wasn't shifting. But the awareness that he got me to look at was that: When I first rang him, he asked, "What can I do for you?" and I told him that I have created shingles. He said, "Who does it belong to?" I mentioned at this point that I had asked that millions of times. He said, "It's not yours, because you telling me you created shingles doesn't match the energy that you created them. You didn't create them." He asked me if I was taking them out of someone's body. And I got, "yes." Then he asked me, "Do you know this person?" and I said "no" and he said, "Is it in this reality or a different reality?" and I got "different reality" and he said, "past, present or future?" and I got "the future." He cleared all of that for me and within 24 hours, the shingles were totally gone. Asking questions will always bring awareness.

Welcome to the world of bizarre with Access Consciousness. But it's amazing when you are actually willing to ask empowering questions. What can change with your awareness of what's appearing?

Everything all of that brought up in everyone's Universe, how weird it all is, and how could you be facilitating someone else's body in a different reality, in the future and someone you don't know and all the bizarreness of all of that, will you uncreate and destroy it all? <u>Right and Wrong, Good and Bad, POD and POC, All Nine, Shorts, Boys and Beyonds.</u>

"Wherever you or someone else is facilitating anything going on in your body for someone else in this reality, some other reality, past, present, future, whether you know the person or not, will you destroy and uncreate it all?"

<u>Right and Wrong, Good and Bad, POD and POC, All Nine, Shorts, Boys and Beyonds.</u>

The intensity of the energy that came up with this whole thing was "what?

How can we do that?"

We are infinite beings and anything is possible. And our bodies are just amazing and especially for those of us who are healers, you've got to be present and aware that our bodies just jump in and want to facilitate bodies because we can and it's actually easy, but you have to be aware of whether that's working for you or not and you have to be present and aware in you doing that. Is it actually allowing the other person to have their own awareness? And that's really the gift of consciousness and awareness; it's being present to all of that.

It is weird for a lot of people to even ask that question, but when you're actually willing not to go into the logical mind and just go with the energy and trust your awareness, it's amazing what can be facilitated and changed.

Body Processes

Question:"If you are actually taking on stuff of others and you've been working with the question "who does this belong to?" and it's not really shifting would running the body processes help at that time?"

Absolutely! At the same time, you have to be aware that you can. Clearing the being with the clearing statement and the body with the body processes assist to create a communion with the body and being so that they can work together to create more consciousness. The body processes definitely make a massive contribution, but you've also got to be clear anywhere where the being is playing a role in all of that as well, which is asking questions, bringing up the energies and then using the clearing statements to clear all the energies that come up with the question.

"Are there any other questions you could ask except for the ones that you've just shared to clear the energies?"

What is this? What can I do with it? Can I change it? How do I change it? These are all great questions. These questions in themselves should shift anything that's not working. And I always say if you can really be present when you facilitate then you will create an amazing change. Being really present with the person that you are working with and talking to the energy was something that I had no cognitive concept of when I first came to Access Consciousness about eleven years ago so I watched Gary and his brilliance with talking to the energy, and I just made a demand every day that whatever capacities that he has, which is talking to the energy, what would it take for me to also have those capacities?

When you ask for something and demand something, it always shows up and I'm so grateful because now I know that that allows my facilitation to get such a fast, amazing shift when you're totally present with the energy and talking to the energy at every moment.

Nilofer: "What would it take for me to have those energies? How does it get any better than that?"

Just ask for it to show up and it will show up.

Working With Many Things At Once

Wherever you are doing everything from the linear concept, I know for me my life is getting faster and I'm actually working on many more projects. I've only been home for two days and I'm leaving again. I had a friend who came in from New Zealand and he said, "I've been watching you for two days, you do more in a day than most people would do probably in a month." I'm really aware of it and to always follow the energy.

Wherever you are trying to do from a linear concept or your to-do list that is actually what slows you down. You are just doing it from the way everyone else is. When you are actually willing to do it from question, choice, possibility and contribution, you're actually functioning from the mutable laws of creation, not the immutable laws of this reality. Wherever you are functioning from the electrical vibration and from fitting and benefitting, winning and losing, you're doing the immutable laws of this reality. Immutable means unchangeable, it's about changing from the mutable laws of creation, which is where everything is done from the question, choice, possibility and contribution and it's very much following the energy. It's really the willingness to follow that and don't make you wrong, because you'll find you'll complete more projects when you function from that.

Everything all of that is and anywhere you're refusing to step into the question, choice, possibility and contribution and to truly trust and know that you do know how to follow the energy, and anywhere where you've bought into the limitation of the linear concept and that you're making time real. Everything all of that brings up, will you un-create and destroy it all? <u>Right and Wrong, Good and Bad, POD and POC, All Nine, Shorts, Boys and Beyonds.</u>

Time is not real, it is a concept of this reality and people use it to destroy themselves, to slow them down and to be the same as everyone else. The true magic is in your willingness to follow the energy and to choose, keep choosing, stay in the question, be and receive the contribution and know that there are infinite possibilities.

"Do you like being the same as everyone else? Destroying you and your body, trying to fit in"?

When you're trying to do your life the same as what everyone else says you are supposed to, does any of that truly work for you. When I look at people relationships, for instance, how many people are just destroying themselves trying to do that, "Am I now supposed to get married? Do I now have to have two and a half children? Now that I have that, I have to have the house and the white picket fence and I've got to have the two cars in the garage and we have to have the money in the bank," and it's this whole destruction of self trying to do what this reality tells us what we are supposed to do. What if you were willing to actually sit down and ask the question, "If I was having my life of choice, what would my life of choice be in regards to relationships?" as an example.

You need to be asking that question around every area of your life. "If I was living my life of choice, what would my reality be with money and my finances?" Now when I look at my own life, this is the first time in my life that I haven't owned property since I was eighteen, because I got married for the first time when I was eighteen and my first husband and I worked really hard to buy property, and we had several properties when we divorced six years later. The thing is, and I always bought into the point of view, especially in Australia, the dream is you have your own house. But in the last ten years, since I've been doing Access Consciousness, I've really had the awareness of "it doesn't work for me to own property at this moment." So every time I ask, "would I like to have some property now?" I keep getting "no".

To me, I'm creating my reality around money and finances different to what most people do: for me it's very rewarding purchasing gold, silver and platinum, diamonds, pearls and antiques – things of intrinsic value. I know that when I ask them and talk to them, "If I buy you, will you make me money?" and if I get a "yes" I am aware that they will contribute to me to generate more for me and my living. It is creating my own reality around finances different from the reality that I'm supposed to do.

Anything that doesn't allow you to perceive, know, be and receive what your reality would be in regards to finances and your money flows, will you un-create and destroy all that? <u>Right and Wrong, Good and Bad, POD and POC, All Nine, Shorts, Boys and Beyonds.</u>

Relationships

Now talking of relationships, a little brief example from my own life – At thirty, I was heading into the divorce court for the second time. I had two babies and I had cancer. I looked at it and went, "I can continue making the same choices, on a different day expecting a different result, or I can totally choose something different here," and I chose something totally different. I started to see that doing traditional relationships of what this reality tells you wasn't working for me and I was destroying me in that process to try to have the relationship that you live happily ever after with. For the last almost thirty years, I haven't done relationship the way this reality says I should do. I do it totally different.

To me the way I do it really works for me. I have a lot of amazing men in my life who bring me amazing gifts, gifts of contribution of energy, because in the allowance of who they are and the gifts they bring to me, contributes to me in so many ways that I never got from doing a traditional relationship. I don't get that it's right or wrong in what I choose, I just choose what works for me and most people will destroy themselves in a relationship instead of really just asking the question of "Is doing traditional relationship a rewarding choice? Is this really what I desire? Or do I like to have many different people in my life who bring different energies of contribution to my life?"

"What would you say for people who are already in a traditional relationship? What questions can they ask to create a totally different relationship there?"

It's your willingness to be in total allowance of your partner. I do a lot of work with people in regards to sex and relationships and what I know is that the greatest destruction of a relationship is judgment. Shifting into that space of allowance is certainly not to doormat yourself. Allowance might be 'do that again and I'll punch your lights out.' It's the willingness to be so present and aware of the choices that you are making, the choices that your partner is making and being in that allowance.

The willingness to be and receive the contribution of each other, that's really what this, is all about. It's one thing to have the five elements of infinite intimacy – vulnerability, honor, trust, gratitude and allowance. You must have these firstly for you and then you can have them for your partner. As you keep choosing more of you, your partner will step into something greater of themselves and then both of you will start to become an amazing contribution of being and receiving for each other.

Anything that doesn't allow you to perceive, know, be and receive the energies of what all of that can bring to your life, will you un-create and destroy it all?

<u>Right and Wrong, Good and Bad, POD and POC, All Nine, Shorts, Boys and Beyonds.</u>

These are big topics that we could possibly do a whole session on. Massive topics! Money and relationships are two big areas that people will destroy themselves in.

Elegance, Aesthetics, Pleasure and Play

Orgasmic Living - Orgasmic living is your willingness to create and generate every single moment of your life from the fun, joy and the intensely expansive energies. If you actually get the energy of all of that, and you be that space, you are in the space of possibility and that's where every moment of your life is like a little small child. It's following the energy of the fun and the joy and the more you have that, the more it shows up as well. It comes back to that willingness to be the vibration of what you are demanding and choosing and then more of that shows up.

So if you would like to have more people show up in your life, functioning from the nurture and care of you, the more you are the vibration of nurture and care for you, the more those people show up in your life. When you love you, everyone wants to love you. When you nurture and care for you, you have others who show up who wish to nurture and care for you. If you desire to have more gold and more diamonds and more pearls, whatever it is that's rewarding for you, when you become the vibration of gold and diamonds and pearls, then more of that gets to show up.

Everything that doesn't allow you to receive the intensity of energy of all of that, will you un-create and destroy all that? <u>Right and Wrong, Good and Bad, POD and POC, All Nine, Shorts, Boys and Beyonds.</u>

The **aesthetics** is about the beauty and the beautiful. It's the magnificence and the refinement. It's like being the energy of allowing beautiful things to show up in your life. A few months ago, Gary opened an Antique Guild in Brisbane, and there were two lamps in there that made it very clear to me that they wanted to come home with me, and so they did. I bought them and the day they arrived at my home, I turned them on and kept them on all day. They exude an abundance of aesthetically beautiful and magnificence of energies that are such a massive contribution to me and my body, and at times, I just sit there and gaze at them and the beauty that they are and I am so grateful for the contribution that they are to my living!

What if you were willing to allow more of that to show up in your life? Whatever that is for you.

The **elegance** is about the purity and the grace and the ease. It's about everything flowing with that ease. When you have that time in your life when it's like all the doors are opening for you and there's this flow of energy and it's like you've got a glass of great champagne in your hand and you're on a skateboard. You're just flowing. That's what elegance is, and it's just such a gracefulness of, and everything showing up with so much ease and what would it take for us to have more of that? That ease, instead of buying into the points of view that life must be hard or life has to be a struggle, where are we refusing to have life as ease, joy and glory?

Everywhere where you are buying into the points of view that life has to be hard, life has to be a struggle, will you un-create and destroy it all?

<u>Right and Wrong, Good and Bad, POD and POC, All Nine, Shorts, Boys and Beyonds.</u>

The **pleasure** is the gratification. It can be the sensuality; pleasure can be the touching of skin. It can be eating amazing, orgasmic food, and your body gets the thrill of every mouthful. That's what the true pleasure is. Pleasure is that gratification of the senses; it's truly with the body. So the pleasure can be, like I explained with the lamps, just sitting and having pleasure of the senses of gazing at the contribution of the lamps.

Pure pleasure can be wearing pure linens and silks. In the first 20 years of my career I was designing and making wedding gowns and high fashion. I got to work with the most amazing fabrics, and I also designed and made my own clothes with beautiful fabrics that when wearing them was such an amazing pleasure for my body. Also include the pleasure of music: what magic that can bring to your ears and having that acoustical vibration adding more joy to your life through the senses as well and the pleasure of what music can be for people.

Even walking on a beach and feeling the sand between your toes, walking in the water and having it splash up onto your skin.

Walking on misty grass that had heavy dew overnight and feeling the coolness and freshness on your feet. There's so much pleasure and joy in everything and yet, most people aren't willing to stop to smell the roses. It's this whole busyness that people are caught up in and the linear concepts of "I have to do this to make sure I've got the money in the bank, to make the house payment and to pay for the food or to pay for the bills." There's this whole destruction of self that takes people out of the simple pleasures and the joy of what is available to us. We are here to have the joy of embodiment. How many people do you know are actually having that and choosing that?

Everywhere we've trained ourselves to be the same as everyone else, then you too are not choosing the fun and the joy and the elegance and the aesthetics and all the other elements that we've been talking about, will you un-create and destroy all that? <u>Right and Wrong, Good and Bad, POD and POC, All Nine, Shorts, Boys and Beyonds.</u>

Exponentialising The Four Elements

"How do you actually add the four elements: hedonism, opulence, decadence and orgasmic living in your life and how do you exponentialize them beyond your imagination?"

It's that willingness to move from the immutable laws of this reality into the mutable laws of creation. When you stop functioning from:

"Where am I going to fit here? Am I going to benefit? What if I lose with this?" shifting out of all of that limitation will take you into the infinite choice, infinite possibility, that's when you really start to be the energies of these elements and this will allow something so totally different to turn up. Your willingness to know that every question that you ask, every new choice you make, knowing that there are infinite possibilities and stepping into the being and receiving of you is what allows these elements to show up with total ease and it is a demand that you have to be willing to be out of judgment of you.

This is what you have to shift into if you truly desire to have these elements show up in your life.

Allowing people to see that there's just so much more available and we don't have to do the limitations of what everyone else is choosing. And just because we bought the lie of this reality, doesn't mean you can't change it and start to live a life that is totally different and it's interesting because I even look at my own life and how different it has been and every day more and more difference is showing up as I'm willing to step in to be more of me.

One of the most amazing books that's available is from Dr. Dain Heer of Access Consciousness called 'Being You And Changing the World' and really that's what it's about. It's about you stepping into all of you and then you become an incredible invitation to others to choose more for them. It's not about getting people to do classes or convincing them of anything; it's just being that space of possibility. People will know that you are different and if they are looking for more they will ask you a question. Everywhere I go, people stop me and say, "You're different, what do you do?" and that's without even having to verbalize anything to them. There's an energy that you get to be that's an incredible invitation. And the more of us that choose that, the more we can actually allow planet Earth to become the most amazing place to live instead of the destruction that's actually appearing right now.

Closing Thoughts

For me, it's like "What would it take for us all to step into all of who we BE? And what would it take for us to be out of judgment?" To stop going down that rabbit hole of wrongness for every choice that we make and every moment of every day. It's something I talk about when I facilitate the three day body classes. Getting participants to pour concrete down their rabbit hole – the place we go to in every moment to make ourselves wrong. Once there is no rabbit hole to run and hide in then we can actually be present and aware and be 'Interesting Point of View' for everything. And that's really when your life will change.

Everything that doesn't allow you to be 'Interesting Point of View' for every single point of view you have, will you un-create and destroy all that? <u>Right and Wrong, Good and Bad, POD and POC, All Nine, Shorts, Boys and Beyonds.</u>

'Interesting Point of View' is a gift.

"What contribution can we all be to each other to create all this with total ease in all of our lives? And everything that doesn't allow that, will you destroy and un-create it all? <u>Right and Wrong, Good and Bad, POD and POC, All Nine, Shorts, Boys and Beyonds.</u>

123

Let's now tap into the energy of everything and everyone of the planet and on three, let's contribute, be and receive the contribution of everything that can now allow some massive change and transformation to show up everywhere.

WHO IS MARGARET BRAUNACK

Margaret has worked in the Personal, Professional Development and Natural Health fields for over 30 years. She is a dynamic Lifestyle and Business Coach, Published Author, International Keynote Speaker & Facilitator of Seminars and Workshops. She is a Naturopath, Trainer of NLP, Master Hypnotherapist and National Values Trainer. She engages her audience & invites, empowers and inspires them to new possibilities. She has travelled the world extensively facilitating and seeking consciousness.

Over 12 years ago she discovered Access Consciousness. Since then her life and living has changed and transformed more than at any other time choosing hundreds of other modalities. As a Facilitator of Change & Transformation, she is willing to assist you to greater possibilities more than you could ever imagine. Are you willing to live in the question to allow greater possibilities to show up? What would it take for you to choose more for you? Are you willing to have the freedom, fun, joy and adventures that your life has to offer? Are you willing to be the magic and miracles that you truly BE? She is willing to travel anywhere for classes. Private Sessions are also available, either in person or over the phone. Please email or phone for further details.

**CREATING A FUTURE FOR YOU AND THE EARTH....
WHAT DO YOU REALLY KNOW?**

By Katherine McIntosh

Your awareness can change the future of the planet (Native Americans looked at every choice they made based on what that impact would create for 7 generations into the future) The future might be undefined, and your awareness can contribute to the creation of a future and a kinder, gentler Earth. Energy is a universal language we all speak...the Earth speaks every day and you and your body can contribute to playing a role in creating a different future. http://www.magicofbeing.com

CHAPTER EIGHT

❖

LIVE BY DESIGN NOT BY DEFAULT

By Vanitha Subramaniam

Access Consciousness Certified Facilitator,

Psychologist, Transformational and Leadership Coach,

Author and CEO of Conscious Solutions

Perceiving Knowing Being And Receiving Energy

I love the Middle East. There is something about the energy of the place that keeps me coming back. There is so much space and possibility that's not tapped into and what would it take to wake all those beautiful people up so that they can become the designers of their life instead of living their lives by default. The other energy which is here which we had loads of fun with the last time in the classes is the energy of abundance with gold and money. As a certified Access Consciousness facilitator, I facilitate the Core Classes; which is Bars and Foundation. All these classes are about you accessing you; your talents, capacities and abilities. These classes are not about telling you what you should do with yourself, but about empowering you to know everything you know, but how do you access that knowing? And how do you access that knowing when everything that you are living your life from right now is based on other people's points of view?

Whenever you attend these classes you learn to perceive, know, be and receive energy and how every element has a different energy. When I was in Abu Dhabi, I took the class participants on a field trip to work on an exercise on the topic of how to know and access the energy vibration of gold. In Abu Dhabi, there are all these beautiful gold shops in a row, so it is pretty easy to do these exercises here. I got the participants to stand in front of each shop – now we didn't even go into the shop – just perceive the energy of gold from outside each individual shop. They were surprised to find that there were some shops where they could not perceive any energy. We ended up buying gold coins from the shops that we could perceive the energy of vibration of gold to it. The whole idea was when you are able to read energies, i.e. perceive, know, be and receive these energies – and you get to do a lot of this – your life suddenly becomes magic. And how does it become magic? It becomes magic when you actually start looking at everything that doesn't work in your life and begin to ask questions with everything.

When you access you, you access the magic that you are and be and for me, my target is consciousness. I go anywhere consciousness requires me. And it is so fun generating and creating consciousness in the world and out of which magic shows up all the time. You become the magician… the Harry Potter; and honestly, I love seeing people access that magic they truly be. Every person is different. Every person has their own talents and abilities and capacities and to see the magic awaken in them is something else and the beauty is- it is not difficult!

We have this thing of getting sucked back into being unconscious again. It's only when we are being consciousness and when we are continuously using the tools that it is truly magical. Things start appearing for you that you didn't even know that you needed and they appear and you realize you needed them.

I see so many people in this reality walking around almost like they are sleepwalking and most people are actually functioning from looking at their past and taking that as a reference point to create their future and what happens when you keep looking at your past to create your future, you are almost going to get the same result with a slight variation, which is the definition of insanity.

With Access, what we are doing is, we're giving you the information like "If this is what you've been doing for such a long time, ask if it is still working? What are you actually not willing to know about your life? What are you not willing to be in your life? What are you not willing to know about you and what's possible for you?"

So here's a tool. Everybody has a toolbox. We all have a toolbox. And when we're faced with adversity or a problem or an issue that we cannot solve and we are looking for solutions, we tend to go into our toolbox and rummage through it to find a way out. But the trouble is, if your toolbox is full of reference points of your past and you have always used the same tools, either you have had no shift, or a slight variation. Instead to create and generate a different reality and possibility, you have got to ask a question as simple as – *What is going to work for me? What is it going to take to change this?* And this is how you get out of living your life by default and getting into the life of design.

You Are The Designer Of Your Life

One of the reasons why I picked this topic was I did this class back in Malaysia– "Live By Design, Not By Default" and it was such a huge shift for the people who came to the class and it was so much fun. I felt this would be a great way to get people to see where they are not being the designer of their life. It is like they have taken a blueprint, or they are given a blueprint of this reality but they don't know how to create outside of this blueprint. Most people are lost in the process."

Living In The Question

One of the first tools that we teach in Access is about living in the question. Everything, and everywhere we have been made wrong in this reality is when we have been in question. For example, when you were in school and you were one of those kids who wanted to ask a lot of questions, you are probably the one who was made wrong the most. Or they shamed you in class or they made you feel stupid because you put your hand up to ask questions. To the point that when you become an adult, and you are sitting in a room with lots of other adults and you want to ask a question, you put your hand up and all you can hear is your loud heart beat and you feel nervous and anxious. All of which is so unrequired, because one of the fundamental things to begin to create and generate your life is **being in question**. To ask questions will always empower you to awareness and to function from answers will always disempower you to conclusions. The way this reality controls people is to judge people who are questions and get them to function from answers."

When we ask a question, we go looking for answers. But the Access way of asking questions is very different. Will you tell a little bit about that?

The way we ask questions is to actually ask a question without a conclusion attached. It is a very interesting thing. When most people ask a question, they have already decided what they would like to see show up in their life. It is almost like you are asking a question with a conclusion attached. The whole idea is when you actually start asking questions with a conclusion attached, what happens is that you are not allowing for something different to show up in your life. You are already putting the question out to the Universe but you are also determining and deciding exactly what you want.

So if something magical and something beyond what you know and experienced shows up, you cannot see it or receive it, because you are already functioning from judgment of what you decided is the answer to your question. Judgment kills all energy of awareness. When you are functioning from judgment, you actually go automatically to the answer. The question is meant to open up more awareness; and every awareness opens up more possibility, and more choices and questions in your Universe. How do you actually ask a question?

I will give an example. I love using this example because I think this one speaks to what I am trying to actually talk about. You know Dr. Dain Heer? He is such a phenomenal facilitator, healer and author. His book- **"Being You, Changing the World"** is changing the world out there. He came to New Zealand a couple of years ago when I used to coordinate Access in New Zealand. He was coming to New Zealand to launch this book called **"Right Riches for You"**. When he came over, I got a journalist to do an interview with him on the topic, the launch of the book and about Dr Dain etc. The next day when the interview was supposed to come out, something completely different was written up. I called her up and asked, "Where is the interview that you did with Dr. Dain Heer on 'Right Riches for You'?" and she told me that when she was doing the interview with Dr Dain, towards the very end, she asked for some personal help for herself from Dr Dain. She told me that she was the editor of a magazine and she was having some HR problems with her management and things were not actually working out the way she would like them to. Dr Dain gave her a question, a tool – **"What would it take to change this?"** And asked her to keep asking this question. And all of the way back to work in her car, she kept asking **"What would it take to change this?"**

By the time she got back to work at her desk to write this article up – the interview – everything had changed. Within the an hour and half of her asking this question and getting back to her desk, everything that she wanted to show up in her discussion with management, showed up. She was so thrilled, she wrote the whole article on this one question/tool, **"What would it take to change this?"** And this question went viral across New Zealand and people started calling her up saying things were changing for them as a result of just asking that simple question. Get the energy of that one question. Notice there is no conclusion to it. You are not deciding or concluding or computing what should show up. You are asking the Universe and if you use this one question, any issues that you have right now, at this time for you could change. Just be with it and be with the energy, with no conclusion and no expectations.

My advice is *"Get Out of Your Own Way"*. I find people are always trying to control the situation to show up the way they think they would like it to look like. And the moment they step away, step out of the way, somehow rather the energy of possibility starts showing up in their life.

Let me give another example. I was supposed to be coming to UAE for classes going to Dubai first. After paying for my flight and getting my ticket issued, my travel agent texts me saying *"I've undercharged you by a RM1000, I forgot to charge you the fuel charges and therefore, now you have to pay another RM1000. What are you going to do?"* She always messes up my flight bookings. I was getting really upset with her as it is RM1000 and since it is just before my departure date, the charges are more and she did not even call me sooner to inform me. I used the Access clearing statement and started "POC and PODing" myself.

I then asked questions including the one above. *"What would it take to change this? And what else is possible here?"* *"What is so right about this that I am not getting?"*

Immediately when I got to work the next day, I texted her to call me and she called and said *"I will pay the difference and I have also seen an alternative route with Qatar Airways instead of Etihad, which gets you into Dubai directly at 9 o'clock in the morning. If you fly with Qatar Airways, it is only RM 100 difference and I will pay the difference."* So I thanked her for offering an alternative airline and her willingness to pay the difference. I offered her half the sum on it and that made her happy and that made me happy and it all worked out. What I am eluding to here is that by **being in question,** and one of my question was **"What is so right about this that I am not getting?"** allowed for everything to change. I could have been really angry and I was justified in being angry with her, but was that going to create any change and possibilities for me?

You cannot create change and possibilities from confrontation. Like when I asked her to call, she said, *"Ok, you are going to scold me, right? I am ready for it"* and I said, *"I am not interested in scolding you. I have only got a question for you. Am I the only one who you have messed up flights with?"* She admitted, *"There are two of you and I don't know why in all my years of being a travel agent why I do this with both of you!"* By the way my travel agent does not know anything about what I do, so I ran a clearing -

All our relationships in this lifetime and past lifetime, could you please destroy and un-create it all? Right and Wrong, Good and Bad, POD and POC All Nine, Shorts, Boys and Beyonds.

Default Or Design

What are some of the limitations that you perceive as keep people stuck in that state of living by default instead of choosing to create what they want in their life?

Living your life from default is the programming you took on from the time you were born in this world. Were you ever taught how to choose? You don't even know how to make a choice for yourself because you have never chosen for you. Everybody tells you how to choose and everybody wants you to be someone they think you should be. From the time you go to school, your teachers knock the question-mode out of you and you get programmed to live your life from answers because that is exactly what you are told- how to think, how to feel, how to emote. Then you go to university and you come out with a degree and you are told exactly what kind of job you should take on. In some cultures, you are told who you should marry.

It is like being in a box and every box looks a particular way. Box A, Box B, Box C and that is what you should look or be like in this reality. You are told when to get married, you are told to have kids as soon as you are married and then you have grand children and then it is time to die. And that is living your life by default- living from the matrix of this reality.

Where are you in creation of your life? Where are you in creating your life? Where are you being the designer of your life? What if your life could look completely different? My desire is for everybody to be able to access their potential, their possibilities and be the greatness of their embodiment whatever that looks like.

What if you are born to be the greatness of your embodiment? What does that look like? You have to actually go out there and design what that looks like for you. Let us say- you are on a boat and for the first time in your life you are going on an adventure called 'you' and you don't know what is ahead of you. And you don't have to know either. It is not a predictable life. Most of us are looking for the predictability of life- "the charted course." How many of you are always reading what the astrologer's prediction about you or your star sign? Most people out there are looking for answers so that it will give them an explanation about them. Does it really work?

My question to everyone is – ***What if you could be the designer of your life? What if you could get on a boat and go on an adventure called 'you' and you don't have to know what that looks like?*** You don't know where you will steer your boat but this is not a chartered course, your life is not chartered. ***What if you could have an adventure with your life?*** Following what everybody else does is not being a designer of your life, that is just living your life by "default".

Actualizing Your Reality

You actually do know what you would like to create in your life, but how do you actually get to that point where that thing starts to actualize in your reality?

Gary Douglas, the founder of Access Consciousness usually says in all his classes – *"You don't really know how to create your life. No one has ever asked you this question. "What would you like to create your life as?"*

What if your life is the way you want it to be? It is never the blueprint of what you desire, but your life up until now has been based on everybody else's points of view on life.

Everywhere that you are creating your life based on other people's points of view about what your life should look like and this reality's points of view on life, will you revoke, recant, rescind, reclaim, renounce, denounce, destroy and un-create it all? <u>Right and Wrong, Good and Bad, POD and POC All Nine, Shorts, Boys and Beyonds.</u>

Most people ask this of me: "Tell me what you think about me?" Have you ever done that?

That is because a whole lot of who we are, what we are, how we are, where we are, why we are and that we are, is created from what other people have told us or think about us.

Judgments

How do you deal with their points of view or judgments?

It has been quite amazing and the tool I have been playing around with is **"being in the question"** and what I am starting to really be aware of at this point of time is that there are so many places in my life where I just go on "living by default". I wake up in the morning and I am like a programmed robot and I just keep going and doing things. There are things that I look at, and think that they are not working for me but I just get into the "default mode" and just resign to however that thing is working out. Sounds familiar? The times when I actually don't do that and I actually start asking the question, **"What would it take to change this? How does it get any better than this?"** Everything starts to change. I have actually printed out these questions and I have stuck it all over my house. If I am feeling a bit off and I feel I am stuck in this limitation, I look at those questions and I start saying those questions over and over again.

I would like to run some clearings right now about how we function in this "default" reality, about where we buy into this reality's view of life, and about how we create ourselves, our lives and our reality based on other people's points of view; and how everything is based on validating other people's points of view, because that is the other thing too. We spend so much energy validating how people view us, to the point that we will change us to fit into their reality of how we should be.

"I have been noticing how we start to act different around different people. Especially around people who have known us for a very long time, you suddenly start behaving in a way that you have behaved a long time ago and you wonder why you are not like that anymore. Could it be a result of what expectations and judgments that they have about us that we start behaving like that?"

Absolutely, because you are busy using so much energy to be different with so many people, where are you being true to you? Who are you being with every person you are in contact with? Are you being yourself?

Everywhere you divorce you in the process of validating everybody else's points of view and everywhere you have been functioning from there that doesn't give you the ease and joy of being you, will you revoke, recant, rescind, reclaim, renounce, denounce, destroy and un-create it all? <u>Right and Wrong, Good and Bad, POD and POC All Nine, Shorts, Boys and Beyonds.</u>

I think a whole lot of people do that. *What if you could be you?* – Just be you. It does not matter what that looks like to everybody else, but you be true to you and you acknowledge what is true for you, everything will change for you. Dr. Dain Heer not long ago posted on his Facebook post *"If you acknowledge what is true for you, everything would change for you."* I had a lady who came for a personal session with me and she was not willing to acknowledge what was true for her. Her point of view was "If I don't look at it and if I don't have to buy into it, it doesn't affect me." But the reality was everything that was a problem in her life was based on that one judgment that she had. Exactly what she wasn't willing to look at was exactly what was showing up in her life. Getting her to acknowledge that, started to shift something in her Universe. And then followed by her asking the questions, **"What is this? What I do with this? Can I change this? How do I change this? What else is possible here? What can I be or do different to change this for me right away?"** Some of these questions that we know and which are tools that we give in Access, can actually change anything in your life if you are willing to use it. You are so phenomenal. You are the designer of your life, but you have never allowed yourself to be that because all your life, you have programmed yourself into "living by default of this reality".

What stupidity are you using to buy into the default programming of this reality you are choosing? Everything that is, will you destroy and un-create it all? <u>Right and Wrong, Good and Bad, POD and POC All Nine, Shorts, Boys and Beyonds.</u>

When I say the word 'stupidity', I am not calling you stupid- just to be clear. There is an energy about stupidity; and it is where you would cut off your awareness of what is possible for you. When you cut off your awareness of what is possible for you, it is almost an energy of stupidity and this has been one of the processes in Access that have been creating amazing shifts for people around the world.

Can you perceive that energy that came up? It is almost so solid and heavy and that is why we want it cleared. You can run this process until it starts to lighten up, so you will start to have a sense of ease and space in your Universe.

It is clearing everywhere you have bought the lie of this reality that the default programming that you are living by is actually working for you. Everything that is, will you destroy and un-create it all? <u>Right and Wrong, Good and Bad, POD and POC All Nine, Shorts, Boys and Beyonds.</u>

If you just get to see this reality as it is, you will see the lies you have bought into. Look at the financial reality and the social reality around us; look at every way governments are asking their people to buy into these lies about society and money; and you want to get past all that. You want to get beyond what is being said and get to your own knowing of what is true for you. One of the tools in Access we talk about frequently is that **"the truth will always make you feel lighter and a lie will make you feel heavy"**. And this is the beginning of you being able to perceive energy. What is true for you may not be true for me; you have to access what is true for you. Access your own knowing. You are an infinite being with infinite capacity for knowing, being, perceiving and receiving. You are infinitely connected to everything around the world and the Universe. You have a sense of what is true for you. When I speak of light and heavy, you can perceive the energy the first time you run the clearing and how it changes as you run them a few times. Was it heavier when you started? Did it get lighter as you ran the clearing?

What stupidity are you using to buy into the lies of this reality are you choosing?" Everything that is, will you destroy and un-create it all? <u>Right and Wrong, Good and Bad, POD and POC All Nine, Shorts, Boys and Beyonds.</u>

What stupidity are you using to buy into the lies of this reality as if it is true for you are you choosing? Everything that is, will you destroy and un-create it all? <u>Right and Wrong, Good and Bad, POD and POC All Nine, Shorts, Boys and Beyonds.</u>

What stupidity are you using to create the invention of the predictable lies you are choosing? Everything that is, will you destroy and un-create it all? <u>Right and Wrong, Good and Bad, POD and POC All Nine, Shorts, Boys and Beyonds.</u>

Invention has a different energy and creation has a different energy. So we run the process slightly different with these two. They actually work on a very different strategy. You would invent something so that you know how good you are to try to clear it. We take money as an example. Many people would have these ups and downs with money. They would do seemingly great at creating money and when they get to the top, they have to get rid of everything they have. They go to the bottom again and start again.

What stupidity are you using to create the invention of stop and start with your financial reality you are choosing? Everything that is, will you destroy and un-create it all? <u>Right and Wrong, Good and Bad, POD and POC All Nine, Shorts, Boys and Beyonds.</u>

It is an invention. It is like you have to prove to yourself that you are really good at doing this. It is insane but this is what you do. Before I came to Access and I used to ask myself, *"What am I doing here? Why do I always have to create my financial reality again, and have to start from scratch?"* Like zero money in my bank account. Then I came to Access and I began to do all the Access classes and the core classes with Gary and Dain, I began to see where I was functioning from that created the limitations. And so much of that began to shift for me because the whole idea is when you become a designer of your life, you tap into your ability to create and generate your life with choice and possibilities; and everything opens up with new doors of possibilities, with new questions, and new choices".

Default In Relationships

People go into that default mode with relationships. And what would it take to actually start creating and generating relationship by design?

Relationships is an interesting concept because a lot of the way we are creating our relationships right now, for everyone out there, it has really been based on other people's idea of what a relationship looks like. You never asked yourself the question, *"What would I like in regards to a relationship?"*

My question is *"How many of you are even having a relationship with yourself before even considering having a relationship with somebody else*? That will be a "no Bob". Everything that is, will you destroy and un-create it all? <u>Right and Wrong, Good and Bad, POD and POC All Nine, Shorts, Boys and Beyonds.</u>

The good thing about questions is that they start opening up a lot of awareness in your Universe because most people who are in a relationship would either go into the wrongness of them or wrongness of the person they are in a relationship with. Everything you have known about relationships, you have learnt from somebody else. *How many people do you know out there who have great relationships? A little, a lot or almost none?* Almost none. You could probably count on one hand, even then you probably know one or two couples who have great relationships out there.

Since being in Access, I have seen the people who are in Access who change so much that their relationships also changed. They either come to the awareness that their relationships are not working out and they use the tools to create something better or choose to leave; or their relationships change along with them and became amazing. They are constantly looking at working out their relationships with the people in their life.

You see a lot of people go into a relationship with expectations. It is the default programming of relationships- expectations. "It is someone else's responsibility to make me happy, to provide for me to, to take care of me for the rest of my life". It is like you have to almost start by clearing all your expectations about what you want out of a relationship before you can even venture into.

All your projections, expectations, separations, judgments, and conclusions about what relationships mean to you, whether it is a relationship with yourself or with someone else or with your family, will you now revoke, recant, rescind, reclaim, renounce, denounce, destroy and un-create it all? <u>Right and Wrong, Good and Bad, POD and POC All Nine, Shorts, Boys and Beyonds.</u>

Gary once said in a telecall, **"You have to create from what is, not from what ought to be"** and most people make that mistake in relationships. A lot of people go into a relationship with the fantasy of what the relationship should look like.

I remember there was this cartoon, not long ago someone posted on Facebook and this girl is asking her new boyfriend, "What are you going to do for me?" because they had just gotten into a relationship and he thinks to himself, "What do I talk about? I am damned if I do. I am damned if I don't. How am I going to answer this question!" and instead he says to her, "I will take you to the beach." They are teenagers. "I will buy you flowers and I will walk with you in romantic moonlight." And then she says, "Aww. I like you already."

So that is basically where people begin with their relationships. They have a fantasy reality about what their relationship should be, but not only that, their expectation is also that their happiness is based on what the other person can provide for them. Moreover, people only speak to what they think the other person wants to hear.

Everywhere you have that expectation that your happiness is based on someone else providing for you, will you now destroy and un-create all of that? Right and Wrong, Good and Bad, POD and POC All Nine, Shorts, Boys and Beyonds.

In the Foundation class, we actually facilitate you to the awareness that in order to have a phenomenal relationship you have to begin with the relationship with yourself. You have to begin to have the vulnerability with you, the trust with you, the honoring of you, the gratitude for you and the kindness, the caring, the nurturing for you because when you don't have these things for you then you cannot see it and receive it when someone is willing to gift that to you. I can always hear this question popping in my Universe from all of you out there, what is my point of view of a phenomenal relationship?

My point of view of a phenomenal relationship is where two people come together to contribute to each other and how does that contribution look like? There are no expectations. The contribution is a question – *"What can I contribute to you today and what can you contribute to me today that will expand each other and our life together? What fun can we have?"* How many people do you know are not having fun in their relationship?

It is like people get into a relationship and it starts of fun in the beginning and then fun is lost in time. They get really serious. Did you know that marriage is very serious? You sign on a dotted line on your marriage certificate, wear that little necklace around your neck or a ring on your finger, which states "ok, I am married now. I have to be serious". We are married now. We are husband and wife. We have got to run a household. We have got to be the managers of our family and we have got to bring up our children and we have got to whip them into shape so they become good citizens of this reality.

Nilofer: I have been in this question, "What would I like my relationship to look like?" and one of the things I became aware of that what I really find contributes to me is to have fun and to have adventures. We have been to this weekend trip- off-roading. And it has been so much fun. One time we got stuck in the desert. That wasn't so much fun but one weekend, we went with a group of four hundred and fifty four off-roaders so there were twenty eight vehicles and we went into 'waadis' and it was adventure and fun galore. I have been in the UAE for seven years and we never ever thought of joining a group and doing something like this and now suddenly I start asking questions and all of this is showing up. How does it get any better than that? What I want all of you to get there is that you can change anything. There's nothing you can't change and it's as simple as asking a question like you just did. "When I first started asking that question "What would I like my relationship to look like?" for a few days I was just in that question and I was just blank. I didn't even know what I would like to have in my relationship. I have become really good at being the question and I was continuously being in the energy of the question and after that all kinds of things started to show up and I look at them and I thought that is not what I have ever expected. It's like it brings me to another question which I keep asking – "What is possible here that I didn't even think was ever possible?"

Let me share some tools. I have been working with a lot of people with these tools. So one day I was exploring on how can we take the energy of a limitations in our life and change it into possibility. Because it is only a limitation as long as you look at it as a limitation- correct? What if every limitation in your life – whether it is in your relationship, whether it is in your life, whether it is your money, whether it is your body, whether it is your job, whether it is your family, whether it is anything – *what if every limitation is a possibility you are not willing to receive?* When I was playing with this, I came up with an awareness that if I was to look at the energy of limitation in my Universe and started to look for possibilities that could show up from those limitations, things would start to change.

EXERCISE:

Take the energy of a limitation in your life. It can be a relationship, it can be money, it can be your family, it can be a job or it can be your body. Anything right now that is not working for you. What if we could change that energy – the energy of limitation – into possibilities? What are you not willing to receive from the energy of limitation that could create possibilities for you? By looking at it right now, ask this question – *What is possible here? What can I be or do differently to change the situation right away or this issue right away with ease? And how does it get any better than this?*

When you can bring yourself to this point of continuously being in the question, it just shifts everything. "What can I be or do different here to change this right away?" or "to change this with ease" Say it three-four times then things will start to change and everything starts to show up.

Use these tools. These tools really work. They work like magic. Nothing about Access is cognitive. It is about accessing the consciousness that you be and the awareness that is possible and available to you.

What energy, space and consciousness can I be to access all the generative and creative energies that are available to me? And everything that doesn't allow that to show up, destroy and un-create it all? <u>Right and Wrong, Good and Bad, POD and POC All Nine, Shorts, Boys and Beyonds.</u>

You could run this process for yourself. All the creative and generative energies that are available to you, but you have never asked for it to show up in your life. So how do you become a designer of your life? You access all the creative and generative energies that are available to you. The moment you do that, you begin creating and generating your life differently. It is not just talking about incremental change here, if you want to become a "designer of your life", you have to create your life differently. And how do you create your life differently? Do you have to know what that looks like? Not necessary.

All you have to do is just **be in the question**. By just asking a question, every day *"What can I be or do different to create and generate my life with total ease?"*- begins to start changing your life.

What you want to get here is the "different"- different Universe and different reality; not choosing something that already exists. To choose something that already exists is choosing "the default programming". If you were the designer of your life, you get to paint the canvas called your "life" whatever colors you want. You get to paint your relationship differently. You get to paint your financial reality differently. You willing to choose to be you regardless of what everyone else thinks of you; you change your world and that changes this world as well. You then become the invitation for others to choose to be them too.

Up until now, it is like everyone has been on a "conveyor belt" of this reality. Someone has put you in a straitjacket so you cannot get off the "conveyor belt" and you are looking at what everybody else is doing and therefore, you think that is what life is, so you sign on to the blueprint of this reality. And no matter how you try to fit into this reality and create your life from the default of this reality, notice how it doesn't work for you. It may work for some people but it doesn't work for you because you are special, you are unique and therefore, you are different. *"What if its okay to be different?"*

Everywhere you have judged you because you are different and you could never fit into the "default programming of this reality" no matter how much you tried and you made yourself wrong and this reality right will you now revoke, recant, rescind, reclaim, renounce, denounce, destroy and un-create it all? <u>Right and Wrong, Good and Bad, POD and POC All Nine, Shorts, Boys and Beyonds.</u>

If you don't ask that question about creating and generating a different reality for you, you are actually setting yourself up to die or you are setting up your relationship to die or your business to die if you just want to maintain it the way it is. Everything in the Universe is mutable and changeable and you are a mutable and changeable being- you are infinite. You are connected with everything. You are connected to all the molecules of consciousness and everything is there wanting to support you and wanting to contribute to you but you have to choose to step into that possibility to change everything. Receiving is not a one-way street. Receiving is not sitting on your chair, putting your head down and saying, "When am I going to get the Ferrari that I'm asking for?" No, that is not it. That is called the 'law of attraction'.

Receiving is stepping into that possibility- the flow- stepping into everything you can receive. You are the creator and the generator of your life and you have to institute your life. You have to go out there and just create and generate and institute all possibilities. You have got to be the designer of your life. Being the designer means you get to paint whatever colors you would like to paint on your canvas and that too can change – Anytime- based on what works for you in that moment. It is like you are painting the colors on your canvas called your life and you are simultaneously connecting to all the molecules of consciousness and what gets created is often times way beyond anything that you ever thought was going to be the result.

That is where you begin to be the designer of your life. You come out of you controlling everything. You come out of controlling everything to show up the way you think is going to show up, but remember everything you think you know has been based on other people's points of view; or based on the your past reference points. When you choose to step into the possibility- it is from that place that you are actually creating and generating your life and that is how you actually begin to design your life. For me when I am in that space of designing my life, it feels like I am standing on air. And there is no ground under my feet and if I can be ok with that discomfort in that place that I am at, everything starts to open up from there.

What if that discomfort is only because it is something you have never experienced before? It is like a new phase of being you, you are experiencing- and you call it "discomfort".

Everywhere you have misidentified, misapplied the discomfort as if it is really uncomfortable when it should be the most comfortable space because you are in a space of creating and generating your life, your living, your reality so different from everything that has been programmed in this reality, will you destroy and un-create it all? <u>Right and Wrong, Good and Bad, POD and POC All Nine, Shorts, Boys and Beyonds.</u>

It is only discomfort because it is not familiar. And what if familiar no longer works for you? It is like everybody is looking for that familiar place, thinking that the familiar place is what is going to create something different. By just asking a simple question like "*Is this working for me? Is this still working for me? What works for me? What will work for me?*" Ask those kinds of questions. Gary always says, "Only do what works for you and do it until it works for you. And if it stops working for you, do something else." And I like that. Because it means that I am not defined by what I choose. Because a lot of people choose something and they think that it is a choice for life. There is no such thing as a choice for life. Even your choices change."

Question: *"I am right now in the process of changing my maid actually. I can see my resistance to changing her even though she has been with me just for a month. It is like "you are familiar." I want to hold on to her even though she is sort of been creating a whole lot of mess in my life."*

Everything that is and everywhere you have bought that as yours, will you destroy and un-create it all and return it all back to sender with consciousness attached? <u>Right and Wrong, Good and Bad, POD and POC All Nine, Shorts, Boys and Beyonds.</u>

One of the other tools that we teach is Access is called **"Who does this belong to?"** 99% of your thoughts, your feelings and emotions do not belong to you. You are like a psychic sponge and you have the capacity to actually pick up other people's thoughts, feelings and emotions. Ever walk into a room full of angry people and you find yourself being angry? Welcome to actually perceiving what other people are feeling. A lot of judgment is like that. You almost think that the judgment you are hearing in your head is yours and then you beat yourself up for thinking it is yours. Like what you mentioned, what if it was actually the maid's? What if the maid is not willing to leave? Perhaps she has found herself a nice comfortable place with your family. But you know that the maid is not working for you, what you are getting is like this conflictual Universe going on.

All the conflictual Universes that you are creating in your Universe as a result of not asking a question "Who does it belong to?" will you destroy and un-create it all? <u>Right and Wrong, Good and Bad, POD and POC All Nine, Shorts, Boys and Beyonds.</u>

"Who does this belong to?" How do you use this tool? By asking the question for every thought, every feeling and every emotion that you have, you ask this question – *"Truth, who does it belong to? Is it mine?"* Remember, the truth will make you feel lighter and a lie will make you feel heavy. So if it lightens up, it is yours. Then you say "Destroy and un-create all the points of view that are creating this, all the lies spoken and un-spoken". <u>Right and Wrong, Good and Bad, POD and POC All Nine, Shorts, Boys and Beyonds."</u>

If it is someone else, and most of the time it is somebody else's points of view that you are hearing in your head, you say, "Return to sender with consciousness attached. <u>Right and Wrong, Good and Bad, POD and POC All Nine, Shorts, Boys and Beyonds.</u>" And don't be afraid to return to sender, because when you return it back to the sender, it shifts for you and for that person and you don't know how many people had this one thought that could have bounced around. It could have bounced around with a thousand people, or a million people.

If it is something else, it is always to do with the Earth. When it is to do with the Earth, you put your hands out, and flick at your wrists to gift energy to the Earth on the count of three. What you do is you fling your hands with the energy of gifting to the Earth. Before we do that with everyone on the call, I want you to go to a place in your body that you might have a pain or an intensity that you haven't been able to get rid of. Take your focus to that place, put your hands out and on count of three you just flick the energy, the gifting to the Earth. And see whether that begins to shift the intensity of the pain in your body. So on the count of three, everything that the Earth requires from us- 123, and so as many times until you can sense the ease in your body.

"Are you gifting to the Earth or are you gifting to change the intensity in our body?"

"We gifting to the Earth. By gifting to the Earth, you change the intensity in your body. Your body is connected to the Earth and vice-versa. When the Earth requires a contribution from you, it shows up as pain or intensity in your body. That is the Earth actually knocking at your body, saying "Gift to me! Gift to me!" We are going to gift to the Earth on a count of three again. **"Let's gift to the Earth everything that the Earth requires from us right now. It doesn't matter what it is. We are just gifting energy. One-connect with Earth, two and three and again."**

Laziness

Question: *"I have a lot of dreams. Also I'm very lazy. So how can I move forward?"*

How much of that laziness is yours?

Everywhere that you are picking up that as an energy and thinking it's yours and therefore creating that as yours, will you revoke, recant, rescind, reclaim, renounce, denounce, destroy and un-create all of that points of view, all the lies spoken and unspoken, and return it all back to sender with consciousness attached? <u>Right and Wrong, Good and Bad, POD and POC All Nine, Shorts, Boys and Beyonds.</u>

This laziness is not even yours. A lot of it is what you pick up from people around you and you think it is yours. You have to start asking a question – *"What would I like to create my life as?"* You have to start creating your life. You want to shift and change this.

Regarding things that you would like to do with your life, your dreams –

What are you not willing to choose for yourself? And everything that doesn't allow you to perceive, know, be and receive what could be possible for you, will you destroy and un-create it all? <u>Right and Wrong, Good and Bad, POD and POC All Nine, Shorts, Boys and Beyonds.</u>

And another question you can ask is *"What would it take to change this? What can I be or do different to change this right away for me?"* Those are some of the questions. A lot of people are not willing to work on themselves, they want everybody else to work it out for them and unfortunately it doesn't work like that. You want to get on your boat and you want to get into designing your own life, and you got to start creating and generating and instituting what is possible for you!

Fears

The way we look at fear in Access is that, firstly, fear is a lie. So if you get the energy of fear, is that heavy or light for you?

Anything that is heavy has a lie spoken and unspoken attached to it. It is a lie because it is heavy.

Everywhere you have bought into the lies spoken and unspoken about fear and have been actually functioning from that, will you revoke, recant, rescind, reclaim, renounce, denounce, destroy and un-create it all? <u>Right and Wrong, Good and Bad, POD and POC All Nine, Shorts,</u>

Boys and Beyonds.

Secondly, fear is what we call a 'distractor implant'. It is implanted to distract you from actually creating and generating your life. It is to distract you from seeing everything that is possible in front of you. It is only a limitation of your mind.

All the distractor implants underneath fear, will you destroy and un-create? <u>Right and Wrong, Good and Bad, POD and POC All Nine, Shorts, Boys and Beyonds.</u>

And thirdly, who does it belong to? Because 99.9% of all the fear that you all are experiencing out there is not yours, and I can tell you that for a fact! Because the way this reality is programmed, the way people are controlled in this reality is by implanting fear in them. So when you sense fear over something, it is almost like there is nothing to be afraid of but you are afraid of it anyway. You have picked up on that energy which never was yours to begin with.

Everywhere you bought the fear from other people and all the points of view spoken and unspoken and all the lies spoken and unspoken running under that, will you now destroy and un-create? <u>Right and Wrong, Good and Bad, POD and POC All Nine, Shorts, Boys and Beyonds.</u>

Return it all back to sender with consciousness attached. <u>Right and Wrong, Good and Bad, POD and POC All Nine, Shorts, Boys and Beyonds.</u>

Anytime you perceive the energy of fear or panic attacks- In the middle of waking up in the morning and you are suddenly having panic attacks and you wonder where it is coming from.

Don't wonder- "Return it all back to sender with consciousness attached. <u>Right and Wrong, Good and Bad, POD and POC All Nine, Shorts, Boys and Beyonds.</u>" And automatically, it is gone and you will realize that it was not yours.

I will share this funny thing that happened to me – This one time, I had a general happy day with lots of sessions with clients and on Skype and personal one-on-one sessions and I came home and had dinner with my brother and his family and played with my little niece and read her story books. And I went upstairs to bed and I just burst into tears. I felt depressed and I was just crying in the middle of the night, and in the midst of the tears I am asking: "Who does this belong to?" and whether it is mine or someone else's, I will just return it all back to sender with consciousness attached followed by the clearing statement, "Right and Wrong, Good and Bad, POD and POC All Nine, Shorts, Boys and Beyonds" and immediately, it was gone!

Be aware that 99% of your thoughts, your feelings and your emotions don't belong to you. Ask a question as simple as "Who does this belong to? Is it mine? Is it someone else? Or is it something else?" and see whether that begins to give you freedom in your life.

Closing Thoughts

Keep running these processes every day. I run these processes on myself every day. All these questions I give you and all these tools, I use them every day to change, to create, to generate my life differently. What I am sharing here today is what I use on myself, what Gary uses on himself every day, what Dain uses on himself every day. You have to diligently use this or you get almost trapped by the default of this reality. You fall into the programming of this reality because majority of the people, where they are choosing from- where they are functioning from is from the default of this reality.

When you are willing to be the designer of your life you will have more freedom, more choice and possibilities will open up for you like magic. Why not just give it a try? You never now how everything will show up unless you are willing to choose it! You are the creator of your life so get on that boat and start your journey, start designing your life and having the adventure called You."

GENERATIVE ENERGETIC DENTISTRY

By Dr Tom Kolso

What joy of embodiment & communion with the Earth can we enjoy with our mouths? What else is possible when we release limitations around eating, speaking, and pleasure with our mouths? What dormant generative systems can we activate for gum, bone and teeth regeneration and plaque dissipation?
http://www.magicofbeing.com

CHAPTER NINE

❖

BE THE LEADER OF YOUR LIFE, BE YOUR OWN BEST FRIEND

By Vanitha Subramaniam

Access Consciousness Certified Facilitator,

Psychologist, Transformational and Leadership Coach,

Author and CEO of Conscious Solutions

"Leadership is you choosing continuously to create your life"

~ Vanitha Subramaniam

Leadership

From the pragmatic Access point of view, Gary Douglas founder of Access, talks about leadership as "not about creating followers but creating leaders." For me personally, my whole life... my life journey to date has been about leadership. You know how you sort of choose things in life and you don't necessarily define it as leadership, but looking back, everything I choose when possibilities presented themselves, I felt guided towards leadership.

For example, the first time I was invited to a leadership conference was back when I was still at University studying in New Zealand. You know, they say things happen...magic happens? I got a call from the University Registrar's office and they said, "Hey Vanitha, would you like to go for a leadership conference?" And I was thinking to myself-Me? Out of everybody on campus, you are inviting me? I said, "Cool, where is it?" "Oh, it's in your own home country- Malaysia." "We will buy you an air ticket, give you pocket money. You will even get to visit your family. So would you like to go?" and I said, "Yeah cool, I will go!" and so I went and it was actually the *South East Asian Students Leadership Conference* and they invited university representatives from New Zealand, Australia and Japan to participate.

When I arrived at the conference which was held at a university in Kuala Lumpur, they put the New Zealand flag in front of me and I went "Holy S@$#, am I actually representing the country?" I am a Malaysian representing New Zealand! It was in that moment, I realized my life and reality, as I know it was changing, and I knew right then this was going to prepare me for something far more in the future.

A few years later, I was an international advocate for women's rights and young people's rights and enjoyed my time at the United Nations where I felt incredibly lucky to have met and worked with some of the renowned feminists who have been champions of women's rights for years. So everything that I did then was actually about choice. It is about choosing and the best way to say how Access defines leadership, is that *you are willing to be whatever it takes, no matter who follows you or not, no matter whether there is somebody else behind you.*

This is why today I wanted to talk about being a leader- being your own best friend. When we were kids, we always kind of wanted to hold our best friend's hand, or ask our friends "do you want to go with me to the toilet?" Do you remember doing that in primary school? "Or do you want to go with me to the canteen?" It was always like taking along your best friend, right? "Or you want to go to the movies with me?" How many people do you know who go to the movies on their own? I do and that is only because I love my own company.

"We are always looking to have somebody along with us, and it is so rarely that you actually step into choosing you and what I have realized is that since I have come into Access is I am choosing to make choices more and more just because I enjoy them and I don't need to have anyone around me."

What Is Being A Leader

What is being a leader? What is being a leader mean to you? It is a question that every one of us needs to ask of ourselves. One of the tools in Access, the very first tools you will ever learn in any class is about being in the question. So when you ask a question *"what does being a leader mean to me?"* and if you can destroy and un-create everything that starts to show up then you begin to get a sense of what being a leader truly means for you. Like for me, personally, being a leader means having the **courage** and the **choice** and being **inspired** every single moment to create whatever that is required or whatever I would like to create in my life. For me, being a leader is being an inspiration. When I look back at my own life, I grew up with very little inspiration. Did you have any inspiration when you were growing up?

Look at the kids today - the children of our future. We expect so much out of our kids but is there anyone there to inspire them or even say "Hey, you know you can choose this, you can choose that, or you can choose a multiple menu of choices available to you. You can succeed at anything you choose." There is not enough inspiration in the world. We do have some phenomenal leaders but very few that inspire the world.

Being Seen

I get a lot of clients who come to me and they talk about wanting to be successful, and somebody who wants to be successful- *you have to be willing to be a leader*. True? You cannot be successful if you are not willing to be a leader of your own life. So for a lot of these people, I ask them a question, "So how successful would you like to be?" and they say, "Oh, I would like to be as successful as Richard Branson, the guy who owns Virgin Airlines" and I ask "Ok, cool. Are you willing to be seen and heard?" Then they say, "What do you mean?" The point is you cannot be successful from behind your barriers. How can you be successful when you walk around with all your barriers up? No one could actually be in communion with you, communicate with you and have an interaction with you, because all they get are your barriers are up. So you have to be willing to push all your barriers right down.

This is a tool you can use. It is literally putting your hands up in the air and pushing all the barriers down to your cute little toes, right down and then you get a sense of like "Phew! No barriers." And what happens is, you begin to actually be present and you begin to have a sense of possibilities and a sense of awareness and a sense of choice and sense of courage, because so many people are afraid. When you ask most people "What it is that you are afraid of? They say, "I don't know. All I know is I am afraid." *So what are you afraid of?* What if you stopped being afraid and created a different reality? The Access point of view about fear is that it is a distractor implant.

Everything underneath the distractor implants, all the fear, can we please destroy and un-create it all? <u>Right and wrong, good and bad, POD and POC, all nine, shorts, boys and beyonds.</u>

The second point of view is that 98% of our thoughts, feelings and emotions do not belong to us and Access has this phenomenal tool **"Who does this belong to?"** What if 98% of what you feel, which is fear, is not even yours? What about all those times you were sitting in a room and you wanted to speak out but all you could sense was everybody's fear about speaking out? So what do you do? You take your whole infinite being and the vibration that you be, and you make it small and contract yourself so you would fit in with all those people who are all sitting right next to you in fear.

Everywhere that that has been your functional reality, would we please destroy and un-create that and return all of it back to sender with consciousness attached? <u>Right and wrong, good and bad, POD and POC, all nine, shorts, boys and beyonds.</u>

The other thing about fear is it is always a lie spoken or unspoken.

So all the lies, spoken and unspoken about fear, everywhere you made it yours and everybody who took it from somebody else, will you destroy and un-create it all times a godzillion? <u>Right and wrong, good and bad, POD and POC, all nine, shorts, boys and beyonds.</u>

Courage And Choice

My point of view is that the recipe for leadership is courage and the recipe for leadership is choice and the recipe for leadership is the willingness to be seen and heard no matter what that looks like and the only way you can have this beautiful concoction that creates this amazing sense of the leader in yourself is when you come out of judgment. That's the biggest barrier. Self-judgment.

Mahatma Gandhi talked about it – *"Be the change that you would like to see in the world."* Most people had it as a caption on their emails or social media at some point. "Be the change that you would like to see in the world." What does that mean? What does it truly mean? Is it about running out there and doing something or is it really about being? Dr Dain Heer wrote the book **'Being you and changing the world'**. At the end of the day, if you were willing to be you, no matter what looked like, with courage – because it takes a lot of courage to be a leader, and the willingness to go where nobody follows, that is truly functioning from the *Kingdom of We*.

Kingdom Of We

What is the *Kingdom of We* and what is the *Kingdom of Me*? From the point of view of leadership, *Kingdom of We* is where we are not willing to have any followers; we are not creating any followers. In the *Kingdom of We*, every one of us are stepping up and being willing to be the courage, the choice, the possibility, the question and the contribution we can be and receive from one another. The *Kingdom of Me* is where you are not inclusive of everybody else and you are willing to create followers. For example, Dr Dain was talking about it recently, how on

Facebook and Twitter, people think the value of them is based on how many likes they get. "Yeah, I have two thousand followers on Twitter! Woohoo! I am a leader." Seriously? No, I don't think that is the definition of true leadership. True leadership is not about having to go out there and proclaim to the world, "Hey, look- me leader, you follower! Follow me!" It just doesn't work like that, and I think I have seen the breakdown of that reality more and more, even in organizations and corporates with the implementation of change management processes. It no longer works. It is no longer a top-down approach saying "I am the CEO and therefore, you listen to me." It is not working because every person has to be recognized as a contribution. Every person is a contribution- if you are willing to look at every person's contribution and be willing to receive that contribution and we become the invitation for more people to step up and be more of themselves. I think that's true leadership.

A Leader Is Born To The Greatness Of Their Embodiment

One of the gifts I got from Access when I first came was just the validation that I have always known all my life- that every one of us are born to the greatness of our embodiment. What if we are the brightest 'star' against the infinite canopy of the Universe? And what if for the Universe to be in its infinite phenomenal glory, in its moment of creation and construction and inspiration that it requires every star- every person to shine? We cannot choose to become a 'dimmer star', dim our light and let the rest of them shine because every light will also get dimmer by the very nature of the law of vibration. This is the whole concept of the *Kingdom of We*.

I truly believe that we are all born to the greatness of our embodiment. We all are born to shine the brightest when we come on this planet. And what if that is what keeps the planet alive and keeps the planet going and that is the contribution to the continuous creation and 'orgasmicness' of this planet? However, we come into this world and we look for inspiration from everybody else around us and no one wants to shine. Everyone is looking at everybody else. It is as if we are all looking for "Is it okay for me to step up or not? Be seen or not? Be heard or not?" "Ok, you know what, I will just dim my light." And based on that- how much are you really creating your life? or are you destroying you?

What if you are born to the greatness of your embodiment? And what if it is different from everyone else? If all of us were willing to shine, would we not be the brightest star (planet) in the whole Universe? The choice is always yours. People who constantly ask: "Why God? Why me? Why does my life suck?" are not aware that they are in control of their lives and that they can change anything by simply choosing a different choice that could lead them down a different path - one that could work for them. So if you want to be seen and heard, you have got to choose to shine brightly with no barriers. You are not the only being with a body on all the planets of this galaxy and beyond. I mean, get over that point of view. You have been on so many planets and all across the Universe, am I right? We all have. We can sense that and that is what I mean about being born to the greatness of our embodiment.

Uncharted Territory

Another example I use in my classes is the analogy of being on a ship. Go back to those years when people discovered countries. They were pioneers who went on uncharted courses of discovery. They didn't have a chart to follow; they charted their own course. What if life is just that- a journey of discovery? What if life is about coming across a few obstacles, and having the tools to take you to the next course? "Bummer, I hit a sand dune. I will use some tools to get me off the sand dune and then ask *how does it get any better than this*? What would it take for the water to rise so my boat can keep going?" *What if life is about charting your own course?* We all need to know that we can be adventurous. Let us have an adventure with life. We cannot know the future but we sure can create a greater future if we choose to.

Recently in one of my classes a woman asked me, "Can you please tell me how is this going to show up in my life? Then I will know what to choose." And I said, "Really? Wait let me look for my crystal ball. Oh, bother, I don't actually have one." I asked her "How am I supposed to know how it is going to show up for you?" How many of us have been looking for the answers from others? Continuously- as if someone else has the answer that is going to validate what we have already decided and concluded and judged that we really want.

Everywhere you have been doing that seeking answers from others, can we please destroy and un-create it all times a godzillion? <u>Right and wrong, good and bad, POC and POD, all nine, shorts, boys and beyonds.</u>

What if we are all here to have an adventure with life? It is not about defining ourselves as – "Oh, I am a leader, you are a follower; or I am this, I am that." What if all the definitions were irrelevant? It is not about defining yourself as a leader, it is about **being** a leader.

"Oh, I want to be just like them"

"What happens when we look at someone who is being a leader and who is shining their light and we literally want to duplicate that and we would like to create ourselves as that and we would like people to validate us and to approve of us?"

I guess a lot of us tend to fall into this category.

This goes back to where people are not willing to "be themselves", so when they are not willing to "be themselves", what happens is they are constantly looking for validation whether they are *doing* the 'right thing' or 'the wrong thing'. "Are they being the "right leader" or the "right follower"? Or the validation seeking behavior of "do you approve of me?" You seek approval when you are not willing to have the greatness of you. So where are we all looking for approval?

Everywhere you are looking for approval, as if getting the approval, it gives you the permission to step up and be you, but you never get the approval because everybody else is walking around with their own judgment about themselves, can you please destroy and un-create all of that times a godzillion? <u>Right and wrong, good and bad, POC and POD, all nine, shorts, boys and beyonds.</u>

Being A Different Leader

Gary once talked about being an opinion leader and it resonated with me. *What does an opinion leader mean?* An opinion leader is one who is willing for people to ask them "Hey, what is it about you and what do you do that is so fantastic?" Such a leader is one who shines with their own knowing and there is no doubt in their awareness. Most people walk around with "Oh my god, something must be wrong with me because I am not measuring up to that person." We see this even in Access among the facilitators. Every one is measuring up against somebody else. Most people measure themselves against Gary and Dain; and I remember when I first came to Access, Gary actually said, "Please, don't measure against me. Don't measure against Dain. Don't try to be like us when you are facilitating. Out-create us. We will be the most happiest people in the world."

When you BE you and you find what works for you, then what happens is you create a different reality for yourself. It is not about what someone else is creating. Sometimes you have to completely block out all of that stuff that is going on out there and one of the ways to do this is by using this tool, which I have been teaching a lot in my classes and I have used for myself is *"how much space can my body and I occupy to have total ease with all of this?"*

You step into more awareness as you do these classes, and you become more aware. It is a very fine line between what is your awareness and what you "think" is yours. Does that make sense? It is like you become aware of where other people are functioning, but just because you think it, just because you feel it, just because you can emote it, it does not mean it is yours. Just ask *"Hey, is this my awareness or is this mine?" "Am I judging or am I being aware?"* So all these tools, all these questions start to create greater awareness.

When you become an opinion leader, you are not creating followers. Being an opinion leader is not about superiority. It is not like "Hey, look at me, look at me, me! Me! Me! I am an opinion leader!"

It is about being willing to have the courage to say what works for you but never expecting other people to follow you; and never expecting someone else to do what you do. I personally do not think that is leadership. It may be leadership in this reality, how it is defined. But it is not the kind of leadership we are looking for and I think the world is requiring a different kind of leadership now.

The Access Classes Contribute To Leadership

I see people who come to Access to do a bars class and they come and do the core classes and they are choosing and they are becoming more and more of themselves and it is like, "wow, what an inspiration you are just by being who you be." All that stuff which you think is creating you is really a pile of shit when you kind of just let go of that stuff and you are just willing to be more and more and more. It is like people are becoming leaders and it is so amazing to watch the journey that people are taking.

As a facilitator the greatest gift of facilitating the Access Core Classes– the bars and the foundation– is seeing people change instantly. Those of you who have done these classes don't get to see how much you do change, we do. In fact we should take a before and after photo because it is a physical transformation and beyond the rest of the transformation which is so amazing. It is like they step out and their whole being is just shining. They are shining. You get to be the shining. The shine. And it is so easy because all you are doing is choosing you.

What if the shine we are talking about is every time you choose you, you shine a little bit more brighter?

I had this guy once who came for a personal session with me back in Malaysia and he was one of the guys who was in the very first Malaysian Idol singing competition. However, he made it to the finals but lost. He came out the first runner up. He lost his confidence after that because he was so aware of all the judgments he was receiving from the audience throughout the country. He felt really stuck and could not sing for more than 10 years, which ruined his whole career. He just felt he was horrible, that he was useless. He made himself so wrong. I asked him, "What if that was not yours? What if everything you perceived was just judgments that were impelled on you? What if that wasn't about you? That was about everybody else who was in the audience, judging you. It is a competition. People are choosing you or someone else." When I asked him, "Would you just destroy and un-create everywhere you are making yourself wrong and you have bought those judgments?" He immediately said, "Oh my god, I can't see you. You are too bright. I need my sunglasses."

Was he referring to me or to him? And today, he is singing again, which is amazing. What if it is that simple? This is why I love the Access tools the information and processes, because it is that simple. It facilitates you to access you instantly. There is nothing out there that is that easy. Trust me, I tried it all. Being a psychologist I have used many different tools to facilitate people and none worked as well or as fast as the Access tools. Facilitating someone and having to listen to their stories about their issues can be a long drawn out process but when you ask- "Will you POC and POD all your stuff?" And it is gone! I mean, *how does it get any better than that?*

Questions and Answers

Q- "I hired a team and asked their energy to contribute to the project with the best of their skill. And I focused on my part only, but in the end, it turned out that they didn't do good work at all. I have seen magic with this tool but this time it didn't work. Problem is now I have to do all of this again. What to do in this situation and asking the question didn't help. That's so weird. How can I be the leader in this situation?"

How could you have done this differently? What if it is not about the question that you ask, but it was about where you went into conclusion?

The conclusion here was that there was almost a sense that it didn't work, and that the sense of separation that got created, because that was the energy that I got, that everybody was working in isolation.

Everywhere you think that's a contribution and that you don't have to contribute your energy to all those people on your project even though they had their various tasks at hand, will you destroy and un-create it all, times a godzillion please? <u>Right and wrong, good and bad, POC and POD, all nine, shorts, boys and beyonds.</u>

In the past, before Access, I managed really huge project teams. It has been one of my strengths- project management. I have even managed 15 different organizations on regional projects continuously for 2 years. These are organizations that had a history of never working together. What I found was the key to successful managing projects is when you are inclusive of people, where you invite people to contribute their ideas and continue to keep the conversation going on and also doing a bit of conflict management in the process. Your contribution is important here. With the Access tools you can POC and POD what is not working and you keep asking *what else is possible here I haven't considered? What else do I know? What do I know that I am pretending not to know, that if I allowed myself to know it, it would change my reality and all realities?* Then that should contribute to this project and it doesn't become your project. It is the other part of it. It becomes a project that everybody has ownership over. When you empower people and you allow them to be empowered in return. They have a sense of ownership- then it is a different contribution altogether.

Q- *"What are some of the tools for working with smokers and addicts. If they are in the team, how do you get the best out of them, without the side-effects of feeling drained, etc.?"*

I am an anti-smoker plus I worked to get Smoke free on legislation a long time ago. Even got blacklisted by the tobacco companies. I know a lot about people who smoke. Firstly, everybody has a choice so you cannot take choice away from those people and this topic gets people always defending for or against. So if you went up to a smoker and said, "I don't like you participating because your smoke is affecting everyone- can you stop smoking in the process?" They are not going to take that lightly. They are going to feel offended and they are going to react. That is not going to work. What you need to do is to see how can you approach the person by asking a question. Firstly ask yourself- "How can I approach this differently?" Then ask- "What is going to create more ease for you guys? You have to smoke? Well, ok, go."

Where have you made smoking so significant? That would be a good way to place a start. Everything that is, times a godzillion, will you destroy and un-create it all? <u>Right and wrong, good and bad, POC and POD, all nine, shorts, boys and beyonds.</u>

All of you who can't receive people who smoke, and where you have made them so significant, where you have made your body being affected by the cigarette smoke significant, and all of that, will you destroy and un-create it all, times a godzillion please? <u>Right and wrong, good and bad, POC and POD, all nine, shorts, boys and beyonds.</u>

So, see where your judgments about people who smoke sit. So you POC and POD all your judgments because if you have got a group of people who are smokers, then you have to also POC and POD your judgments about them and their behavior and what their addiction is.

Secondly, teach people to expand the energy, space and consciousness of their body so that the body has more ease. I had a guy who was smoking in my Foundation and Level 1 class, and every time he went out to smoke, it was because he stepped into so much space that he had this need to create density in himself again. So he would say, "Oh my god, can I please go and have a smoke? I have a point of view." "Ok, go."

Every time he came back, he created more density and solidity in his Universe, and until he came to his own awareness of his own behavior, which he did eventually, is the space that you have to allow them to have the choice, because where you are not willing to be in allowance of people who smoke?

I never thought I would say that, being an anti-smoker myself but what if we could be in allowance and have the ease. Be everything with no point of view. I am also willing to POC and POD everywhere that nicotine is creating that addiction in their body.

All the chemical compositions of nicotine that is making them smoke, destroy and un-create it all, times a godzillion? <u>Right and wrong, good and bad, POC and POD, all nine, shorts, boys and beyonds.</u>

The other thing about smokers is how many people are actually projecting at them and how much are you aware of those projections and you think, "oh my god, I don't want this.

As a leader be aware of where you are projecting someone else's points of view.

All your projections, expectations, rejections, separations, judgments and conclusions about what a leader is, what a leader must do or how a leader must be seen, how a leader must speak, how a leader must talk, communicate, everything else, will you destroy and un-create it all, times a godzillion? <u>Right and wrong, good and bad, POC and POD, all nine, shorts, boys and beyonds.</u>

I always say this to people, "Please don't try to be like me. Don't try to be like Gary. Don't try to be like Dain. Don't try to be like all the Access facilitators that you did classes with". Everyone of us are unique and you have to find what your uniqueness is. I always say every person who comes to Access is like an uncut diamond. It is like the classes polish them and that is why they shine; especially, after Foundation and level 1 and more so after Level 2 and 3 and it carries on depending on all the classes that they do thereafter. You become that real, clear, beautiful, whole diamond of this reality. How does it get any better than that?

Q- *"I teach and people ask me questions looking for answers. I like sharing what I know yet I would like to empower them. How do I teach, which is giving them information and empower them to know what they know?"*

The easiest way is to only speak to what they can hear. Not everyone is able to receive. Receiving is a huge thing. We have all this awareness- "Oh my god, I am so aware- I can say this, I can say that. I can say everything." But not everyone is willing to receive. One of the best questions that you could probably use all the time is **"What information do I require here? What can I speak to that this person can receive?"** And what you will find automatically is that you will speak to what they can hear and they will go back thinking- "Wow, I got the best answer" but you didn't give them an answer. You were actually speaking to awareness.

A question will always empower you to more and more awareness and an answer always disempowers you to conclusions. So if you love teaching, please carry on doing that but teach from a place of questions, not from a place about answers. In fact just today, I was talking to the Kitchen Manager of this hotel before I left Mumbai- I ordered a piece of toast and coffee. It came in a dirty tray, with just 2 pieces of toast, no butter, no jam and I waited another 10 minutes for the butter and jam to arrive and by that time, my toast was like a stone. So the manager comes running, "I am sorry, madam. I had an accident and we did try to tell these young people what to do, but they are all new and untrained. We are training the staff." And I said, "Well, if you are going to 'tell' them they are definitely not going to listen. What if you were willing to ask a question?" He said, "What do you mean?" I said, "Well, ask them a simple question like what would you do? How would you serve the tray? Would you, as a customer, be willing to eat something presented like this? What would you do differently?" So I always say teaching with a question creates far more awareness than teaching with a purpose of giving people answers.

"That's brilliant. It is because when you ask them a question and they come to that awareness themselves- it is theirs. But if you try to tell them something, they have to fight you over it, because it is your point of view."

Q- *"How do you bring out the leader that is within you?"*

It is not inside of you, by the way. I would love to say, "Oh, you know what, the leader is inside of you and I can just pull it out like that." No, it doesn't work like that. You are a leader and it is everything about you, including the action you take and the choices you make. What if you are an inspiration to yourself? How many of us inspire ourselves? Maybe that is the mistake. We are always looking outside of us when looking for inspiration. We look for role models; we read autobiographies of all these famous people, thinking that is going to inspire us to step up and be more. But we are losing the true essence of what leadership is here. I think leadership starts with your own worship.

"And also when you are looking outside of you, when you are looking for people to inspire you, it is like a double edged sword, because when you read about a person, you also have to judge you. That "I am not all of that" and for me, I think that creates the greatest amount of contraction in your Universe."

It is that whole 'wrongness'. You look for what is wrong about you because you are constantly measuring yourself against those people, right? So here is a process Gary recently shared:

What energy, space and consciousness can you and your body be to become the celebrity, focal point and spokesperson for a different reality for all eternity that you truly be? Everything that doesn't allow that to show up, times a godzillion, will you destroy and un-create it all? Yes? <u>Right and wrong, good and bad, POC and POD, all nine, shorts, boys and beyonds.</u>

What If We Were All Celebrities?

What have you made so vital, valuable and real about never possessing the total leadership of a different reality that keeps you in judgment of and in wrongness of you for all eternity? Everything that is, times a godzillion, will you destroy and un-create it all? Yes? <u>Right and wrong, good and bad, POC and POD, all nine, shorts, boys and beyonds.</u>

These are two good processes. If you put it on loop and keep listening to it, it might take away all that funky stuff. The stuff that you keep telling yourself that only other people are capable of being a leader of a different reality, not you. *What if every one of us is a gift and what if each of us were willing to step up and be a leader?* It does not mean it has to look like something. Just be you and change the world. What if that is all it takes?

Q- *" I need your assistance about my home. I have been living on rent for the last 15 years. I really long for my own house. Bored and tired of changing apartments every now and then. I can't stay anywhere for more than 2 to 3 years. Agreement is just for 11 months. I have been asking 'what energy, space and consciousness can me and my body be to buy a 3 bedroom house with total ease?' and a few more questions. It has been a year I am asking, so far nothing. I really want to enjoy this experience. I do feel everything is my home, so how do I create magic here?"*

Where are you not in the computation of your own life? Where are you not including you in your life?

Everywhere you are not in the computation of your own life and everything that you are making solid and significant about moving houses, about changing houses will you destroy and un-create it all, times a godzillion, please? <u>Right and wrong, good and bad, POC and POD, all nine, shorts, boys and beyonds.</u>

What if it only worked to the degree that it just worked? Which means what if you just enjoyed the hell out of where you are for the period of time where you are? What are you making so significant? I mean, at the end of the day, we make everywhere we live, who we are with, what we are wearing, how our life is, so significant that we almost miss the boat. And what I mean by "miss the boat" is when choices and possibilities show up, we do not even see it. So what you have got to do is you have got to keep running a process. Like this is what you do every day, when you wake up in the morning, you are going to:

Destroy and un-create all your projections, expectations, rejections, separations, judgments, conclusions everywhere that is your functional reality? <u>Right and wrong, good and bad, POC and POD, all nine, shorts, boys and beyonds.</u>

And keep asking questions- *what else is possible? What would it take for me to have an amazing place?* It is not just running an energy, space and consciousness process. It is about really knowing what you truly want. Have you truly asked for what you really desire? Or what you are asking is just randomly showing up? That is probably what is happening here. So ask- is now the time for you to own your own house? How about inviting the house that would like to own you to show up rather than you having the point of view that you have to own it? Gary always used to say this- "you don't own things, things actually own you. That is why you have to go out there and earn money." So, you need to ask a question, *"What would it take for the house that would like to own me to show up and is now the time?"* and keep checking with it energetically and keep adding, *"What would it take for the house to have all the ecstatic of living?"* rather than focusing on the cost of it or the look of it. Ask yourself- what would you like in house? Personally, I like lots of windows, lots of natural light coming in, a place that is so energizing, a place that is a contribution that brings the caring and nurturing energy for me, my body and my family. Perhaps you need to ask that for yourself. Start looking at the way you frame your questions. I hope that will start you off in a different way or path.

Q- *"I keep creating a life through other people only. Most of everything I get is that way only. I don't seem to break the pattern. It is as if no matter how amazingly magical I am in what I do or be, things, that is, money, home, food, etc., come to me through others. Not a wonderful condition too. So how do I change it? What is happening here? How do I be the leader of my creation? Receiving from others is good but I would like to receive directly too. That way somewhere feels dependent and limits me."*

What if you are a leader of receiving? I mean, where have you made it so significant? It is amazing. I always get questions from people who are not receiving. Here you are receiving so much that people want to contribute to you, so are you truly receiving here or are you making it so significant?

Everything that you have decided is your functional reality including standards of judgment, will you now destroy and un-create it all? <u>Right and wrong, good and bad, POC and POD, all nine, shorts, boys and beyonds.</u>

So look at what your standards of judgments are. At the end of the day, it is just choice, my dear. It is a matter of just choosing what is going to work for you and what you would like to create as your life and if it is fun for you to receive from others, I say why not? Why make it so significant? Enjoy the hell out of it!

The other place I really see people constrict themselves, is they go to this place of "it has to show up by this time" and if it doesn't show up by that time, they have to judge that it is not happening. And what if it was that moment at which the next moment it was going to actualize in your Universe and just the moment before you went, "it is not showing up" and you just killed the whole process? What would it take for you to choose something different? And I remember Gary talked about something once. He said, "I never take no." and he says, "no matter what it is and even if it is not happening in the moment, I am continuously asking for it to change." So what if you could be that? And what if you could be in that energy of what else is possible always?"

Instead of actually contracting yourself, why don't you expand yourself? What if you could expand the energy, space and consciousness of your receiving more, and keep asking what else is possible? What else that can be a contribution to you? And how can you be a contribution back? By the way please acknowledge that you are a leader because people will not contribute to you if you are not a leader. Unless they 'see' you, they won't be contributing to you.

Where have you decided and concluded that you are not a leader? And everywhere you have, will you destroy and un-create it all times a godzillion please? <u>Right and wrong, good and bad, POC and POD, all nine, shorts, boys and beyonds.</u>

And if you are aware of that energy of magic that you are creating where others are contributing to you, where else can you use that energy? Where else? Who else? What else? How else?

Who, what, where, when, why, how you are, are you not willing to ask more? More receiving, more contribution, more magic? Everything that is, times a godzillion, will you destroy and un-create it all? <u>Right and wrong, good and bad, POC and POD, all nine, shorts, boys and beyonds.</u>

What have you made so vital about magic that you are unwilling to be so magical, so potent, and just enjoy the hell out of it? And everything that is, times a godzillion, will you destroy and un-create it all? Yes? <u>Right and wrong, good and bad, POC and POD, all nine, shorts, boys and beyonds.</u>

Sometimes it is just the willingness to choose. *What if being a leader begins with choice?* What if it is not about all the processing? What if it is all choice? "I'm going to demand." **A choice and a demand.** Make the choice and make the demand that no matter what it takes, you stepping up and being you, and enjoying the hell out of you, and enjoying the creation of you, and enjoying creating everything that is going to keep adding to your life and a contribution to your life, and you are not at all discounting anyone else but including everyone else. You are not creating followers, you are also inviting people by saying "come along. Let us have some fun." Well, that is what leadership is. How does it get any better than that?

THE MAGIC OF BEING

My Interesting Point Of View On Leadership

I think we are at a time where every one of us has a job to do. So fire yourself from all the other jobs, ok? And it is not a doing, but it is a matter of **being**. And the willingness to be, no matter what it takes, to be the invitation to step up and embrace the greatness of our embodiment, because the more we embrace the greatness of embodiment, the more magic we step into, the more magical we become, the more courage and inspiration we become– and we inspire courage in everyone else. Instead of just one person's voice having to create a different reality- voices from the *Kingdom of We* will create a different reality! I know the planet requires that and I reckon that is why we are all here. We are here to inspire, to create and to choose and to be. What if that is all it takes? What do you know? What do you all know?

WHO IS VANITHA SUBRAMANIAM

Vanitha Subramaniam is an Access Consciousness Certified Facilitator, Psychologist, Transformational and Leadership Coach, Public Health Specialist, Speaker, Author and CEO of Conscious Solutions. Vanitha travels the world inspiring and empowering people to create change and transformation so they can become more aware of what they would like to generate and create as their lives.

Vanitha has a Masters degree in Clinical Psychology and Health Development and Policy. With more than 15 years of experience in leadership and management. Vanitha has worked internationally in public health, health promotion, women and child health, sustainability and mental health; including in partnership projects with UNIFEM, UNFPA and UNDP. Currently she coaches clients, teaches classes on various topics, conducts workshops internationally and spends her time writing her books.

WRITE A BOOK & MAKE IT AN AMAZON BESTSELLER

Have you written and published a book?

Are you writing a book?

Do you have a book in you that would like to be written and published?

Would you like to write, publish and make your book an Amazon Bestseller?

From coaching on getting started, to helping you with the publishing process to getting your book to be an International Amazon Bestseller, Nilofer offers it all. Contact her to explore the Infinite Possibilities with your book - nilofer@illusiontoilluminationsummit.com

CHAPTER TEN

❖

BEING DEFINITELY DIFFERENT

By Sophie Mihalko

Access Consciousness™ Facilitator
Comedian
YouTube Specialist

Definitely Different

Since I started using the tools of Access Consciousness® about 3 years ago, my breasts grew 1 size larger. So when I heard Gary Douglas, the founder of Access talk in class about "You are Double D", I thought "Well, it may not be my size but seeing how everyone suddenly looks at me, I sure feels like it."

So what does Double D stand for? Definitely Different.

How many times have you been made wrong for being Definitely Different? What if being definitely different was actually what was right about you?

The truth is, we don't see how different we really are. I go through my day and I always assume that people think like me, act like me, are going to react like me. I just don't get that I'm different, until something happens and I'm like "wow, I really don't think that way!" I realize how really unique and special I am. Everybody really is. But it's not until we look at it, not until we acknowledge it that we actually can step into it.

The reason why I love the expression "you are Double D" is that it makes it not so serious. It's not because we are different, that we don't fit, but it's not that because we are different that there's something wrong with us. Once you know how different you are, you can actually use that to your advantage and you can create so much more than resisting and trying to fit into somebody else's mold.

For instance, I love technology and it's very easy for me to build websites, and start using the new online tools pretty quickly. But I am aware how many people think it's weird. However, when people ask me questions about the technical tools, they often go "Wow, it actually looks easy. Maybe I can do it too." So I become an invitation for other people to acknowledge how different they are and the gift that they be.

That has only become my reality since I have acknowledged how definitely different I am.

Being Definitely Different With Me

I used to make myself wrong for everything. I was wrong for the way I type on the computer. I was wrong for how I say hello. I was wrong for the way I brush my hair, and so on.

Access Consciousness® talks a lot about judgment and how judgment is not real. I realize that many of these thoughts were not real. I brush my hair the way I brush my hair, there is really no wrong or right way to do it.

I have been an actor since I was 15 years old and I remember one day I was on stage and I didn't have any lines to say. I was one of the characters in the background and the main character was supposed to say something but he forgot his line. So I decided to be me and be as funny as I could be, and I bumped into the lead characters to make the crowd laugh. And that changed everything. The main character suddenly remembered what he had to do and everything started to flow again. As an actor, you are not supposed to do that, if it's not in your script or if it's not what you rehearsed, you don't bump into another actor. It was weird. But I just knew something different was required and by me being me, I was able to help others, to invite others to be them. To be everything that they could be. So that's my invitation and that's what I love about being a Double D – Definitely Different, is that we are a living invitation to consciousness. We are being a complete invitation to creating more with no judgment.

It was the first time that I made an audience laugh and I got hooked. I realized that loving to make people laugh was how different I was . So I became a Comedian.

We also spend our lives defining ourselves. We take on the labels of woman, man, child, adult, parent, employee, business person, healer, artist, lover, etc.... What if we had no definition? Being definitely different means that you are willing to be anything you choose to be at anytime. This is the space of being.

When I ask people to let go of any label or definition of themselves they sometimes think it feels like empty or blank. They suddenly have no reference points. Is it true or is it a misidentification and misapplication of space? Which one is lighter? Which one creates more possibilities for you and your life?

The space of being allows you to choose joy at anytime. Joy is not excitement; it does not have to be "Yay! Woohoo!" all the time (although it can be). Joy is simply the space of infinite possibilities, where no limitations can continue to exist.

Being Definitely Different with Energy

I used to do a lot of video editing and one day I got footage that was completely out of sync. I had to re-sync audio and video for a video that was 2 hour long. Usually, it would take me a whole day to do this. But I started seeing that my hands knew exactly where to stop and go with the footage to sync it all up. I was following the energy of the two pieces and matching them by energy! It was so much easier than trying to figure it out! It took me less than 1 hour!

Following the energy means that I can match two things that don't look the same but have the same energy. I do this a lot when I facilitate classes or work with clients. I will let people talk until they say something that has the energy they are looking for. Then I will ask questions about that energy. They always think I am psychic but truly, I am simply matching the energy of what they are saying with what they want to create in their lives.

I had to start trusting my body more. I just ask my body to show me this energy or that energy and I get a sensation or an image sometimes. Our bodies can communicate with us clearly if we ask them to show us how.

Being Definitely Different In Relationships

For a long, long time, anytime that I would do something for a man, I felt like I was weak. I felt that I was less than men. So it was very frustrating because I love being a contribution to people, but when I was a contribution to men, there was this weird heavy feeling coming up. Finally, last year, I asked Gary Douglas (Founder of Access Consciousness®), "What is this?" and he says to me, you know, that a lot of men want to do things for women, so when a woman does something for men, the men feel weak, or pathetic.

He made me realize that I was aware of how they were feeling when I was contributing to them. It was not me feeling weak like that, it was them. Now that I know this, I act differently toward men. I do not feel frustrated with them anymore, I actually adore them and how much they truly care.

I am also aware that I am different in the way I express my emotions. I have pretty intense emotions right away. I told my boyfriend I loved him after our second date for instance. I was aware he would be fine hearing it, which is why I said it, but if he had not been ok with it, I would have just acknowledged it for myself.

When I acknowledge my emotions without making myself wrong about it, people that I am in relationship with don't feel like I am hiding something from them. The energy is clear. They know the deal.

While I may not hang out often with someone who is not comfortable around my strong emotions, when I meet people I am aware of what they can or cannot receive. It would not be a kindness to them if I simply dump it on them.

In Access we have a saying "just for me, just for fun, never tell anyone". It's sometimes a lot better to just keep it for myself. I don't need validation; I just need to acknowledge what is true for me. So always ask first: What can I say to this person that would create more for both of us? Not just for me, not just for them, but for both of us.

And it's not about censoring yourself. It's about getting out of the auto responder systems you have bought from everybody else and truly looking at what you want to create with that person. May it be a romantic relationship, a professional relationship or someone in your family.

Being Definitely Different with Sex

Because I am French, people assume some things about me. They assume I know a lot about sex for instance, or that I sleep around. I am actually the opposite. So I resisted people's judgment of me around sex for a long time. I decided that I really didn't want to know anything about sex. And I kept finding myself in really weird, crazy sex situations. What I decided I could not have kept showing up. But when I started taking Access Consciousness® classes, I started having a lot of spontaneous orgasms for no reason. I thought there was something wrong with me. Finally, I started using the tool "Who does this belong to?" and that's when I realized I was actually perceiving everyone around me who was sexually attracted to me and all the thoughts they were having in their heads about what they would do with me. Pretty funny, right? It changed everything. Suddenly, I was not wrong anymore. I was just really aware. It changed my body. It changed how much joy I allowed myself to have in life. And now, I actually work with people who would like to have more sexualness in their life. Now, I realize that this yummy, creative energy that we call sex is just that, an energy and it is available to all of us at any time.

That, I know, is Definitely Different.

Being Definitely Different With Business

I use energy a lot in my business, and that's different. For instance, I pull energy from the Universe through the people looking for what I am offering through the websites, online tools and traditional marketing I use.

I also send my energy to these people too. But for this tip to start creating business I had to really acknowledge my talents and abilities. People were not looking for me as a friend or a good person, they were looking for the results that I create with my clients.

Here is a great Access Consciousness® clearing I used:

What do I know that I am pretending not to know that if I allowed myself to know it, would create the business I want to have? And everything that is, will I uncreate and destroy it all? <u>Right and wrong, good and bad, POD and POC, all nine, shorts, boys and beyonds.</u>

Once you acknowledge how awesome you are, the world gets to know it too.

When I looked at the creation of my business, I saw that people in my industry did not like to advertise. They felt they were too "different" to advertise. I thought the same too and then one day I was tired to struggle to get clients or class participants every month. So I did the unthinkable: I started advertising.

I started with the good old traditional advertising of knocking on people's doors. I got some great connections that brought me enough business for a year. Then I started using signage: on my car, on my lawn and

I even had buttons made for my jackets, just like politicians.

Being the nerd I was (I love being a nerd), I started to look into advertising online. I did not like a lot of what I saw, and that was another sign of how different I be. It's not because it works for others that it will work for me. I am using the platforms they are using, but the content is very different than most.

I started playing with my business. If I did not have to follow everyone else's rules, then I wondered what I could create. The space I now have is so much more fun than anything I could have thought of before.

I do business to create my life, and that's definitely different.

Being Definitely Different in Creating

Most people function from doing when it comes to creating anything. They have the point of view that if they want to create something they are going to have to do a lot.

Being definitely different I know that I create by Being. So when something is not showing up the way I want to, I ask "Who am I being?" Doing is included in being and through being lots of actions will occur but not of it will feel like work or effort. It will all be me.

Here is a great exercise: look at what you would like to change. Acknowledge you have created it. Then ask, who was I being? Get the energy of that. Is this who you want to be? Does it match the energy of what you want to create?

I am truly grateful to Gary Douglas and Simone Milasas (worldwide coordinator of Access Consciousness®) for coming up with the expression of "Joy of Business". I really did not want to be in business for a long time because there was no joy in it for me. And when I ask: "Who was I being in business?" I saw that I was being my dad. My dad is a very successful businessman but he always came home stressed and angry. I did not want to be that so I did not choose a successful business for a very long time.

If I look at my business and decide it is a success or a failure because of this or that, I am limiting what my business can be.

Everywhere you are judging yourselves for being a success or a failure because of the size of your bank account or mailing list, would you please uncreate and destroy it all? <u>Right and Wrong, Good and Bad, POD and POC, All 9, Shorts, Boys and Beyonds.</u>

Considering yourself a success can be a limitation too because we tend to not outcreate it. What if you chose to create more every day?

What if being definitely different did not mean you were different but what you create looks different than what anyone else creates? Everybody is unique, so you are different by nature. It is how you function in the world that's different. NO ONE can be you. Being you surpasses everything and makes everything so much easier. There is nothing to define and nothing to defend for or against. Hey, there is nothing to do!

Want to learn to be you? Start by sensing your feet on the ground, the temperature around you. The sounds you can hear. Right there, you are being you. Being you is much easier than you think! (Because it does not require any thinking).

Being Definitely Different With My Body

I almost did not talk about the body because I have always been so different, it has become "normal" to me. I was born 3 weeks premature and the doctor did not think I was going to live. So I grew up thinking I was fragile but somehow I always wanted to do what I was not supposed to do. (Are you like me, do you feel like you HAVE to do what other people say you can't do?).

I was very skinny so I was allowed to eat anything I wanted. It really worked for me body, until I started buying the point of view that what I was eating was not healthy. How many points of view about food have we bought from other people?

Today, I started again eating whatever my body wants to eat and whenever it wants to eat. This is how I lost 10 pounds in 30 days over one summer.

How do I know what my body wants to eat? I ask before I eat or drink anything. And I stop eating when it does not taste good anymore.

Also, what if you were being definitely different when you felt pain? What if instead of calling it pain you asked your body what it is? Is it an awareness? What is your body communicating with you?

Not calling it pain or illness allows your body to shift it much faster than if you buy into any diagnosis. Traditional healing methods may still be required but you may be surprised how fast things change when you don't make the diagnosis solid.

Finally, another way I am definitely different with my body is before, during and after sex. I notice who my body wants to sleep with but I ask more questions: does my body want to have sex with this person or is my body telling me that this person wants to have sex with me? Will it be easy, fun and will I learn something?

During sex, sensations may come and go and be very intense. Whether I do not "feel" anything or I am having a complete orgasm I also don't go in the conclusion that what my partner is doing is working for me or not. I simply be in the moment, with the sensation and ask my body to expand. (Expanding will always increase the pleasurable sensation or allow for new pleasurable sensations).

My body is now a great companion in gaining more awareness. It no longer reacts from adrenaline and is often the space I need it to be. Without being the weight.

People cannot tell how old I am by just looking at me. I have no points of view around age so my body no longer to choose to appear my age unless I want it to. Yes, my body changes the way it looks and functions as required.

Steps toward allowing yourself to being definitely different:

Look at where you function on auto-pilot and, in those areas, ask, how could I do this different today? May be it's changing hands when you brush your teeth, may be it's writing a blog on a completely different topic than what you usually write about.

Dare yourself once in a while. Share your dares with people.

Change things around. Be as different as you are willing to be.

Being definitely different can also mean that you have things in common with people that you have not acknowledged yet.

Choice creates awareness. You can make a different choice every 10 seconds or choose the same thing. No choice is wrong. If you make a choice that does not work for you, make a different choice.

Choose space. Feeling good means that you have to judge something as good. Judgment limits possibilities. Instead of looking for what feels good, look at for what creates more possibilities, more space for you to be anything you choose to be. When you are the space of being, this is when things start falling into place. The Universe can now deliver more than anything you could think of asking.

Drop all your points of views. Often, people who say they are "different" compare themselves to others: "I am not like that". But if you have the point of view that you are right or wrong for being different, you are still functioning from the polarity that everybody else is functioning from. Being definitely different means having no point of view, or having total allowance for all that is (does not mean you have to choose everything but you don't have to have a point of view about it). For the next 3 days (at least, if possible longer), say "interesting point of view I have that point of view" for everything.

For instance, I used to react with anger and frustration when someone said to me "you have to work hard the first year in business". I had the point of view that if I worked hard, I would be like everybody else and

I wanted to be special. I said "interesting point of view I have that point of view, interesting point of view they have that point of view and interesting point of view I have the point of view that they have that point of view" over and over. Now I don't react. Sometimes I work "a lot" and sometimes I don't.

Choose to be you, no matter what that looks like. When you are being you, there is nothing the Universe cannot deliver. Being you is like having your arms wide open and receiving everything there is to offer (with no point of view).

When you are being you, the world wants to have what you have. There will be more people who will want to have sex with you, more people who want to pay you or create with you. How does it get any better than this? ®

When you being definitely different, you start tapping into the infinite being you truly be. As an infinite being, you change the world by simply being you. What if being definitely different was everything you could ask for and more because it is also including possibilities that you don't even know exist yet?

WHO IS SOPHIE MIHALKO

Born and raised in France, Sophie never let anything stop her. When she heard in high school that there was a film school in which Steven Spielberg could not get in she wondered what it would take for her to get in? She got in (did you doubt it?) and ended up producing large scale musical events throughout the world.

A few years later she was working for Fortune 500 companies, transforming their workflow so that more could get created in a shorter amount of time. All while being a stand up comedian! Today, she travels the world facilitating people into more ease and joy in their business, relationships and bodies. Her target is to get everyone laughing and creating the world we truly know is possible to create.

THE ARTLESS ART OF ALLOWANCE

By Bhagyalakshmi Murali

A doorway to possibilities. "To be or not to be, that is the question" Allowance is not a synonym for doormat. The doors one must choose to close first. http://www.magicofbeing.com

CHAPTER ELEVEN

❖

THE ART OF CREATING BUSINESS FROM THE EDGE OF POSSIBILITY

By Steven & Chutisa Bowman

Pragmatic Futurists

Thought Leaders on Benevolent Capitalism

Authors & Speakers

Prosperity Consciousness And Business

The whole narration of Prosperity Consciousness really underpins how you choose to create your business. A lot of the work that we have done both in our own business and also the many hundreds and thousands of CEOs and senior executives and directors that we deal with around the world, it all comes back to the point of view. If you have the point of view that there is abundance out there, there is prosperity out there, then funnily enough, you start looking for it. If you think there is a scarcity and a lack out there, well, then guess what? You get all the evidence to prove the rightness of that particular point of view.

As you create your life and your business from the energy that you create from, so if you create the energy from lack, from scarcity that is how you would actually create your business. It is important to be aware that when you start creating or generating your business and your life, from what energy or space you are creating from so whenever you go into the space of scarcity, be sure that that is a space you are creating your business from. Everywhere that you create your business from scarcity, you have to be willing to destroy and un-create all of that energy and step in to create from prosperity and abundance. And that is the foundation of your business.

In creating your business from scarcity or creating your business from prosperity, you have to be really vigilant about what you are doing at every point of time because you could start off with creating from prosperity and then very insidiously slip into scarcity. Because this world and this reality, the business world is functioning from scarcity. Everyone functions from lack. Basically, when you ever think that you have to compete to get something, you are already coming from scarcity and lack anyway because if the world is an abundant place and there are plenty of things, do you have to compete or do you just choose to create your business whatever way you would like it to be? You do not have to compete with anyone really, you just have to out-create yourself and out-create everyone in every moment, because there is plenty to go around, you just have to choose. And you have to be willing to receive different possibilities. And the key thing is about who you are choosing to be.

No Judgment

A practical tool for everyone is do not judge yourself when you find you are getting into scarcity. I do it at least once a day in different areas, but I am much more aware of it now than I used to be. So when you get into scarcity, your body starts to hunch up a little bit, you start to feel it is all too difficult, there is not enough of something out there and you can go on about the lies of scarcity, but one of the great questions to ask of yourselves or your colleagues is simply this question, "So what if that was not so, what would need to change?" What if it was not what I thought it was, what would need to change? So it is just a very simple tool and this is something that we teach the chief executives and the directors. Whenever they come across something where they feel, "Oh god, this is going to be really hard" or "There is not enough money to do this" or "There is nothing I can do about it because I am just a chiropractor" or whatever it might be.

What If It Was Not So

Then the next question you just ask yourself, "What if that was not so, what would need to change? What if this was actually easy what would need to change? What if there was plenty out there what would need to change?""What if what I had already decided was in fact was not what would need to change?" Most people will have intention to start off from the prosperity space but before you know it, the trauma and drama of the world actually steps in front of you and you buy into the reality that it is true. The key thing is to be aware that you are actually stepping into someone else's trauma and drama that does not belong to you, unless you are able to allow yourself to have that awareness, then you could be a victim of this contextual reality because everyone else around you is functioning from that space, so you have to make a conscious choice to say, "I am going to create my life and my business from prosperity consciousness." And the second thing is, you have to truly perceive, know and trust that the world is an abundant place and there are plenty to go around because you could say that I am functioning from prosperity consciousness space but if you do not truly believe that the world is an abundant place, of course, you are going to buy into the scarcity, the lack that everyone else telling you that is real. So two things are, to actually choose to be in that space and the second one is you have to totally trust that the world is an abundant place, before you even do anything else.

Out-Create Your Competition

Someone I know has this amazing business that they are going to close down. And the reason they are going to close it down is that there was a competitor who opened up near them. The competitor opened up and copied the name of the business and copied all the stuff that they were selling in the store. The person with the original business went, "Oh my god, he is taking away all my customers and business is not working anymore" and I just realized he had such a thriving business and just in a few years, it has kind of come to this. Most people think that when there are competitors, they are going to take things away from you.

What if that is not true? What if you can out-create them? And out-create yourself? Because the thing is, if someone else comes and copies you, can they be as good as you? So if they can be as good as you, then you can say, "What can I change? What can I do different that will create a different possibility for me? Because there are many other spaces I can function from. I do not have to actually maintain or try to be in exactly the same space." And maybe that is what they think, that they are already successful therefore, they have to keep on doing what they have been doing before. What if this is a great advantage or opportunity for you to start being in the question and say, "Okay, there are these people coming in to do and be in my space, what else can I be? What else can I do that will create greater possibilities for me? I do not have to keep on doing what I have been doing." And most people think that they have been successful in that space, they cannot do anything else. And that is a lie, really, because you can do anything you choose to do. If someone else steps into your space, step into another space and create greater than that.

If you have a really successful restaurant and then another restaurant which is similar to yours opens up next to you, you can actually say, "Oh, another restaurant opened up. I am going to close down now because obviously, there only needs to be one restaurant in this space" and can you feel that? That is a lie. If another restaurant is opening up, it is so, so good what they are doing. You can also say, "What else is possible for me? Is it still expansive for me to keep on doing restaurant the way I am doing it right now? What else is possible? What else can I add to my business that will create different possibilities for me?" and once you are in the questions, you know whether you want to maintain the same business or you want to add something else to your business to create different possibilities.

How many people really want to ask questions in their business? And how many people are functioning from judgments and points of view how they built their business? Are you using the questions to create?

Most people miss out on when they hear the word "question" and think "Oh, I have to ask a lot of questions" and they then absolutely do nothing. Questions will create awareness. Awareness creates the ability to do things in a different way. Do not forget, there is a little bit of doing in all this too, so you cannot just sit down and ask questions of everything and do nothing different, because then you will be insane, which is doing the same thing again and again. You will not get any different result. It just does not work.

The above example is a fantastic case study of that business owner who has got themselves into that particular area, that particular view of the world. One of the things that we do is we work with businesses, getting them to look at things from very different points of view and what we have found is that once they are willing to look at things from different points of view, they can actually recreate their business, recreate everything that they want to recreate and also add to their life. "So do I need to get into something totally different?" No, but you can do things different and you can be different and still have the shop but it will just be a different shop that does things in a different way.

4 Key Points

1. BE INNOVATIVE

Now what the heck do we mean by that? Well, constantly look at what else is happening out there? What else do I need to do? Who else is being innovative? What can I learn from other examples? Because every situation that you face as a business owner, someone else has faced it somewhere and really turned it to their advantage. Why not start to look for some of those and find out so what is the innovation that we can do here? What can we do a little different?

Now also, the example of another business coming in and just copying the first business. I will guarantee that second business is not going to be successful because they will think they found the answer by getting someone else out of that particular area. If the original business owner then says, Ok, so the first thing is, I want to look at innovation. What can I do in my shop that no one else is doing? What can I do in my shop that is just a little bit different than what everyone else is doing? What are other shops like mine doing that is different?" And then that starts to lead to the questions we have been talking about.

2. GIVE UP BUSINESS MODELS THAT ARE ACTUALLY NOT TRUE

And then the second point you can look at is – "So let me give up any business models that I have already subscribed to that actually are not true. So a business model for a small shop might be "My shop has to look this way". No, it does not. It is only that you have decided that it has to look that way. "How do I want my shop to look like? What are the different things that it could look like? How are the other shops that are being set up? What are they looking like around the world? What can I learn from them?" So if you think, "I have got to do it this way", you are screwed. You have absolutely, already bought into a business model that actually is not true. Just because everyone else does it, does not mean it is right for you. It just means that is what everyone else does. So look at relinquishing any business models you have got in your mind. Maybe is a chiropractor. Well, then, for example, you do not have to actually be a chiropractor like everyone else is. You can do it different. Now what would that look like?

3. BE A PRAGMATIC FUTURIST

This thing is making new innovations, and the third point is, you could be a pragmatic futurist. Chutisa has a fantastic blog called The Pragmatic Futurist and have a look at that and read that and say, "Now what does that mean for my business? How can I turn that to my advantage? What is it that I could do that would enable people?" And one of the simplest things you could do, even take something like Chutisa's blog and go to your clients and say, "Here is a great blog. What can you do in your business?" So you can actually help them think differently using this different way of thinking and you can think differently about having them think differently so that they think differently and do things in a different way. All of a sudden, there is a point of difference.

4. CULTIVATE A PROSPERITY CONSCIOUSNESS

And then the last point, the fourth point is, looking at this whole notion of prosperity. It is part of the puzzle. Do I choose to look at everything as easy? There is abundance and it can be any way I want it to. Or do I choose to look at it from the scarcity view point, which is, there is not enough out there, it is really hard and there is nothing I can do about it. It is just your point of view.

Be The Question And Don't Look For An Answer

Most people misidentify, misapply that when they ask questions they are going to get the answer that will allow them to create their lives different, their business different. It is not the case. It is about creating the space for you to be aware of different possibilities, so it is not like asking the question and getting the right answer. That is a limitation. So ask questions, let it go, allow yourself to be and you might be aware of different possibilities by just living your life and doing things and something will pop up and say, "Maybe I could do this. Maybe I can change my restaurant to another type of restaurant."

And for business above, maybe they can still do that business, but add something else totally different to make that business, offering different services, different products. I have got a wicked thought for this business. What if they put the word "Not" in front of the name of their business. So the new business has been set up in their name, printing all their stuff, and so their business will say "Not..." The name of the business and it would make things different. It would make fun out of the whole situation and also create a great buzz in. And the other part of it is they made this so significant, "Oh my god, that business is doing that and as a result my business is not working." And now they are now creating the business so everything that is showing up is exactly from that place.

Asking For Change And Instituting It

Question: "When you are asking questions and it is starting to change, the phase before it is instituted, before you see it, how you deal with that when your mind wants to stop it or basically judge that it is not working? That is what I am seeing a lot of people do. When they are in the question or have started creating something and they are like "Yes, but I do not have more customers. I am not selling any more. I am not getting any more money in my pocket." That is a key thing. Judging that it is not working because you obviously have an expectation about what working is supposed to look like.

The overlight on top of that is also – "And what else can I add? And what else can I add? And what else can I add?" And if you are constantly asking yourself, "What else can I add to my business? What else can I add to my business? What else can I add to my life?" then if any one particular thing doesn't particularly work, it does not matter, because there are so many things going on. So the interesting thing is, let us say you have had an awareness of some sort, you say, "Ok, I am going to try this to create more clients" and then as soon as you think that is the answer and you stop looking at other ways as well, you have bought back into "Well, this is the answer" and "If it does not work, I am also a failure."

What if you actually said, "Here are the different ways I can add more clients. I have got to try this one. And here is another one and I will try this one as well. And here is another one and I will try this one!" And I guarantee you will get more clients. It just will not necessarily be because any of those three things that you have done.

None Of This Is Linear

People have got to get it is not linear. What the big difference is that your sense of curiosity and your sense of excitement and your sense of possibility will start to get you to look at things differently and then you can institute each of these new things but it does not matter whether it works or not. That is not the point. The point is you are looking at things differently. You are looking at things with a sense of curiosity and you are constantly adding to your business and your life.

People judge that something is not working. When people are actually judging that something is not working, they have decision and conclusion and also expectation about what the thing is supposed to look like if it is working. What if the thing that you judged was not working actually is really working well but because you judged that it is not working, you are actually not receiving what is actually happening or occurring and you are not using it as a statistical advantage. Whenever you are in business and you start jumping into, "Oh, this is not working" maybe it is going down another path that would create greater possibilities than the path you think it should be and is not working.

I see how quickly we just say, "This does not work, let us stop it" and then there is nothing else after that. And it is just kills everything if they stop.

One key tool that I would like to give to people when they are actually in that space is to stop. Catch yourself and stop and say, "What conclusion am I being here?" You obviously go into conclusion when you think it is not working. And if you are not being a conclusion, you might open up yourself, open up the space to receive different possibilities. "Oh, ok, it does not have to be a red car, it can be a blue car." It might be even more expansive to get the blue car instead of the red car if you are looking to buy a car.

Failure

Are people more determined to show or prove that they are a failure than willing to include that they might be successful? The joy of failure is a big thing. People really have a joy of failure and that seems to be a part of the collective unconsciousness in this world. Not everybody gets that. How can you enjoy failure? And it happens all the time. Joy of failure is where people have got a point of view that they are likely to fail at things, they are constantly looking for the evidence to show that they are actually failing. And if you look for evidence, guess what, you start to find it! And everything that you do is then created around to prove that particular point of view, so the joy of failure is, "Yes, see I was right!" It is the rightness of your point of view again.

Now if nothing could be a failure, it was just different than what you had already decided it should be, and you recognized that this is just different then you start to look at "Now, how can I turn that to my advantage?" People too often get into, "Oh, I know this is going to be hard, I know it is going to be difficult and float in a big, horrible ball of mist. Yes, it is joy of failure when they are constantly looking for evidence that they are going to fail at something and ignoring everything else around them. So if you have got a joy of failure, then you have also got the point of view that if you are a success, then it must look like this.

If it does not meet this – whatever this is – then by its very definition, it must be a failure. So it is the black and white view of the world? What if there were 450 other really cool outcomes from that, that are knocking at your awareness for you to take note of, but because you are so convinced that it has either got to be this or it is going to be a failure, that is all you ever get to see and you do not look to see all the other really amazing potentials out there that could triple your income because you are not willing to look at it because you have already decided how it should be, so the joy of failure is thinking "I was right. Screwed it again. Did not work. Oh, god, it is hard out there."

And the thing is the failure is a lie anyway. There is no such thing as failure.

You only fail if you have a certain expectation about what it is supposed to look like. What if everything is supposed to be the way it is creating? The thing is, if Thomas Edison had enjoyed the joy of failure, we would not have had lights right now because he failed so many times according to our reality, before he actually came to his discovery of the light bulb.

If you keep looking at different people, if you are even looking at Apple, if you read the history, people would judge that they fail with so many beings, so many previous computers, but look what they are creating now. So they never judged that anything failed. It was just giving them different possibilities. So failure is just a lie.

What will dispel failure, what will make failure disappear from your view of reality is if you function from a sense of curiosity, if you function from the sense of question, if you function from the sense of possibility. Functioning from those three things, failure does not even bloody well exist! Because it is irrelevant. It does not exist. So if you actually look at your business from that point of view, from the sense of curiosity, from the sense of fun, from the sense of joy, creating the business that works for you has got nothing to do with money. Money is a by-product of all these other things – a sense of fun, curiosity, joy, possibility.

For example, many of the people who are reading this will be running seminars or running workshops or doing something with clients. We run these public playgrounds of 2000 people, slightly different version will have 60 people, sometimes we have got 10. Now if we have got 10, is it a failure? No, because you do not see it as a failure. One of the more recent ones that I had was where we had I think 6 people and I had fun. It was a sense of curiosity. The people that were there were absolutely having a blast and 2 days later, one of them gave me a $20,000 job. Now do you think I went into that expecting that? No! But what were they buying? What do people actually buy? What they buy is a sense of curiosity, a sense of excitement and a sense of possibility.

That is what people buy. And if you are willing to be that, that is what people are going to buy. Then you add on to that your particular skills or your particular business, but people will buy curiosity, possibility, excitement.

Success never looks the way you want it to look anyway. Like our example when we do Master classes, sometimes we get 100-200 people, sometimes we get 50. So when we get 50 and if we judge that that is failure, we might not be able to receive what might transpire from those 50 people and quite often, when we have the small number, if we did not judge that that did not work, we often find 2-3 other people will actually come to us and say, "Could you please come and work with our board? Could you please come and present these to someone else?" So the outcome is never what the number of people sitting on the seats in that moment in time. The outcome from that 50 people versus 200 people is that, it is more expansive. You have more 100 jobs. Ask more people from that space if you are willing to not judge that what is right or wrong and what is success and what is failure and we are going to say, "Ok, I wonder what is getting created from this space? I know that something else is happening or occurring and what would it be for me to receive all that?"

I am just going to make a comment, that I encourage people to ponder over the next 18 months because it is one of these wedge and walk comments.

We know there is an infinite amount of money out there. We know there is an infinite amount of all sorts of different resources. It is just very different than what we have already decided. So what if your point of view about what money was, about what success was, what if that point of view was what you were actually creating? So if something is not occurring that is creating the life that you desire then look at some of your points of view about this, because that is what is actually creating it. Often we find that the Universe is knocking at our awareness door, just saying, "Hey, look at all these wonderful things that are available to you" and we refuse to see the damn things because we have already decided whatever it is – what it should look like. So if you really want to create a business that works for you, do not have any point of view about what that business should look like.

What If Business Were Just About Life And Living

What if business is not just purely to make money, it is about life and living? So if you are functioning from that space about you doing business from living and from life, what else can you create and generate from that space? And if you could do everything just for the fun of it?

A lot of people have a weird point of view about business, how you are supposed to feel or how it is supposed to be and how serious and that it is tough and it takes a lot of years to be successful, and not many people talk about joy. I was fortunate to have parents that decided to change their career and do something they really enjoyed doing, even if they were not happy with it every day, but they had this eager joy and expansive life. But I see a lot of people who are like, "It is a big thing to do. It is not fun. You are going to work a lot. You are not going to be successful for a long time." This is so different, and being willing to choose to live in a different way. If somebody asks me when do I work, I am like, "Always, and never" because it never feels like work. Very rare it does. Once in a while, yes, but I was like wow, this can be very different if we are willing to choose from living. What would it be like if we chose everything *from that space*?

And how often do people actually buy into the lie that you really do have to work hard for your money and you have to really work hard in your business and if you do not work hard then you will not make a successful business. It is just crazy. What if you change from having to work hard? If you put joy and having fun with it and all of that in place, you would create from a different possibility in your life. I will not do anything if it is not fun. That is the only criteria for me. If it is fun, I can get up at 2 o'clock in the morning just to do it. So doing everything from fun is a space.

And the interesting thing about fun is, what creates fun? Your point of view about what is or is not. So if it is fun, it is just your point of view about it. If something is not fun, then you have got a couple of options. Change your point of view so it is fun. Change something else so it is fun or do something else.

Non Contextual Reality

Being functional within this contextual reality and not buying this contextual reality as real and true. If you get this, this is going to change your business. You have got to understand what is happening out there in your sector, in your profession, in your business. You have got to understand it, you have got be aware of this. So that means you have got to read about things, you have got to see what other people are doing, you have got to look to see what other businesses are doing, but at the same time, you cannot buy any of it as real. It is not real, it is just how they are doing it. So if you understand what is actually happening out there, this means you have to understand things like book-keeping, you have got to understand things like finances, you have got understand things like how some businesses work but none of it is real.

This contextual reality says that there are certain rules and regulations you have got to follow. Cool! Follow them, but do not buy them as your reality. It is not how to do business, it is just some of the rules and regulations. The next question is, now how can we turn those to our advantage? Now I do not want to have to spend time learning how to do bookkeeping, so how can I do bookkeeping without having to do bookkeeping? Oh, I know, shocker, I will get a book-keeper. Oh, but I cannot afford them. Well, what if I could? What would need to change? What if I could actually deal with a book-keeper so that I could provide them with clients and they could give me pro-bono work?

There are a hundred and one million different ways of how you can do this. But the contextual reality will say you have got to pay someone to do this. Non-contextual reality would be "Ok, I know I need to use this. What if I could do this in a very different way?" So people have said, "Oh, you just need to function outside of this reality." No, you need to understand or be aware of this reality, use it to your advantage but do not buy any of it as real. So this is how you can actually leverage off, this is how you can manipulate, this is how you can look to see what is happening in this reality. This contextual reality, because everyone else functions from it. Be aware of what they are doing and then do something different as well.

What contextual reality actually means, it is that when people function from "Where do I fit? Where do I benefit? How do I win? And how do I not lose?" that is when you step into contextual reality and that is what all businesses are functioning from. So if you know where other people in the business are functioning from, you can use that to your advantage. You need to understand or need to get the awareness and knowledge about different aspects of business, not that you have to do it yourself but you have to have the awareness that if you use the book-keeper, you are not giving your power totally away to your bookkeeper and your accountant. How many people do we know in business that totally collapse because they think, "Ok, Ill find a great book-keeper, I'll find an accountant, I do not need to know any more about money and about finance and they give the power totally away to the accountant and to that book-keeper. Then they pull energy out of anything to do with money and finance and that is when they hit the fan. Because things will happen behind your back and you shut off your awareness totally not perceiving, knowing, being or receiving what is going on. So when you are being functional in this reality, understand what needs to be done to make a business successful but use awareness to be aware when you have to put the energy into that place. You do not have to do anything yourself.

Cutting Off Awareness

I have been working with a lot of women in business. Most women that I talk to are so brilliant in every aspect of their life but they tend to give their financial reality over to their partner, over to their accountant because they think, "Oh, I do not know how to do it. It is too hard. I am not interested in finance." So when you are in that space, you have to stop and say, "Ok, everywhere that I am giving my power away, I am willing to stop doing that" and ask the question, " What would it take for me to get more awareness, to know more about financial reality?" Not that you have to become an accountant but you have to be willing to receive the energy of the finance and that will be a totally different possibility for you and will create, generate more money and more possibilities, more success.

And if you are willing to receive the energy of finance, for example, then you start to ask different questions."So, what do I need to know?" And you can ask your accountant, "What do I need to know?" or you can ask your bookkeeper, "What do I need to know?" You can ask colleagues that run successful multi-million dollar businesses, "What do I need to know?" You just need to know that you need to know. And you keep asking, "So what do I need to know now?" It is going to be very different than what you needed to know six months ago and it will be different again in six months time. So what do I need to know? Is that a bad question? That will turn you into a financial expert without having to be a financial expert because you've got access to financial expertise just by asking the question "What do I need to know?"

Your Point Of View Creates Your Reality

Question: "I have been a strong self-starter and a successful small business operator in earlier years of life with a shop front business. Now I choose to create a business from home and I am having problems getting started. I struggle with the social media concept of creating a business even though I know it may be the key to success. What energy, space and consciousness or action is required to create on a low budget? And what is the greatest contribution I or anyone can be to create and generate a business of ease?"

It would be really interesting for you to sit down and just list down all the points of view that that question has brought to the surface. First point of view that "I used to run a successful business". That is the first point of view. Second point of view, "I am not interested in social media", second point of view. Third point of view, "So what is it..." – and this is probably the only one worth listening to – "What do I need to change?" Ok, go back to the first two.

Change those points of view. It all starts with the point of view. It all starts with the point of view. So list down all the points of view and then work through each one and change. And have fun with it. In that question is a two day workshop to just work through those points of view. So first point of view, "I had a successful business in the past." Ok. What if you looked at that and said, "Hang on a second, I've just defined what successful business is! Wow! What if it was not successful? What if it was just a different business that I really enjoyed?" Now the next question would be, "What did I enjoy? What can I take from that enjoyment into this next one? Ah, what I enjoyed was my point of view that it gave me the freedom, it gave me access to clients, it enabled me to play with different products. Oh, I wonder if my online business could do the same thing? But I do not know how to do an online business." Well, the next question would be, "Who would I need to ask?"

I have a key question for this person that asked the question and if you keep asking that question, it would change your reality totally and the question is, "What can I be or do different today that would create more than I ever thought was possible right away?" And if you keep asking that question, you will create a totally different possibility. When you start going into, "Oh, I am only working from home and I hate social media and things are not working and lives are tough and business is not successful," stop and ask "What can I be or do different today that would create more than I ever thought was possible right away?" And keep on asking that. "What energy, space, consciousness can I be that would allow me to create different possibility for my business right away?" You know, either or. They are both wonderful questions.

What Can You Be Or Do Different

Question: "When things take time and it does not move much then I feel it may not be meant to be so I change the career. It is happening again and I am now using Access tools, asking questions. Every career I have chosen comes naturally to me, makes me happy but does not grow outside the small box. I know I am an infinite being so even if I do not create something, does not matter to me." "What can I be or do different today that would create more than I ever thought was possible right away?" It is a really cool question for anyone and everyone. Start asking that question. Some awareness will come to you sooner or later. And never come to conclusion. And all of those is a conclusion, you know. As soon as you go into any of conclusion, you already kill different possibilities. The other thing that comes from that question too is again, the point of view that I have changed profession. Now what that tells me is that whoever is asking that – many people do this – this is the way that profession has to be. They have already built it into a business model. They have already bought into a business model. This is the way the profession has to be. What if you started asking the questions.

"This is the profession I am in. what are the 4 different ways I can create money out of working in this profession?" That would be a different way of looking at it. What that does is it gets you to start looking at different ways of creating using the profession as a platform, but not the answer. And so "What are the 4 different ways that I can make money out of being an artist? What are the 4 different ways I can make money out of being a therapist? Or the 4 different ways I can make money..." And as soon as you think, "Oh, no, there is only one way. I can only be a salaried employee", then you have already bought into that business model.

There are millions of different ways you can make money out of it. Well, let's make it a bit easier and narrow it down to 4. Do not complain if you only come up with 3.

What Else Is Possible

Question: "I have a business that was quite successful for over 4 years and after having a relationship break up, I let it go. I seem to be more drawn towards investing my time with Access rather than my business. So how can I continue to keep my business successful and continue having time for Access as this is one of the things that keeps me sane."

If you really love and enjoy Access, and that gives you the vitality and life, you could ask, "What else can I do with Access that will create a different possibility for me?" You obviously found something that you really love doing and that creates a new possibility for you. You do not have to let go of the other business either. But you can say "Ok, this is something that I really love. What else is possible? What else can I be and do with Access that will create more than I could ever imagine?" Because quite often most people do not know what they actually love or what they enjoy doing. You already know what you love or enjoy doing, so now ask what can you be and do different to allow this thing that you love doing to create different possibilities for you.

Tools To Expand Your Business

The key tool that we use ourselves every day of our life really, is be in the questions. I be the question as soon as I open my eyes.

"Who am I today? And what grand and glorious adventure will I be having today?" I always start my day with that question because that question in itself allows me to destroy and un-create everything that I was yesterday and allows me to create everything new, totally new today. So that is the first question that I always ask. And also un-create and destroy your relationships, because it does not work with the question. Un-create and destroy your relationship every day, what would that look like? Who do I want to be today?

Just start off being in the question and do not try to get the answer. And be willing to receive all of the awareness and possibilities that might be available in that moment. Never come to the conclusion about anything. And instead of asking questions that try to create result, ask, "What do I have to be or do today to expand this business right away?" or "What can I do or be today to expand my life right away?"

If you have a lot of business or a lot of projects going, which I do, so after I ask myself those questions when I wake up, I will always ask "Where do I need to put my energy today?" So I will put my energy to the thing that I get the awareness of otherwise you get overwhelmed. Otherwise you will be thinking, "Oh my god, I have so much to do. I do not know which one to do. I do not know what to do." If you ask yourself, "Where do I need to put my energy today that will create greater possibility for me, for my business and for the world right away?" The key tool to change business - It is very simply this – Your point of view creates your reality. So literally, most things come back to that. Your point of view actually creates your reality, so if something is not working for me, then I have a look at what my point of view is. Now often I will talk with Chutisa about it. Sometimes the point of view that I have got, I have not even articulated, I have just got it. So exploring what point of view you have got about something and then saying, "Ok, I am over that" is not a bad tool. "Great, I am over that. What next?"

I wonder what would happen if everybody would use questions because they would be very different for everybody around as well. So yes, what if we would challenge ourselves to ask more questions and see what happens? Like every time you have a point of view or you feel stuck, ask a question. See what happens. Be curious.

It is interesting. I posted on Facebook that about 3 days ago. No, probably about a week ago now and a CEO responded to the post because the post was something about being in the question and the CEO said, "Yes, but you have got to find an answer sometime?" and I said, "Ok" and I wrote back 3 words. I wrote back "Question. Do.

Have." Question. Do. Have. Be a question. Do something. Have it.

Then be a question again. Do something. Have it. Do not forget the doing bit. The doing bit comes from the question. Never in there is the word answer because as soon as you have got the answer, you stop to question. So "Question. Do. Have. Question. Do. Have." And then I think I wrote, "Stir and repeat." I did not hear from him again.

Quite often it is fun talking about all these tools and things but you are going to have to deal with difficult people and difficult projects and things in life. I tend ask the question, "Who am I being?" When I feel really irritated and annoyed with people I just stop and ask, "Who am I being that if I change it, will create a different reality?" Because it is energy creating within myself that creates that space to be annoyed with people or for the business and not doing well or the project is not working out the way it is supposed to be according to my conclusion. I stop and I say, "Oh, ok, I got into conclusion again. Who am I being? What needs to change here?" We are all so fast at going into conclusion. would love to stop going totally into conclusion and that I think is my target. "What would it take for me to stop functioning from conclusion?"

Beliefs As A Business Model

Question:"I have a belief that you need to be in a group of people like-minded to have the best rather than being alone and changing at a slow rate. So I am aware that this the truth with a lie attached. What question can I ask here to change this?"

I lost interest after I heard the word "Belief". And I do not mean to be rude here, but as soon as I have a "belief in", it means "Ok, I have already decided how something should be" and it is irrelevant what comes after that. It is totally irrelevant what the rest of that sentence was, because as soon as you have an "belief in" then you have already decided that is the way it should be. So please destroy and un-create all beliefs that you have got. What if it just was in any way that it needed to be?

"I need to be with a group of like-minded people." Oh, oh, there is no one like you. That is the point. And there should never be anyone like you, because what you are as a person is the sense of excitement and joy and curiosity and it is irrelevant what other people are like. Be this yourself. Do not expect anyone else to be it. And that is another business model. "I have got to around like-minded people." No, you do not! You have just got to be this yourself and guess what that creates in everyone else's Universe? It creates possibility and it creates a sense of joy. If you are being joy, that is either going to – Number 1: Piss off some people, which creates even more joy in my life. The more people you piss off that do not like joy, the more fun that is. And then it creates a sense in their life, a sense of possibility, and if they do not see a sense of possibility in it, they go away, which again creates joy in my life. There is nothing better than someone going away if they cannot see any of this.

The word 'like-minded' is contextual reality. As soon as you say 'like this' or 'like minded', it is "Where do I fit?"

What if you do not have to fit anywhere? What if you just being you and be the catalyst that creates a different possibility wherever you are or wherever you be? If you start being in the group and like-minded, you already buy conclusion in that. That is the only space that you can be the greatness you can be. What if you can be the greatness that you truly be just by choosing to be that?

Here are some great questions to consider – "What if I was the CEO of my own life? What would that look like?"

"What if I was the Chief Financial Officer of my own life? What would that look like?"

"What if I was the chairman of my Board of Directors in my life? What would that look like?"

"What if I was the joy and the energy and the fun in my life? What would that look like?" If you are willing to be that.

"Am I a leader in my own life? And if not, why not? And who is the leader in my life if I am not the leader in my own life?"

And just ask those questions because having the belief that you have to surround yourself with like-minded people means you have got to put yourself in a very small box and go insane very quickly.

Closing Thoughts

I just say that really, enjoy the questions. The point behind asking questions is not to seek an answer, it is to seek different insights to enable us to look at things in a different way. Every question that someone asks gets us personally to look at things in a slightly different way too. Every question creates awareness. There is no such thing as a dumb question. There is no such thing as a question that does anything other than create greater awareness both in the person who asked the question and also the person who is receiving the question, which is not a bad way to finish this off because actually being the question can then lead to the sort of questions that you can ask, which can then lead to different sorts of questions, which then changes both your reality and the reality of everyone else around you. I would like to leave everyone with this question to ask, "Are you a leader in your own life?" And if you do not get a yes, the next question could be, "What would it take for you to be a leader in your own life? What needs to Change?

WHO ARE STEVEN & CHUTISA BOWMAN

Steven and Chutisa Bowman are global business advisors, authors and speakers who have spent the past 10 years working with many top society changing companies and entrepreneurs of our time.

They are recognized worldwide as Pragmatic Futurists and "thought leaders" on: strategic awareness; prosperity consciousness; business transformation in a period of economic uncertainty; and Benevolent Capitalism.

> **ROMANCE WITH MONEY**
>
> **By Nirmala Raju**
>
> What if money is not about "earning" but receiving? Are you willing to be so seductive to money that it falls in love with you and never leaves you? What energy can you be that would allow people to flock to pay you money with total joy? What would it take to have millions as pocket change?
> http://www.magicofbeing.com

CHAPTER TWELVE

❖

MY BODY BEAUTIFUL

By Nilofer Safdar

Bestselling Author, Speaker, Money and Prosperity Coach

Access Consciousness Certified Facilitator CFMW

Host Illusion to Illumination Summit

Judgment

One of the things that has been in my face is a lot of judgment about my body. I have been in question about it. I interviewed Katherine McIntosh last year. One day she realized that every time that she judged herself, she cut off her receiving from her beautiful child. I said to myself, wow, that is great and right now, I would love to have a tool that would help me with judging my body. So, every time I started judging my body, I would go to this question - What is right about my body I am not getting? That seemed to change a lot of things for me and the judgment would fall away. I would really start to get the energy of what my body was. The other question that I would love to ask you is - What does a beautiful body mean to you?

What Does A Beautiful Body Mean To You

I asked a bunch of people this question. Here are some of the responses-

- Something that is external, the so called appearances, the look, external beauty, ignoring the inside

- It means feeling more comfortable and not being ashamed of your body
- Having fun, being happy in the body
- Having a healthy body

If you look at each one of these, is it a judgment of your body? Is it a judgment of how you would like your body to be? Isn't it a shouldor-shouldn't with your body? Is any of that real? Or do you buy it as real and lock it up in your reality? How is that working for you?

Would you like to let each of these judgments go?

We use judgments in this reality to create. Does it really create? Or do you just create what you are judging?

For example, if you judge that you have flabby arms, do you create skinny arms? Or do you just create more flab in your arms. Judgment then becomes a self-fulfilling prophecy.

What Beauty Is Your Body Being

One day I woke up with this strange awareness. What if my body was already beautiful? What a strange and novel concept! I started exploring this further.

Body show me what beauty you are being!

As I started being in this question, people started complimenting me on my looks. I started feeling more beautiful. At random moments in the day I would pass by a mirror and just feel more beautiful.

What if it was all about acknowledging the beauty that my body was already being?

What beauty are you being that you are not acknowledging? Everything that doesn't allow you to perceive, know, be and receive that will you destroy and uncreate it please? <u>Right and Wrong, Good and Bad, POD and POC, All 9, Shorts, Boys &Beyonds.</u>

What energy, space and consciousness in you and your body being to be the infinite beauty you truly be with total ease for all eternity. And everything that doesn't allow that will you destroy and uncreate it all? Right and Wrong, Good and Bad, POD and POC, All 9, Shorts, Boys &Beyonds.

What was interesting was that every time that I would run these clearings on myself, my body would start to be happy, to have ease and peace inside and what was amazing was that people would just compliment me on my looks and they would say, "Oh, you are wearing a great dress" or "you are looking very pretty" or things like that.

What if beauty was not what we thought it was, what if it was something totally different?

Everything that you have misidentified and misapplied beauty as will you destroy and uncreate it please? Right and Wrong, Good and Bad, POD and POC, All 9, Shorts, Boys &Beyonds.

Everything that you thought that beauty was which it is actually not, will you destroy and uncreate it please? Right and Wrong, Good and Bad, POD and POC, All 9, Shorts, Boys &Beyonds.

Everything you didn't think that beauty was that it actually is, will you destroy and uncreate it please? Right and Wrong, Good and Bad, POD and POC, All 9, Shorts, Boys &Beyonds.

What Does Your Body Know About Beauty

I wonder what does your body know about beauty that you are not willing to know?

What does your body know about beauty that you are not willing to know? Everything that brings up will you destroy and uncreate it times Godzillion? Everything that doesn't allow you to perceive, know, be and receive that will you destroy and uncreate it please? Right and Wrong, Good and Bad, POD and POC, All 9, Shorts, Boys &Beyonds.

I started to ask this question - Body, what would you like to look like? Every time I would ask that question it did not really feel expansive to me and it felt as if there was something missing there. One day I changed the question a little bit and I asked, "Body, what would you like to **be** like?" The energy completely changed and I had this awareness of my body which I had never had before.

What if beauty was not to do about what your body looks like but rather what it BE?

What Would You Like Your Body To Be?

Ask this question - What would I like my body to be like?

Write down everything that comes up.

Now look at everything on your list. My question to you is - Is your body already being that?

You can only ask for something when you are already being it. When you acknowledge it, you can ask for more of that to show up.

What would you like your body to be like? Is your body already being that? Would you like to acknowledge that please? Everything that doesn't allow you to perceive, know, be and receive that will you destroy and uncreate it times Godzillion? <u>Right and Wrong, Good and Bad, POD and POC, All 9, Shorts, Boys &Beyonds.</u>

What Would Your Body Like To Be?

Body, what would you like to be?

The body has its own point of view about what it would like to be? Everything that the body desires is about creating it as an Infinite Body.

Would you be willing to be in allowance of everything that the body desires to be? I wonder what that would create?

Do you have a knowing of what that could be like?

THE MAGIC OF BEING

What do you know about your body that you are pretending not to know or denying that you know that if you would allow yourself to know it would create your body as everything you always knew was possible and did not think would ever actualise? Everything that doesn't allow you to perceive, know, be and receive that will you destroy and uncreate it times Godzillion? <u>Right and Wrong, Good and Bad, POD and POC, All 9, Shorts, Boys &Beyonds.</u>

What would your body like to be like? Everywhere your body is being that will you acknowledge that please? Everything that doesn't allow you to perceive, know, be and receive that will you destroy and uncreate it times Godzillion? <u>Right and Wrong, Good and Bad, POD and POC, All 9, Shorts, Boys &Beyonds.</u>

What else would your body like to be like?

What else would your body like to be like?

Whispers

Question: My body would like to move more. It is probably not moving as much as it would like to because of the time I spend on the computer. It would like to move more.

How would your body like to move?

Go for a walk, not just walking because it is required but just for the fun of walking. It is movement, just movement.

It is beautiful weather where I live right now, it is cold and it is the winter. It is a beautiful time and when I wake up in the morning my body goes, "We have to go out, we have to go out, we have to go out." The moment I move out of the house, I can hear the birdsong and feel the breeze on my face and listen to the sound of the leaves rustling in the wind and my body goes ahh, it expands out and relaxes. I don't care how much work I have or what is to be done, I am just willing to listen to my body and go out when my body requires it.

Everything that doesn't allow you to listen to the whispers of your body will you destroy and uncreate it times Godzillion? <u>Right and Wrong, Good and Bad, POD and POC, All 9, Shorts, Boys &Beyonds.</u>

Everything that doesn't allow you to know what your body requires and desires will you destroy and uncreate it please? <u>Right and Wrong, Good and Bad, POD and POC, All 9, Shorts, Boys &Beyonds.</u>

Body And The Earth

One of the things which has actually shown up for me very strongly in a way in which I just cannot deny it any more is this awareness of the Earth. I can just feel the energy of the Earth in my body. When I actually go out of the house, even if I am driving in the car, I can feel the energy of the trees and the birds and all the critters, I can feel my body pulling in that energy.

Everywhere that your body is aware of the Earth and everywhere your body is aware of the contribution of the Earth will you acknowledge that please? Everything that doesn't allow you to perceive, know, be, and receive that will you destroy and uncreate it times Godzillion? <u>Right and Wrong, Good and Bad, POD and POC, All 9, Shorts, Boys &Beyonds.</u>

I always knew that I was really happy when we drove down certain roads, and I always said, "Wow, this is so beautiful," Now it is physical, it is visceral in my body. When I drive down those paths I can just feel that energy flowing from all the trees and all the nature around me into my body. A couple of days back I happened to go into the industrial part of the city where there are a lot of big trucks and buildings. As we were driving through one little bit there were a few trees. Even though if you look at it, these were a very few trees in that huge area. Those trees were talking to my body and they were going, "Hi!" My body was going, "Hi!"

Everywhere you are aware of the nurturing of mother Earth for your body will you acknowledge that please? Everything that doesn't allow you to perceive, know, be and receive that will you destroy and uncreate it times Godzillion? <u>Right and Wrong, Good and Bad, POD and POC, All 9, Shorts, Boys &Beyonds.</u>

This is a two way street. As you are receiving contribution from the Earth, your body is also contributing the energy to the Earth.

All the places and spaces which you have locked up in your body, that could be contributing to the Earth will you unlock them please?

Let us do this, "I am the lock, I am the key, I am the lock, I am the key, I am the lock, I am the key, I am the lock, I am the key, and let me open each and every cell and molecule of my body to the contribution and the gifting and receiving with the Earth. Hold your hands out, and a thunderbolt of energy 1…..2………3…... 1, 2, 3, 1, 2, 3, 1, 2, 3, 1, 2, 3, 1, 2, 3.

Projections, Expectations, Separations, Rejections, Judgments

A couple of months back I was in this whole conversation with myself, "Oh, I have put on so much weight and I have to lose weight from here and there and blah, blah, blah, blah, blah." I even went to the extent of creating this whole clearing loop for losing weight, that was designed to get me 10 kg lighter. I had this awareness that this is where I am impelling my point of view on my body. What my body would actually like to be is way beyond that. I got the energy of what my body would like to be and it is way greater than what I could ever think about.

Everywhere you are trying to override your body and everywhere you are trying to be superior to your body and trying to impel your point of view over your body will you destroy and uncreate it times Godzillion? <u>Right and Wrong, Good and Bad, POD and POC, All 9, Shorts, Boys &Beyonds.</u>

All the projection, expectations, separation, rejection and judgment that you have about your body or anybody else has about your body, that have been impelled upon your body would you like to destroy and uncreate it times Godzillion? <u>Right and Wrong, Good and Bad, POD and POC, All 9, Shorts, Boys &Beyonds.</u>

Everywhere you have aligned and agreed with all of this or resisted and reacted to this which allowed you to be implanted or explanted with all this will you destroy and uncreate it times Godzillion? <u>Right and Wrong, Good and Bad, POD and POC, All 9, Shorts, Boys &Beyonds.</u>

What Else Would Your Body Like To Be

Can you perceive that your body is actually talking to you? You are perceiving the energy of it and you may not necessarily have the words to it right now.

What energy, space and consciousness can you and your body be to be everything that your body would like to be with total ease for all eternity, everything that doesn't allow you to perceive, know, be, and receive that will you destroy and uncreate it times Godzillion? <u>Right and Wrong, Good and Bad, POD and POC, All 9, Shorts, Boys &Beyonds.</u>

So, I wonder what would it be like to be everything that your body would like to be?

What does everything your body would like to be mean to you? Everything that brings up will you destroy and uncreate it times Godzillion? <u>Right and Wrong, Good and Bad, POD and POC, All 9, Shorts, Boys &Beyonds.</u>

What does being everything with your body mean to you or what does being everything that your body would like to be mean to you? Everything that does not allow you to perceive, know, be and receive that will you destroy and uncreate it times Godzillion? <u>Right and Wrong, Good and Bad, POD and POC, All 9, Shorts, Boys &Beyonds.</u>

What energy, space and consciousness can you and your body be to be everything that your body would like to be with total ease for all eternity? And everything that does not allow you to perceive, know, be and receive that will you destroy and uncreate it times Godzillion?

Right and Wrong, Good and Bad, POD and POC, All 9, Shorts, Boys &Beyonds.

Communication With Your Body

Everything that you have misidentified and misapplied as communication with your body will you destroy and uncreate it times Godzillion? Right and Wrong, Good and Bad, POD and POC, All 9, Shorts, Boys &Beyonds.

In how many ways is your body communicating with you that you are not acknowledging? Everything that does not allow you to perceive, know, be and receive that will you destroy and uncreate it times Godzillion? Right and Wrong, Good and Bad, POD and POC, All 9, Shorts, Boys &Beyonds.

Listening To Your Body

In how many ways are you actually listening to your body that you are not acknowledging?

There is a difference between hearing and listening. You might hear what the body is saying but may not actually listen to it ie follow what it says.

What invention are you using to create the need for overriding your body you are choosing? else before you and your body. Everything that is will you destroy and uncreate it times Godzillion? Right and Wrong, Good and Bad, POD and POC, All 9, Shorts, Boys &Beyonds.

How many oaths, vows, fealties, communities, swearing, binding, bondings, contracts and commitments do you have through all time, space, dimensions, reality to never listen to your body and always override it? Everything that is will you now revoke, recant, rescind, reclaim, renounce, denounce, destroy and uncreate it timesGodzillion? Right and Wrong, Good and Bad, POD and POC, All 9, Shorts, Boys &Beyonds.

Everywhere you have been implanted and explanted to believe that you have to always override your body and everything you have aligned and agreed to or resisted and reacted to which allowed you to be implanted and explanted in the first place will you now revoke, recant, rescind, reclaim, renounce, denounce, destroy and uncreate it times Godzillion? <u>Right and Wrong, Good and Bad, POD and POC, All 9, Shorts, Boys &Beyonds.</u>

All the algorithms that you have that you will never be in communion with your body and will always override your body, will you destroy and uncreate it times Godzillion?

Let us do a 1, 2, 3, 4, 5 on that. 1, 2, 3, 4, 5, 1, 2, 3, 4, 5, 1, 2, 3, 4, 5, 1, 2, 3, 4, 5, 1, 2, 3, 4, 5, 1, 2, 3, 4, 5, 1, 2, 3, 4, 5, 1, 2, 3, 4, 5, 1, 2, 3, 4, 5.

What is the value of overriding your body? Everything that brings up will you destroy and uncreate it times Godzillion? <u>Right and Wrong, Good and Bad, POD and POC, All 9, Shorts, Boys &Beyonds.</u>

No Time

Question: I would love to be kind and caring to my body but I just don't have the time. I would like to spend more time with my body. What would it take?

If time were not the issue what would you choose?

Everywhere you are buying into the edicts of time will you destroy and uncreate it times Godzillion? <u>Right and Wrong, Good and Bad, POD and POC, All 9, Shorts, Boys &Beyonds.</u>

What energy, space and consciousness can you and your body be to be a timeless being that you truly be with total ease for all eternity. Everything that doesn't allow you to perceive, know, be, and receive that will you destroy and uncreate it times Godzillion? <u>Right and Wrong, Good and Bad, POD and POC, All 9, Shorts, Boys &Beyonds.</u>

Everywhere you are unwilling to be kind and caring towards your body will you destroy and uncreate it times Godzillion? <u>Right and Wrong,</u>

<u>Good and Bad, POD and POC, All 9, Shorts, Boys &Beyonds.</u>

Communion With Your Body

What would it be like to be in communion with your body and what would it be like to listen to your body?

Can you connect to your life at any time when you actually were that total communion with your body, even if it was just for one second? Everything that does not allow you to perceive, know, be and receive that will you destroy and uncreate it times Godzillion? <u>Right and Wrong, Good and Bad, POD and POC, All 9, Shorts, Boys &Beyonds.</u>

If you are asking for that it is because you are being that, you couldn't even ask for it if you were not being it.

Everywhere that you are being the infinite communion with your body would you like to acknowledge that please? Everything that does not allow you to perceive, know, be and receive that will you destroy and uncreate it times Godzillion? <u>Right and Wrong, Good and Bad, POD and POC, All 9, Shorts, Boys &Beyonds.</u>

Everywhere you are judging you for not being in communion with your body will you destroy and uncreate it times Godzillion? <u>Right and Wrong, Good and Bad, POD and POC, All 9, Shorts, Boys &Beyonds.</u>

Oneness With Your Body

What energy, space and consciousness can you and your body be to be the oneness with your body that you truly be with total ease for all eternity? Everything that does not allow that will you destroy and uncreate it times Godzillion? Right and Wrong, Good and Bad, POD and POC, All 9, Shorts, Boys &Beyonds.

What oneness are you being with your body that you are not acknowledging? Everything that does not allow you to perceive, know, be and receive that will you destroy and uncreate it times Godzillion? Right and Wrong, Good and Bad, POD and POC, All 9, Shorts, Boys &Beyonds.

Everywhere you think that oneness is a lofty goal that you can never, ever achieve will you destroy and uncreate it times Godzillion? Right and Wrong, Good and Bad, POD and POC, All 9, Shorts, Boys &Beyonds.

Awareness Bar

Do you know the awareness bar on your head? (The Bars are 32 points or bars on the head including; Healing, Body, Sexuality, Money, Control, Aging, Hopes & Dreams, Awareness, Creativity, etc. Activating these points by lightly touching them and by allowing the energy to flow through these bars releases the electrical charge that holds all the considerations, thoughts, ideas, beliefs, decisions, emotions or attitudes you have ever stored or decided was important in any lifetime. Bars is an incredible technique that is useful for stress reduction, depression, anxiety, clearing the mind chatter, to aid sleep, for ADD and ADHD, for children before exams, pregnant women, etc.)

Would you like to turn on the Awareness Bar now please? Just ask it to turn on.

We are being something and we think we are not being that so we judge ourselves for that. When you run your awareness bar what starts to happen, you start to actually get awareness of where you are really aware of things instead of judging yourself for not being aware enough.

Capacity Shopping For Bodies

What would being everything that your body would like to be be like I wonder? What is everything your body would like to be for you? Once I asked Gary a question about creating your life, "What if you don't know what you would like to create your life as?" Gary said something like, go shopping and start looking at things around you, start looking at how people live, start looking at what people are being and whatever you like you can go, "I would like to have that please." Would you be willing to go shopping for capacities that bodies have?

THE MAGIC OF BEING

It is really interesting, my son, he is 17 years old and he used to be a little bit chubby, 2-3 years back. In the last couple of years he has completely changed his body and he has created a really gorgeous body. He is tall and thin. He loves sports and he has been biking and running, he has been running races and now he is training for a triathlon. Just a few days back I was looking at his body and I said, "Wow! He has this energy where he can change his body just in a blink of an eyelid." I looked at that and went, "What would it take for me to outcreate that capacity in his body?"

That was a lightbulb moment for me. Since then I am aware of bodies around me and I be the question, "What magical capacities do these bodies be?" I start to see these capacities in bodies and go, "I will have that. What would it take for my body to outcreate that capacity?"

Everything that doesn't allow you to perceive, know, be and receive the magical capacities that bodies be will you destroy and uncreate it times Godzillion? <u>Right and Wrong, Good and Bad, POD and POC, All 9, Shorts, Boys &Beyonds.</u>

What magical capacity does your body be that you are not acknowledging, and everything that does not allow you to perceive, know, be and receive that will you destroy and uncreate it times Godzillion? <u>Right and Wrong, Good and Bad, POD and POC, All 9, Shorts, Boys &Beyonds.</u>

What do magical capacities with and of bodies mean to you? Everything that does not allow you to perceive, know, be and receive that will you destroy and uncreate it times Godzillion? <u>Right and Wrong, Good and Bad, POD and POC, All 9, Shorts, Boys &Beyonds.</u>

All the lifetimes that your body was killed for being the magical capacities that it be and all the oaths, vows, fealties, communities, swearing, binding, bonding, contracts that you have, that you will never, ever be those magical capacities will you now revoke, recant, rescind, reclaim, renounce, denounce, destroy and uncreate it please and return it all back to sender with consciousness attached? <u>Right and Wrong, Good and Bad, POD and POC, All 9, Shorts, Boys &Beyonds.</u>

Everywhere that you have locked up the magical capacities that your body be will you destroy and uncreate it times Godzillion? <u>Right and Wrong, Good and Bad, POD and POC, All 9, Shorts, Boys &Beyonds.</u>

Intimacy With Your Body

Your body goes everywhere with you. One of the biggest things that I have been looking at is actually acknowledging all that we are being… we just go into judgment of ourselves that I am not doing this, being this, being that but the truth of the matter is that we are actually being all of those things all the time, because only when we are being all that can we judge that we are not being it. If we aren't being it we wouldn't be able to judge, that energy would not exist in our awareness at all.

What would it be like to be everything that your body would like to be? Your body can be everything it would like to be when you have intimacy with your body.

Having intimacy with your body means having the 5 elements of intimacy with your body. Having honor, trust, vulnerability, allowance and gratitude with your body.

Honor with bodies means honoring the greatness of the body. Honoring the body as the Infinite Body it truly be.

Trust with bodies means trusting that the body will be exactly what it is. It means that if your body likes to eat meat, it will eat meat. And not impelling it with the point of view that it will be vegetarian or vegan.

Vulnerability with bodies means having no barriers to the body. It is being willing to receive all awareness and information from, with and about the body. It is being willing to include the body in everything that involves the body. It is about asking the body what it wants to eat, how it wants to dress, how it wants to move, which bodies it would like to play with.

Allowance with bodies means that everything with the body is an interesting point of view. It is about never judging the body. It is about honoring the choice the body is making at all times.

Gratitude with bodies is having gratitude for the amazing body we have. Having gratitude for the body because it is with us everywhere and every moment that we exist on the planet. It is having gratitude that it has been with us in spite of us using and abusing it and judging it.

When I first started exploring the 5 elements of intimacy with my body, I did not really get what that was.

So I started asking-

What would it take for me to have the 5 elements of intimacy with my body?

I wonder what would it be like to have honor with my body?

I wonder what would it be like to have trust with my body?

I wonder what would it be like to have vulnerability with my body?

I wonder what would it be like to have allowance with my body?

I wonder what would it be like to have gratitude with my body?

Body what would it be like to have the 5 elements of intimacy - the honor, trust, vulnerability, allowance and gratitude with you?

As I was in these questions, my body would start to show me glimpses of each of these energies. And they were not what I had thought the to be. Would you be willing to be in these questions and discover what these are for you and your body?

What energy, space, and consciousness can you in your body be to be the 5 elements of intimacy with your body - the honor, trust, gratitude, vulnerability and allowance that you truly be with total ease for all eternity and everything that doesn't allow you to perceive, know, be and receive that will you destroy and uncreate it times Godzillion? <u>Right and Wrong, Good and Bad, POD and POC, All 9, Shorts, Boys &Beyonds.</u>

Everywhere that you are being the 5 elements of intimacy with your body - the honor, trust, gratitude, vulnerability and allowance would you like to acknowledge that please? Everything that does not allow you to perceive, know, be and receive that will you destroy and uncreate it times Godzillion? <u>Right and Wrong, Good and Bad, POD and POC, All 9, Shorts, Boys &Beyonds.</u>

What energy, space and consciousness can you and your body be, to be the infinite honor with your body that you truly be with total ease for all eternity. Everything that doesn't allow it will you destroy and uncreate it times Godzillion? <u>Right and Wrong, Good and Bad, POD and POC, All 9, Shorts, Boys &Beyonds.</u>

What energy, space and consciousness can you and your body be to be the infinite trust with your body would truly be a total ease for all eternity. Everything that does not allow you to perceive, know, be and receive that will you destroy and uncreate it times Godzillion? <u>Right and Wrong, Good and Bad, POD and POC, All 9, Shorts, Boys &Beyonds.</u>

What energy, space and consciousness can you and your body be to be the infinite vulnerability with your body, you truly be at total ease for all eternity and everything that does not allow you to perceive, know, be and receive that will you destroy and uncreate it times Godzillion? Right and Wrong, Good and Bad, POD and POC, All 9, Shorts, Boys &Beyonds.

What energy, space and consciousness can you and your body be to be that infinite allowance with your body, you truly be with total ease for all eternity. Everything that does not allow you to perceive, know, be and receive that will you destroy and uncreate it times Godzillion? <u>Right and Wrong, Good and Bad, POD and POC, All 9, Shorts, Boys &Beyonds.</u>

What energy, space and consciousness can you and your body be to be the infinite gratitude with your body, you truly be with total ease for all eternity and everything that does not allow you to perceive, know, be and receive that will you destroy and uncreate it times Godzillion? Right and Wrong, Good and Bad, POD and POC, All 9, Shorts, Boys &Beyonds.

What awareness with bodies are you being that you are not acknowledging? And everything that does not allow you to perceive, know, be and receive that will you destroy and uncreate it times Godzillion? Right and Wrong, Good and Bad, POD and POC, All 9, Shorts, Boys &Beyonds.

What energy, space and consciousness can you and your body be to acknowledge everything that your body truly be with total ease for all eternity? Everything that does not allow you to perceive, know, be and receive that will you destroy and uncreate it times Godzillion? Right and Wrong, Good and Bad, POD and POC, All 9, Shorts, Boys &Beyonds.

Closing Thoughts

What if everything you thought as beauty wasn't? What if beauty was way more than what you ever acknowledged it to be? What if beauty were everything your body would like to be? Are you willing to explore this? Is it about the infinite possibilities available to us? Is it about the capacities and talents and abilities that the body has that we haven't even considered? Is it about being and Infinite Body? I wonder what an Infinite Body is? Are you willing to have an Infinite Body?

THE BEGINNING OF INFINITE POSSIBILITIES

By Gary Douglas

Most people believe that if they can get this reality 'right' or not get it 'wrong' that somehow they are creating. How much of what you have been trying to create as your life has been based on other people's ideals of what should be, what could be, what could never be and who you could never be? And what does any of that have to do with infinite possibilities? Infinite possibilities begin when you are willing to ask a question. A question always opens the doors to new possibilities…and then it's your choices that create the reality you would like. What can you be or do different today that will create a whole new reality right away?

-Giving up your ideals and seeing what is truly possible.

-Your Choice Changes Reality

-The Infinite Colours of Infinite Possibilities
http://www.magicofbeing.com

CHAPTER THIRTEEN

❖

CREATING YOUR LIFE FROM CHOICE

By Michelle Edhouse

CFMW, CF, JCF,

Author of Unlocking Unhappy

Nilofer: I love this topic ... I love everything to do with creation and I love everything to do with creating so, Creating Your Life from Choice, what is that all about?

Michelle: Well, it is something I have only come to grips with recently and the seven day event here in New Zealand was a huge step forward for me. The work that we did at the seven day has totally catapulted me into a different level of being me and I am able to look back and see the places in my life where I have been being me. In those times everything has been flowing and easy and joyful and the things I am asking for show up and this has been where I've been creating my future deliberately, rather than in resistance and reaction to what's going on. So that's what I'd love to talk to everyone about today because the possibilities are infinite.

Nilofer: Yeah and amazing things showing up, we all have those occasionally and how do you actually have that as your reality all the time?

Michelle: One of the things that I've started using more often and it's assisting to change stuff is actually knowing what you are choosing. So I don't know about you, but when I grew up it was "so what classes are you going to do next year at school?", or "what sport are you going to play?" And it was all very defined but it was only short term. One of the tools that Access teaches, and Dain goes into it very clearly in his "Being You Changing the World" book, it started to be called the energy ball, but it's not a ball. It's getting the energy of what you'd like your life to be and putting everything into it, not just the house and car but also the energies of living, joy, space and happiness. When you create the awareness of the energy of this you can choose to be that energy in any 10 seconds no matter what else is going on around you. So this is not about having things in your life although they show up too. It is about being aware of the energy you desire to be and choosing to be it not in the future but now!

The other thing have I started doing, is actually creating a list of exactly what I would like to show up. When you sit down and write a list, and I got this from Lisa Murray on Creativity Lab, a list of what you are asking the universe for, it actually tends to be quite small. So what if you had the target of asking for more and more and more? Is the universe going to say "No you are being greedy and you can't have any of it!" or is the universe going to say "Ok cool, you'd like more, awesome, let's create that. Let's have that show up." The universe desires to contribute to you and "ask and you shall receive" is a truth!

So those are the two tools I've been using a lot lately, getting the energy of what you'd like your life to be and being it and also having a list of what you'd like to show up of what you're actually asking for.

Nilofer: What I like about the list is when you have the list you can look at it after a few months and you go ooh that showed up, that showed up, that showed up, so that's so much fun when you can see where you have asked and received.

Getting Out of Stuck

So here is a question from one of my listeners "So thank you for your contribution, my body balloons up suddenly and then in a few hours comes back to normal suddenly. It usually happens when I am fighting with a friend, so what is this, what do I do with it and how do I change it?"

Michelle: Awesome. Would you be willing to acknowledge how awesome your body is, that it can change on a dime like that? And what if you can start using that to your advantage, rather than to your detriment? With the ballooning of your body, there's two major questions I'd recommend you asking.

First is "Who does this belong to?" This is one of the most basic tools of Access Consciousness and Gary Douglas (founder of Access Consciousness) tells us that 99% of our thoughts, feelings and emotions are actually not ours. They belong to not just the people but also the earth and the universe. The way we use this tool is get the energy of what is showing up (so like the ballooning of your body) and ask, "So truth, does this belong to me, someone else, or something else?" Which ever feels lightest and most expansive is what's true for you and your body.

So if it's yours, great, then the four questions that you asked would be the next step. "What is this?", "What can I do with it?", "Can I change it? and if so, how can I change it?" These questions are fabulous to unlock the awareness of what the target you had when you created this was and what is required to change it if it can be changed. This only works if it is yours!

If it's someone elses you can ask your body "Thank you body for this awareness, can we return it to sender now please?". Your body is your awareness unit. Its job is to give you awareness, if it is showing you by pain or other physical "symptoms" what is going on for other people is it wrong? Or is it doing it's job? Good body! Thank you body! What else is possible now?

And if it's the earth, doing some 123's, as contribution to the earth all the energy you have that the earth requires is a great way to dissipate any energy that's creating that symptom in your body.

Nilofer: Can we go over that bit about the earth once again and what is the 123 and how to do that and then maybe we can do it together.

Michelle: That sounds like a great idea. So the thing about the earth, is that we're psychic little sponge bobs. As we are all connected through consciousness and we're all part of the oneness of the universe, we are actually aware of what's going on for the earth and what the earth requires. I know we aren't being taught that in this reality and when I say this, is it light and expansive? If so it is true for you!

So what tends to happen is that we become aware of what's going on for the earth, but we don't acknowledge it is to do with the earth. By asking the "Who does this belong to?" question, we get the awareness that it's something else and 99% of the time that something else is the earth requiring energy or contribution. So to do a massive contribution, we just pull all the energy we have that can contribute to the earth, gather that energy together and gift it to the earth on 3. Don't go into your head and try and work out what it requires or why, literally it is just gathering the energy together and gifting it on 1-2-3.

So just tap into the earth and perceive the energy that it requires that you can contribute. Anything that doesn't allow you to perceive, know, be and receive that, will you now destroy and uncreate that? <u>Good and Bad, Right and Wrong, POD and POC, All Nine, Shorts, Boys and Beyonds.</u>.

Now gather all that energy up, all of the places where you've stuck the energy in your body because you didn't know what to do with it and on three we are going to gift it to the earth.

1 - 2 - 3

Awesome and let's do it again

1 - 2 - 3

Nilofer: Woohooo!

Michelle: One of the things I find that is really awesome to do is if your day seems to be going really wonky and when nothing seems to be working, just go outside and do ten 1 - 2 - 3's to contribute to the earth. Also Dr Dain Heer talks about doing 1-2-3-4's to contribute to changing the future. So tap into the future and lets contribute to creating more ease and joy in the future can we now gift that on 4?

1-2-3-4

So if your day is going really crappy....

Nilofer: You don't have that, right? (laughs)

Michelle: No, no, never, my life is perfect. (laughs)

So if you are having a day when you are just 'rahhhh' go outside, do 10 x 1-2-3's and 10 x 1-2-3-4's and if you still aren't happy, do it again, and keep doing it. It tends to be when we are sitting in the stuck energy that once we start doing the 1-2-3's and 1-2-3-4's it shifts and we are no longer stuck in the miserable hole where we buried ourselves. So then we can create more joy in our lives now and in the future.

Nilofer: And the great thing is you are able to wake up in the morning and do it everyday!

Michelle: No don't do that! Don't do that, you would be a far happier person, your body would be more joyful, you would have less pain and suffering and people wouldn't want you around because you'd be happy. Being happy is just terrible!

(both laugh)

What would it take for the planet to have 100% happy people on it?

Parenting

Nilofer: So Michelle you have said that one of the things that has changed the most for you is around parenting. What do you mean by that?

Michelle: Parenting is a very big topic in my world. I have two boys, and when I first became a parent I did so because I was under the impression that if I didn't give my husband children, he'd leave me. Since I've done Access we've spoken about it, and he's said, "nah I wouldn't". I'm like, "oh you didn't tell me that!" Now I wouldn't give them back, I love them to pieces and they're such a gift and contribution to my life. When I was functioning from that space I was always in a "bluuurgh" around being a parent and everything I had to do for them was from obligation and became a trauma and drama. When other people said to me that I was a kind parent I didn't believe them. How could I be a kind and caring parent if I didn't want to be a parent in the first place? This has all completely changed for me. I now really can see the gift that they be, the contribution that they be both energetically and physically, and I allow them to contribute to me and I allow myself to contribute to them. That is massive in my universe! So from a parenting perspective that's what's changed for me.

That was one of the things that when I started doing Access classes that I thought "Right I would like to change this" and I started to create my future as a more joyful, expansive parent. How? By choosing that! As we were saying earlier, choice creates! Also if you don't choose something it won't show up. I chose to have a different reality around parenting and with my children. I choose to start having more ease, joy and glory with parenting. Through classes with people like Brendon Watt (Totally Different Dad) and Glenna Rice (the Questionable Parent) I have opened up lots of awareness and I really am grateful for those 2 facilitators as well of course the classes with Gary and Dain. Also what are we teaching our kids if we choose to not choose? Are we showing how to create their lives? Are we teaching them that they can create what they desire or are we teaching them to sit around and wait for the world to happen around them and hope it turns out ok?

As my children start to reach teenage-hood I have been asking a lot of questions around how to parent them. Reading books on parenting has never really been light and easy and as there were people in my life that would spend hours pouring through books for new techniques to try I used to make myself wrong for not doing the same. As I have been using the tools and questions from Access more and more I have come to recognise that although books may give you ideas, you require to follow your awareness. What do you know as a parent? What does your child require you to be or do as their parent? Are each of your children different? Do they require different things from you? If so are you willing to be different with each of them?

Another gift I have received from Access is the willingness to acknowledge that the kids know what is required for them. By including them in choices that involve them and inviting them to choose for themselves how much more prepared for adulthood will they be? Even from really young this can contribute to them creating more ease and joy for them and you.

Changing what is stuck

Nilofer: A lot of people I know hate technology and then there are others who even talk about being vibrationally compatible with technology. You are one of the people who love technology aren't you Michelle?

Michelle: I have always have a capacity with technical stuff. I realised I was a little bit different around technology way back when I was 13 (back before Windows even existed - for those of you that are a bit younger than me may not know that there was a time when Windows didn't exist but it's true - laughs) and in those days we used something called MS-DOS which was where you typed in CD to change directory and MD to make a directory, there were no pictures, there was no drag and drop, and I tried to teach my mother how to use it and she just couldn't get it, it was just so far out of her reality, so far out of her possibilities that she just couldn't get it no matter how much I tried. So I asked "Is this me that is different or her?" and I got the awareness that it was me. By the end of my high schooling I was actually teaching the Computing studies class, the teacher was the Dean of our year and she would be off most of the time dealing with that stuff and she would leave me to teach the class because I had that talent and ability with technology.

So I went to University and studied computers because that is what you do! I Hated IT! I bribed other people to do my assignments and all sort of things to get through and kept it fun by being the leader of the student activists and playing pool at the bar. After I graduated I kind of pushed the computing away and when I started doing Access, my first facilitator, Moana, asked me what I had done before becoming a parent and I listed the jobs I had had. She was waiting for something that went ping in my universe, something that sparked me, that was fun.

When I got to that I had done Computer Science at University and she exclaimed "OOOH You know computers. You could build me a website" and I replied "What? How does doing computer science 15 years ago have anything to do with building you a website now?" she responded "Well you now have the tools, you now have the questions, go work it out" Oooh rat bag! So I did. I started using questions like:

1. What is this? (a point of view I can't build a website)
2. What do I do with it? (stop myself for creating possibilities)
3. Can I change it? (YES)
4. How do I change it? Who do I need to speak to? Who do I need to get information from in order to create this?

Literally within 24 hours of her putting that in my space I had started building my first website. That has progressed and I have built many websites since then. It keeps growing and keeps changing and I have even worked on building mobile apps.

Really I created that huge shift for myself where I went from being stuck as an at home mum with no employment prospects to creating myself a business doing something I really enjoy! I love talking to people about what they require, how they would like their website to be and so by asking questions I have opened up this possibility that has now also led to working with Access Consciousness and Simone Milasas, through Joy of Business, doing business tech stuff, which is fun for me. I love doing it. I'm making money doing it and I can do it from home so I can still be an at home mum. It kind of filled all those spaces where I required something added to my life.

Nilofer: This leads into our next question "Since using the tools of Access I have been choosing for myself and things are more fun for me and my body. I'm getting in trouble with others as I no longer live in a limited reality. However everything is insanely busy with my family demands (I need to POC and POD me, what's right about me that I'm not getting?). I seem to be taken over by their point of view, judgments and everything they think."

Michelle: The first thing I would ask this person is "Can an Infinite Being actually be taken over?" A little while ago when I was feeling very buried in the amount of work I had created for myself. I kept asking "What would it take for more work to show up?" and then it all showed up, and on top of that I had the kids requiring stuff, and all over the place I had requirements. I started to ask "Where am I?" so I used this question to get out of it "Would an infinite being ever be overwhelmed? Would an infinite being ever be taken over?" if not why are you choosing it?

Once you have that awareness you can actually start asking "What am I going to choose now?" as choice trumps everything. It trumps POC'ing and POD'ing it trumps everything, because it literally is the liberator.

So the question I would recommend you start to ask is "What choice can I make here that will create more ease?" and another question that Dr Dain Heer gave me was:

"What energy space and consciousness can my body and I be to have total ease and clarity with this for all eternity?" and everything that doesn't allow that will you destroy and uncreate it please? Good and

Bad, Right and Wrong, POD and POC, All Nine, Shorts, Boys and Beyonds.

That particular one I ran it 40 times before I actually started to see possibilities showing up on how I can change things and I could see something different. And that is different. It is not differently - which means the same dress in a different colour. Choosing something different is truly different , not just making a little tweak, it's what else is possible? What else can I choose here? So those would be the questions I would start with.

Nilofer: It is also about being present. What am I choosing that is creating that and what else can I choose?

Michelle: Also, by choosing to be taken over what are you avoiding? I found that when I was choosing to be buried in the amount of work I had to do I was avoiding choosing to create. I was burying myself in the now and not being willing to be present with the future as well as the present. Present with the present as well as present with the future!

Nilofer: Can I ask you something which is totally related to that? I find myself in the place where I have too much to do and also I find myself having large chunks of time on my hands and I don't do anything.

Michelle: Ok so there are 2 possibilities here and it may be one of them for some times and the other one at other times. So when you have been really really busy have you ever said something like "What would it take to have a break? Some time out for me"?

Nilofer: Yes!

Michelle: Great so would you be willing to acknowledge that the times you are not doing anything is where you have actually created what you have asked for?

The other side of it is something that Dain asked Simone and this is more when you have a big list of things to do and all you want to do is lay on the couch, don't move and don't do anything even though you know you have things to do and you don't. "Is your body preparing for what is to come?"

Is it storing up the rest and energy levels because it is willing to be aware that very soon you are going to have a large amount of body input required?

Have I created this so I can have that relaxation time I have been asking for?

Is my body preparing for what is to come in the future?

Our bodies are aware of what we are creating in the future and sometimes it will just say "Please If you want me to do this you need to let me sleep and prepare for it!"

Nilofer: Oh they both seem to be what is going on.

Michelle: How cool are you and your body?

Nilofer: Ok let;s take another question:

"I have been doing a lot to create money, developing websites, painting, writing, all sorts of things. I'm in debt and no matter what I do my debts increase."

Michelle: So the tool that comes into my awareness for that is "Everything is the opposite of what it appears to be, Nothing is the opposite of what it appears to be". This is a great tool to use when things seem to be twisted and running in the opposite direction than what we expect it to. If you say it 10 times it will start to unlock where things are twisted and seeming to function in reverse order to where they "should" be functioning.

Let's try that together, put your attention on something that seems to be upside down or back to front and lets say the crazy phrase 10 times:

1. Everything is the opposite of what it appears to be, Nothing is the opposite of what it appears to be.
2. Everything is the opposite of what it appears to be, Nothing is the opposite of what it appears to be.
3. Everything is the opposite of what it appears to be, Nothing is the opposite of what it appears to be.
4. Everything is the opposite of what it appears to be, Nothing is the opposite of what it appears to be.
5. Everything is the opposite of what it appears to be, Nothing is the opposite of what it appears to be.
6. Everything is the opposite of what it appears to be, Nothing is the opposite of what it appears to be.
7. Everything is the opposite of what it appears to be, Nothing is the opposite of what it appears to be.
8. Everything is the opposite of what it appears to be, Nothing is the opposite of what it appears to be.
9. Everything is the opposite of what it appears to be, Nothing is the opposite of what it appears to be.
10. Everything is the opposite of what it appears to be, Nothing is the opposite of what it appears to be.

There is also something there around an oath, vow, swearing or commitment to someone or something to never have money.

All the oaths, vows, swearing, promises, allegiances, alliances and commitments to anyone or anything in this or any lifetime to never have money and to be indebted will you revoke, recant, rescind, renounce, denounce, destroy and uncreate all of that and return it to sender with consciousness attached? <u>Good and Bad, Right and Wrong, POD and POC, All Nine, Shorts, Boys and Beyonds.</u>

That person may wish to run that a few times and at this point I can't put my finger on the other part right now sorry.

Getting Paid to Have Fun

Nilofer: This is a really good one, "How do you make money when you are having fun?"

Michelle: Yes that was one of the questions that was given to us in the Foundation when I first did my Foundation class and it was "So what do you find fun that you never thought anyone would give you money for?" Just so easy and fun that you can't believe anyone would give you money to do it. I kept asking that question until I finally acknowledged that I was having fun playing on Facebook it wasn't just a time waster as people said. There are also people out there that don't wish to be on Facebook yet they perceive that having a presence on there would contribute to their business. Guess what I got invited to work for someone and get paid to post on Facebook! I couldn't believe it! I got to play with graphics, I got paid to post on Facebook! I mean anyone who loves Facebook would say "You get PAID to post on Facebook?"

So I had been asking over and over again "What is it I love doing so much that I can't believe anyone would pay me for doing?" and I asked that and asked that over and over until something started to show up and about the same time I started to sell some of my paintings as well. In fact l sold 3 paintings to a woman who had randomly walked into the gallery where they were on display and she was buying them to put in her healing center in Europe. I had had so much fun creating those paintings and as if by magic by asking that question I made money by having that fun.

So it is such a basic question and yet how many people actually ask it? How many people have decided that what they have fun and joy doing nobody would ever pay them for and so they don't even see the possibilities when they show up.

How many decisions, judgments, conclusions and computations have you created and are now functioning from that limits you from perceiving the income possibilities? and everything that doesn't allow you to perceive, know, be and receive those income possibilities would you be willing to destroy and uncreate that please? <u>Good and Bad, Right and Wrong, POD and POC, All Nine, Shorts, Boys and Beyonds.</u>

Decisions and judgments stop the future. When you have a decision or a judgment that something can't show up or this is the only way that it is or anything like that then you will find that nothing else can show up. Like for example, I decided that I wasn't going to work with computers any more and so I literally had stopped all possible flows of money from computers because I had made that decision. Now what percentage of the worlds jobs these days actually require a computer? It meant I couldn't go back to working in a call center like I was before I had kids because it would mean working with computers. So when I decided that I wasn't going to work on computers then that stopped any other possibilities showing up. Once I destroyed that point of view the possibilities could start to show up and I could perceive and receive them.

Simone Milasas (the founder and author of Joy of Business) loves to go for a walk on the beach with her dog, but while she is walking she is working; she is coming up with ideas, she is being inspired, she's talking to people on the phone, she is making appointments, she's writing down little ideas that she has that she can do when she gets back to her computer. In fact, Steve Bowman said to her one time when he saw her on the beach "You are the only person I can see lying on the beach and I know that you're working". She doesn't have her computer on the beach but she is always creating. What if, when we go for a walk, we don't stop creating our lives, we don't stop creating our future? What if that could be a contribution to having more fun?

I do it all the time... My body is sitting here going "OMG we are sitting down again, can we go for a walk please?" and I find that if I get up and move at that time, it may just be going and getting an arm load of firewood or it could be going for a walk, but when I get up and move I find that I am far more productive and I get so much more done.

There are so many different ways that energy can create money. You can create future if you are willing to follow that energy. If I was to sit there and go "No! I have to get this done" I am stopping the energy from creating greater.

Nilofer: That is amazing because you have already decided the point of view of how you are going to earn money instead of being willing for everything to contribute to your money flows.

Michelle: While also asking "What would it take for me to get paid for doing the things I love?". Part of my job for Access Consciousness is approving the products that facilitators create. To approve them I actually have to listen to them and I can do that while I am going for a walk! So what if there is a way you can get paid while doing what you love to do?

I remember hearing the story about a guy who had created an online business and he was putting two hours of actual work each month and receiving $3 million per month income each month. So he is off playing golf or doing things he loves to do and still getting paid.

What have you decided about how you earn your money that limits money from showing up in other ways? Let's say you have decided you get paid hours for dollars, can you actually receive a passive income? How many of us ask to win the lottery but have decided that we only earn money hours for dollars? A $10 million payout for a 5 minute trip to the shop to buy your lottery ticket, how many of us are willing to receive that hourly rate?

So how have you decided you earn your money? How have you decided you receive money? From where have you decided you receive money? Everything that is will you destroy and uncreate it? <u>Good</u>

<u>and Bad, Right and Wrong, POD and POC, All Nine, Shorts, Boys and Beyonds.</u>

If you decided any of those things, can the money show up from other ways? I remember doing a telecall series with Curry Glassell (Right Riches for You) and she was talking to us about this and I started POC'ing and POD'ing every morning all the decisions, judgments, conclusions and computations I had around money and how money showed up in my life and I had always decided that money didn't just show up in my bank account so I POC'd and POD'd that. The next day I get a phone call from a very special person ringing to find out my bank account number so she could put a large sum of money in as she felt like contributing to me!

Nilofer: That is so amazing!

Michelle: Now if I hadn't POC'd and POD'd those points of view would I have been in the space of being able to receive it? Would it have felt light and fun for her to choose to gift to me? Or would the idea have felt odd to her when she thought of it?

Where are we limiting our money flows that if we weren't to limit them could create the infinite possibilities of future that truly are possible? Everything that is times a godzillion can we destroy and uncreate it? <u>Good and Bad, Right and Wrong, POD and POC, All Nine, Shorts, Boys and Beyonds.</u>

Just Choose

Nilofer: Another listener has written in "I have been doing a lot of Access in the last couple of months and life has become much easier and expansive but if I seem to focus on what I want to create I don't do anything."

Michelle: Yes this is definitely a space that people get to when they have been doing a lot of POC'ing and POD'ing. Even Gary talks about the time he was just sitting around on the couch not doing anything,

THE MAGIC OF BEING

and this is exactly the time when you need to start choosing what you would like to create and doing it. It may start as small as laying there on the couch and thinking "I'm going to make a coffee" and actually getting up and going and making a coffee. It's about getting into the habit of choosing to create something and doing it or being it. As you start deliberately creating from choice you can start to expand that choice.

Let's go back to that list I talked about in the beginning. Write down a list of things that you would like to have in your life, a list of places you would like to go, a list of the energies you would like to be, the types of people you would like to surround yourself with. Write the list not in the form of an "I want..." list but writing it in the form of a question like "What would it take for me to have more fun people in my life?" "What would it take for me to have a sexy man in my life?" (my husband just walked past *laugh* How does it get any better?).

By asking it as a question you are requesting of the universe to actually contribute to that showing up and until you ask for it you are not actually willing to receive it. It's like what you would like to have is on the other side of the forest and POC'ing and POD'ing sends a machine through which cuts down all the trees and brambles in your way so you can get through. Until you actually take a step and start to create, one step at a time, will you ever make it to the target?

I talk to a lot of people who say things like "I would love to have an Access business. I would love to have more people in my classes" instead of asking "Who can I speak to today to contribute to creating my business?" "What would it take for me to have 100 or more people in my classes on a regular basis?"

Creating that list as questions not only have you chopped down the trees but you are also moving towards the future you would like to be living. In regards to this person's question, some of us have cut off choosing for ourselves so much that we do need to start with "Would I like a drink? Yes I would. What would I like to drink?" and choosing in those 10 second increments "I would like a coffee!" Cool go and make yourself a coffee. When you have made the coffee "Would I like to drink the coffee?" and make a choice, and choose again and choose again and choose the big things, and choose the small things and just keep practicing that choice and that will start to move you forward from where you be at the moment from all the POC'ing and POD'ing to be able to create the future you would like to live.

Nilofer: The other thing is that by actually choosing "OOh I would like to have that in my life" things are starting to show up even if I don't put them on my list. As I am listening to Access classes and I look at when people are having things and being an energy and I would like that or receive that I am asking for those things.

Michelle: Absolutely! The other thing you just reminded me of was about living life in 10 second increments and being willing to be an energy even if it is just for 10 seconds. So what would it take for me to be that and me to have that? Choose and it shows up! "What would it take for me to be that generosity of spirit?" Cool I have it, I be it AND then you keep choosing it. "What would it take for me to be that generosity of spirit in everything I be and do for all eternity?" and keep choosing it and keep choosing it and keep choosing it. Also it is about adding it to your life rather than it just be that 10 seconds instantaneous be it.

My list used to look like this:

- I would like to skydive
- I would like to go water skiing
- I would like to have a leather couch
- I would like to have a white picket fence and 2.5 children.

Those things show up and then what else?

Nilofer: and then the other part of it is that when what you have been asking for shows up sometimes you forget to ask for more, the what else?

Michelle: Absolutely, writing your list is not something you sit down and do once, it is something that you keep adding to constantly and it doesn't have to be a physically written list either, it can be "I will have some of that thanks" and you receive it. Also acknowledging when it shows up "Oh that is me being that, can I have some more of that please" "Oh the leather lounge suite showed up, how awesome am I? and what else can I choose?" It is the constant creation of future that if we are willing to choose it can be so much fun and so expansive and joyful!

I had a friend recently who had had some bad news and was sitting in a down space and I asked her "What could you create to go beyond this?" and she started saying "Oh I could create this and I could choose that" and instantly all of her energy shifted and she started to see possibilities beyond that news she had received. She didn't say "I don't want to think about that I just want to sit in my little hole", she was willing to choose "Oh cool what could I create?" so that is another awesome question to ask yourself and creating a future "What can I be or do today to out create myself?"

Nilofer: You know what you just said is so brilliant and I know it is true for me and maybe it is true for a lot of people is that energy of creation for me is so exciting and so joyful, so expansive. When I am down in the dumps and I get an idea of what I can create and I am like Yahooo! I remember the first time I was interviewing a lot of Access Consciousness facilitators, I did it over a 3 day period and they were talking about the energy of fun and joy and one of them asked me "What is the energy of fun and joy for you?" and I said going for a walk, going to this.. and then I realised "Doing what I am doing right now is fun for me" so how does it get any better than that?

Michelle: And what if you being you is the change you desire to see in the world? My husband and I ran a telecall recently and it is called "What if You're Not Wrong?" and we would love to gift that to the readers of this book if you would like to choose something different in that area www.AccessYou.co.nz/NotWrong Normally it would be $20 but if you use the coupon code "Choicetheliberator" at checkout you will receive it for free.

Nilofer: This is awesome! So many people send in questions to the summit and they are questions like "I tried to create this and but it is not happening" they are creating from the linear do this and get a result. What would it be like if you had no wrongness around it I wonder?

Michelle: Exactly and what if the only thing that you could see was question?

Instead of going to OMG I shouldn't have done that! Look at what I did ARRGGGHHH!

What if you stop and say "ok what else can I choose?"

What else?

What else is possible here?

What can I choose now?

Wow that was an interesting choice, NOW what can I choose?

If you were creating your life today what would you choose?

WHO IS MICHELLE EDHOUSE

Michelle best describes herself as a facilitator of change. Empowering people to quit life long drug addiction through to conceiving a child after months of trying Michelle's CFMW status is well documented. Drawing on life experiences ranging from student activism to office management as well as developing her talents as an artist and website creator, she is well aware that the possibilities are infinite if we choose them.

Michelle always thought of herself as a normal middle class girl with an engineering/mathematical brain. Michelle studied Computer Science, Mathematics and Management Systems at University but she always knew there was more available than what she saw those around her choosing.

Having used the tools of Access Consciousness in her own life, she enjoys helping those that wish to create more. Her own changes have been subtle in some areas but profound in others. *"This ease I have with my children now is something I could never have imagined possible."* The tools and techniques in Access have also opened up possibilities in business (www.WWWebsites.co.nz) and creativity (www.McEArt.co.nz) by clearing out limitations and asking "What else is possible here?"

WHAT IF THAT PAIN WAS THE EARTH SAYING HELLO

By Donnielle Carter

Why does the Earth communicate to you with pain in your body

What if you could hear before it's pain

Does little ole you really contribute to the Earth?

http://www.magicofbeing.com

ACCESS CONSCIOUSNESS COPYRIGHT NOTICE

———— ❖ ————

Access Trademarks and Trade Names:

1. Access Consciousness®
2. Access Bars®
3. Conversations in Consciousness®
4. Energetic Synthesis of Being®
5. The Bars®
6. Right and Wrong, Good and Bad, POC, POD, all 9, shorts, boys and beyond®
7. All of Life Comes To Me With Ease and Joy and Glory®
8. Ease, Joy and Glory®
9. How does it get any better than this?®
10. How does it get any better than that?®
11. The Body Whisperer®
12. What else is possible?®
13. Who does this belong to?®
14. Energetic Symphony of Being®
15. Energetic Synthesis of Being®

16. Symphony of Being®

17. Leaders for a Conscious World®

18. Consciousness Includes Everything and Judges Nothing®

19. Oneness Includes Everything and Judges Nothing®

THE ACCESS CLEARING STATEMENT

❖

The Clearing Statement is a tool you can use to change the energy of the points of view that have you locked into unchanging situations. You are the only one who can unlock the points of view that have you trapped.

Clearing Statement: Right and wrong, good and bad, POD and POC, all nine, shorts, boys and beyonds.

Right and wrong, good and bad is shorthand for: What's right, good, perfect and correct about this? What's wrong, mean, vicious, terrible, bad, and awful about this? What have you decided is right and wrong, good and bad?

POD is the point of destruction immediately preceding whatever you decided.

POC is the point of creation of thoughts, feelings and emotions immediately preceding whatever you decided.

Sometimes instead of saying, "use the clearing statement," we just say, "POD and POC it."

All nine stands for nine layers of crap that we're taking out. You know that somewhere in those nine layers, there's got to be a pony because you couldn't put that much crap in one place without having a pony in there. It's crap you're generating yourself.

Shorts is the short version of: What's meaningful about this? What's meaningless about this? What's the punishment for this? What's the reward for this?

Boys stands for nucleated spheres. Have you ever seen one of those kid's bubble pipes? Blow here and you create a mass of bubbles? You pop one and it fills in, and you pop another one and it fills in. They're like that. You can never seem to get them all to pop.

Beyonds are feelings or sensations you get that stop your heart, stop your breath, or stop your willingness to look at possibilities. It's like when your business is in the red and you get another final notice and you go argh! You weren't expecting that right now. That's a beyond.

(The majority of information about the clearing statement is from the websitewww.theclearingstatement.com)

CONTACT OUR CONTRIBUTORS

❖

CORY MICHELLE
Website: www.meetcorymichelle.com
Email: hello@meetcorymichelle.com

SIMONE MILASAS
Website: www.simonemilasas.com
Email: simone@accessconsciousness.com

LIAM PHILLIPS
Website:www.liamphillips.com
Email:liamrphillips@yahoo.com

Dr KACIE CRISP
Website: thelittleblackbookonrelationsihps.com
Email: drikaciecrisp@gmail.com

SUSAN LAZAR HART
Email: info@susanlazarhart.com
Website: www.rightrelationshipforyou.com

WENDY MULDER
Website: www.kindnesswithgrief.com
Email: swmulder@bigpond.net.au

MARGARET BRAUNACK
Website: www.margaretbraunack.com
Email: Margaret.braunack@gmail.com
Phone: +61 418 877 946

SOPHIE MIHALKO
Website: http://www.SophieMihalko.com
Email: info@breakdownthelimits.com

VANITHA SUBRAMANIAM
Website: http://www.conscioussolutions.info
Email:accessvanitha@gmail.com
Phone: + 60 12 7210705

STEVEN & CHUTISA BOWMAN
Website: http://nomorebusinessasusual.com/
Email: steven@consciousgovernance.com

NILOFER SAFDAR
Website: http://www.nilofersafdar.com
Email: nilofer@illusiontoilluminationsummit.com

MICHELLE EDHOUSE
Website: www.AccessYou.co.nz
Email: Michelle@accessyou.co.nz

WHO IS NILOFER SAFDAR

❖

Nilofer Safdar is a bestselling author of the books, Cracking the Client Attraction Code, The Colors Of Now, Money Circle and Transformations.

She is a Certified Access Consciousness Facilitator CFMW. Nilofer helps people change their reality to generate and create a life they desire and require. Her target is to generate a life that is joyful and expansive for everybody she touches.

Nilofer is a Life Coach, Money Mastery Coach, Public Speaking Coach, Relationship Coach and Weight Loss and Anti Aging Expert.

She is a creation junkie and loves to play with infinite possibilities. The latest bee in her bonnet is videos. You will find most of her videos on Facebook and on YouTube.

She is the host of a TV show which aired on JIA News in India called The Nilofer Show.

She is the host of the First online radio show in the Middle East, The Healthy Living Dubai Show, in which she interviews Speakers, Coaches, Natural Healers from the Middle East which empowers the listeners to Create everything they desire in life.

She is also the host of the telesummit, Illusion to Illumination Summit, in which she has interviewed more than 150 Luminaries, Change Agents, Best Selling Authors from around the world including Peggy Phoenix Dubro, the originator of the EMF Balancing Technique, Gary Douglas – the founder of Access Consciousness.

To contact Nilofer for further information about her books, audios, newsletters, workshops & training programs and consultancy or to schedule her for a presentation, please write to: nilofer@illusiontoilluminationsummit.com

Websites are –

www.illusiontoilluminationsummit.com

www.healthylivingdubai.com

www.nilofersafdar.com

SESSIONS WITH NILOFER

Would you like to have the magic of Nilofer touch you, permeate you and turn your reality on it's head?

Here are some possibilities -

SOP Sessions (Available Online)

Verbal Facilitation on any topic under the sun (Available Online)

Right Voice For You Sessions (Available Online)

Bars (In person)

Bodywork (In person)

Book - nilofer@illusiontoilluminationsummit.com

MAKE YOUR BOOK AN AMAZON BESTSELLER

Have you written and published a book?

Are you writing a book?

Do you have a book in you that would like to be written and published?

Would you like to write, publish and make your book an Amazon Bestseller?

From coaching on getting started, to helping you with the publishing process to getting your book to be an International Amazon Bestseller, Nilofer offers it all. Contact her to explore the Infinite Possibilities with your book - nilofer@illusiontoilluminationsummit.com

WHAT NEXT

Nilofer loves hosting Telesummits. You can visit www.illusiontoilluminationsummit.com to find her latest offerings.

Past Telesummits:

Creation From Joy

Choice The Liberator

Earth! Love It Or Leave It!

Where Is My Doorway To Possibilities

All the tools and techniques from this book are from the body of work called Access Consciousness.

If you haven't already, I would highly recommend you start with the Access Consciousness Core Classes - Bars, Foundation.

Each of the authors in this book can facilitate these classes and are happy to travel.

You can find more information on these classes at www.accessconsciousness.com

MORE BOOKS BY NILOFER SAFDAR

❖

BOOKS BY NILOFER
http://www.nilofersbooks.com

Cracking The Client Attraction Code
By Carla McNeil & Nilofer Safdar
http://www.crackingtheclientattractioncode.com

Transformations
By Nilofer Safdar
http://www.thetransformationsbook.com

The Colors Of Now
By Nilofer Safdar
http://www.thecolorsofnow.com

Money Circle
By Nilofer Safdar
http://www.moneycirclebook.com

Where Is My Doorway To Possibilities
By Nilofer Safdar
http://www.whereismydoorwaytopossibilities.com

UPCOMING BOOKS

Create Your Life
By Nilofer Safdar
http://www.thecreateyourlifebook.com

Choice The Liberator
By Nilofer Safdar

Creation From Joy
By Nilofer Safdar

30 Days Business Bootcamp
By Aditi Surti & Nilofer Safdar

Abundance From Kindness
By Nirmala Raju & Nilofer Safdar

No Form No Structure No Significance
By RituMotial & Nirmala Raju